TITUS LIVIUS

UMBRI

ETRUSCI

SABINI

AEQUICULI

AEQUI

HERNICI

VOLSCI

RUTULI

LATINI

Cures

Trebula Mutusca

Tiberis Fl.

Crustumerium

Cameria

Veii

Nomentum

Fidenae

Medullia

Corniculum

Ficulea

Tibur

Anio Fl.

Caere

Antemnae

Roma

Collatia

Gabii

Praeneste

Fossa Cluilia

Aqua Ferentina

M. Albanus

Ficana

Alba Longa

Salinae

Tellenae

Albanus

Signia

Ostia

Laurens

Aricia

L. Nemorensis

Ager

Laurentum

Apiolae

Lanuvium

Lavinium

Numicus Fl.

Ardea

Suessa Pometia

LATIUM

MILES

0   5   10   15   20   25

Circeii

TITUS LIVIUS

BOOK ONE

EDITED
WITH INTRODUCTION, NOTES AND VOCABULARY

BY
H.E. GOULD, M.A.
AND
J.L. WHITELEY, M.A., PH.D.
AUTHORS OF "A NEW LATIN COURSE"; VERGIL
AENEID I, II, IV, VI, ETC.

Published by Bristol Classical Press
General Editor: John H. Betts

First published by Macmillan Education Ltd
in 1952. Reprinted, with permission, in 1987 by:

BRISTOL CLASSICAL PRESS
226 North Street
Bedminster
Bristol BS3 1JD

ISBN 0-86292-296-8

Printed in Great Britain

FOREWORD

THIS edition of Livy, Book I, has been prepared on the same principles as previous volumes in the Modern School Classics. That is to say, the editors, believing that the annotated classical texts of the past generation give too little practical help in translation, and yet at the same time have their commentaries overloaded with unnecessary information on points only remotely connected with the text, have sought to write notes that will make it possible for the school boy and girl of today to produce, in reasonable time, and without the discouragement of being baffled by difficulties, a correct translation of passages set by their teachers for preparation.

In these times such pupils will need a great deal of help which in the spacious days of classical teaching fifty years ago they were considered not to require, and they will need moreover that such help should at first be given repeatedly, until each difficulty of construction becomes familiar.

The editors, bearing in mind, as they have tried to do throughout, the difficulties experienced by present-day pupils in the study of a subject which once received a much more generous share of the time-table, hope that in the present edition they have done something to smooth their path.

H. E. G.
J. L. W.

LONDON, 1951.

v

CONTENTS

MAPS

INTRODUCTION

1. Life and Work of Livy

WE know very little of Livy's life, and what information we have can be stated in a few sentences.

Titus Livius lived from 59 B.C. to A.D. 17 and was a native of the north Italian town of Patavium (the modern Padua), an important and prosperous place with a reputation for strict morality. Many writers have suggested that it was from such a background of puritanism and simplicity of manners that Livy derived his dislike of the luxury and immorality that existed in Rome.

Livy tells us in his preface that he preferred to turn away his eyes from the miseries of the dying Republic and to fix them upon all that was great and noble in the history of his nation. He seems, therefore, to have taken no active part in the politics of his own day, although we gather from his work that his sympathies were on the side of the senatorial party. Moreover, we learn from Tacitus (*Ann.* iv. 34) that his senatorial bias was so clear in his treatment of the Civil War that Augustus called him a ' Pompeian '.

As far as we can tell, Livy probably settled in Rome about the age of thirty and spent the last forty years of his life in the composition of his great history, a work which had the support of Augustus and his friends and gave him immediately an assured place at the imperial court and in literary circles.[1]

Jerome, who is the authority for the dates of his birth and death, tells us that at the end of his life, he returned to his native Patavium.

The traditional title of the work is *Ab urbe condita libri.* Of the books, which originally numbered 142, we now have only 1-10, 21-45, of which 41 and 43 are imperfect. For all the books, however (except 136, 137), summaries have been preserved and enable us to form some conception of the general scheme and the treatment accorded to different periods from the earliest times down to the death of Drusus in 9 B.C.

2. LIVY AS AN HISTORIAN

If we criticised Livy as an historian in the light of modern historical research, we should have no difficulty in building up a strong case against him. It could easily be shown that Livy disregarded original sources that were available and accessible, that he often neglected to verify his facts and his topography, that he used his sources with too little discrimination, that he was not interested in sifting his information and in making valid deductions from it, and that, finally, he allowed his patriotism to make him un-generous towards his country's enemies. All this and more could be said against him.

But most of this criticism ignores the conditions under

---

[1] Cf. the story of the man from Cadiz who travelled to Rome merely to see Livy, and, having seen him, returned home immediately.

which and the ideals with which an historian of the ancient world worked. Today, the historian is supported in his work by a tradition that has been slowly built up in our universities over the last hundred years and soundly based on the scientific method which has revolutionised the technique of modern scholarship as it has the world of the natural sciences. Today the historian has access to libraries and record offices, to archives and the journals of learned societies, all of which did not and could not exist until comparatively recently. Finally, the historian is aided today by many fellow-workers, all of whom have been trained in and inspired by the same historical schools in our universities.

In a word, Livy is not a modern historian, but a writer of the 1st century B.C., who had well-defined aims in writing the history of Rome which he undertook. He sought, first to emphasise in his story the traits in the national character which had made Rome great, the firmness, the discipline, and the political wisdom of the founders of the nation's greatness, and, secondly, to impress upon his readers that Rome had developed into the mistress of a great empire under divine guidance and leadership. It was, therefore, his purpose that we should learn noble lessons from the lives of the great heroes of the Republic. In both these aims, Livy uses with great literary skill and artistry all the technique of the rhetorician and the poet. Thus Livy may be called an artist rather than a scientific historian, a poet who wrote in prose. Every critic has praised his power of graphic description, his dramatic contrivance, his imaginative skill in the composition of the speeches, his details of character and finally his language, which rarely fails in nobility and pathos to match the events and character of his story.

There are many fine passages in Book I which illustrate the points made in the preceding paragraph. We have, for example, the story of Romulus and Remus, the rape of the Sabine women, the combat of the Curiatii and the Horatii, the coming of Lucumo from Etruria, Tarquin the Proud, the clash between the two strong characters Turnus Herdonius and Tarquin, and, finally, the rape of Lucretia with which the book ends. To read or to re-read these passages is to admit that in the Augustan age there is no prose writer who can be compared with Livy.

3. LIVY AS WRITER AND STYLIST

Just as Livy was writing during the final years of the Republic and at the beginning of the Empire, so his language can be said to partake of the characteristic features of both periods and thus to form a link between the Latin of the Golden and that of the Silver Age, i.e. between the prose of Cicero and Caesar, and that of Seneca and Tacitus. If we examine the dates of the births of these writers, Cicero 106 B.C., Livy 59 B.C. and Tacitus A.D. 54, ,we shall realise at once how Livy occupies an intermediate position between Cicero on the one hand and Tacitus on the other, and we shall not be surprised to find that he displays characteristics of both.

We shall now refer briefly to some of these character-istics and attempt to illustrate them with examples from Book I.

(1) The period, or long and elaborate sentence, which was brought to perfection by Cicero, was adapted by Livy to historical narrative. Many good examples in Book I will illustrate the usual framework : ablative absolute, **cum** and pluperfect subjunctive, nom. of perfect participle of deponent verb, ablative absolute with dependent clauses, sometimes another **cum** clause and finally the main verb. On the whole, as one would expect in an author who wrote to be read rather than to be heard, the periods of Livy tend to be more elaborate than those of Cicero.

(2) On the other hand Livy may be said to look forward to Tacitus in his love of variety and in his introduction into his prose of features which are normally character-istic of poetic diction.

For example, while in Cicero the law of symmetry and balance prevailed, Livy did not hesitate to aim at variety in his narrative, chiefly in his vocabulary and syntax. As an example of the former, Albula in Chap. 3 is in turn called **fluvius, amnis,** and **flumen** ; while **forem** is fre-quently a synonym of **essem**. As an example of the latter, we note the way in which **ob** is combined with **quod** in Chap. 14.

Many examples will be found in this book of poetical usages and vocabulary. Of the latter there are 48 words in Book I, such as **errabundus, glomero, nati, parens, proles,**

strages ; of the former, the most noticeable are the following :

(1) local ablative without a preposition, e.g. **carpento** (34, 8).

(2) abl. of separation, **caelo** (16, 6).

(3) simple verb for the compound, **pono** = **depono** (19, 4).

(4) the dative of advantage or disadvantage = English possessive genitive, e.g. **fusis** (5, 6), **raptis** (10, 1).

(5) albative of manner without a preposition or adjective, e.g. **agmine** (6, 2), **ordine** (58, 9).

(6) modal use of the ablative of the gerund or gerundive (=present participle), e.g. **venando** (4, 8).

(7) use of plural of abstract noun, **amicitiae** (45, 2).

(8) perfect participle passive in agreement with noun = abstract noun with a genitive, **ducta** . . . **Tanaquil** (34, 4). Cf. also 28, 1.

Finally we shall observe as we read Livy's first book his richness and fullness, two qualities which were commented upon by the Roman critic Quintilian (10. 1. 32) as **illa Livi lactea ubertas**. Sometimes, however, these two qualities degenerate into mere pleonasm and tautology ; e.g. **rursus** with **repeto** (33, 3), **saepe** with **iterare** (45, 2), and thereby expose Livy to the criticism made by Caligula (Sueton. Calig., 34) that he was **verborum in historia neglegentem**.

Our last reference will be made to the rhetorical character of his style. Quintilian (10. 1. 101) and Tacitus (*Ann.*, 4. 34) both refer to his **eloquentia** and the modern reader will have no difficulty in noting his frequent use of such figures of rhetoric as personification, metaphor, chiasmus, asyndeton, and alliteration.

The rhetorical flavour of Livy's style and his skill in composing stirring and moving speeches not only enable him in his long history to avoid dullness and monotony but also give charm and distinction to his work.

4. GRAMMAR AND SYNTAX

Livy differs from the usage of Cicero in the following points.

1. The Verb.

(*a*) The subjunctive is used with **priusquam** even where there is no additional idea of purpose or action anticipated.

(*b*) The subjunctive is used after **ubi** in a frequentative or iterative sense.   Cf. 32, 13.

(*c*) The strict rule of the sequence of tenses as used by Cicero is not applied by Livy.   See the note on I. 31.

2. Participles.

(*a*) See (8), p. xiv. See also the note on **inter Lavinium ... conditum** (3, 4).   See also 34. 4 ; 28. 1 ; 45. 3.

(*b*) The perfect participle as a noun, **coeptum** (36. 1), **deditis** (5. 3), **degeneratum** (53. 1), etc.

(*c*) the present participle as a noun, especially in the gen. pl., **condentium** (25. 4).

3. The attributive use of adverbs and prepositional phrases is common ; e.g. **circa** in 14. 7 and 59. 9 ; **deinceps** in 6.1 ; **deinde** in 15. 7 ; **ex plebe homines** 9. 11 ; **erga patriam caritatis** 34. 5 ; **aream ad aedem** 38. 7.

4. The modal use of the abl. of the gerund or gerundive. See (6), p. xiv.

5. Local ablative without preposition. See (1), p. xiv.

6. Ablative of separation without a preposition, **caelo** (16. 6), **finibus** (55. 4).

7. The use of adjectives as nouns especially in oblique cases is frequent in Livy ; **in sicco** (4. 6), **ab coacta** (58. 9).

For the use of the adjective as a noun with a dependent genitive, see **in medio aedium** (57. 9). Cf. also **summa rerum** (36. 6).

8. **ceterum=sed** is common (24. 3).

alius=ceterus (12. 9).

Both these uses are colloquial.

5. The History of the Period

In studying the history of Rome during the period covered by Livy's Book I, i.e. from the foundation of the city (753 B.C.) down to the expulsion of the last of the seven kings, Tarquinius Superbus (569 B.C.), the student cannot do better than read for himself what Mr. H. Last has written in the *Cambridge Ancient History*, Vol. VII, pp. 363-435.

However, an attempt will be made here to give very briefly some of the main points which are made in that work and seem likely to be of interest and help to the student who is reading the first book of Livy's *History*.

Of the foundation legends, Hugh Last (op. cit.) emphasises that they are purely Greek and developed be-

tween the 5th and 1st centuries B.C. the shape in which
they are narrated to us by Livy. He mentions one
difficulty—a chronological one—that as one authority
in the 5th century B.C. made Aeneas the founder of Rome
and Roman tradition knew only of seven kings, this number could hardly be sufficient to bridge the gap between
the Trojan war and the expulsion of Tarquinius Superbus.
Hence arose the necessity to transfer Aeneas and his
descendants to the towns of Lavinium and Longa Alba.

Again, not only are Hercules, Cacus, and Evander
Greek, but also the story of the twins—Romulus and
Remus—exhibits the usual features of Greek legend as
well as the universal theme of the exposed children who
rise to a great position. Romulus is simply an eponym of
Rome, while Remus is the Latin form of Rhomos, an
eponymous name again, known to Greek authors as the
founder of Rome. Hence arose the duplication and the
appearance of the twins, with one or two Italian features
added.

The story of the Rape of the Sabine Women is aetiological, i.e. it is a story invented later to explain an early
custom, practice, or tradition ; in this case we are given
a precedent for the force put upon a bride before she
entered her husband's home. Aetiological also is the
invention of the character Thalassius to explain the cry
' Talassio ', which was raised in Roman marriage proces-
sions.

Of the seven kings of Rome, we have already said on
the authority of scholars that the first, Romulus, cannot

be regarded as an historical figure. On the other hand, we are informed by the same authorities that the stories of the remaining six contain a kernel of fact. A few notes are given below.

To Numa Pompilius (715-673 B.C.), whose name suggests Sabine origin, is attributed the organisation of the priestly colleges and of the religious calendar, and the building of the Regia. Although many of the reforms which are ascribed to him are the result of a long process of religious and cultural development, the general feeling of scholars seems to be that the nucleus of tradition about Numa must be retained, especially so far as it refers to the organisation of the state religion.

Tullus Hostilius (673-642 B.C.) is again regarded as an historical figure, although it has been suggested that his warlike activities (**ferocior quam Romulus**) point to his being a mere duplication of Romulus. His reign is concerned with an invasion by the Albans and ends with the destruction of Alba, two events which can be accepted, although many of the details have to be ignored. For example, it is now believed that the name of the Alban king C. Cluilius is an eponym of the fossa Cluilia, that the combat between the three Horatii and Curiatii is mere invention, that the story of the surviving Horatius is an aetiological attempt to explain the **tigillum sororium** and **provocatio ad populum**. Scholars, however, accept as fact his foundation of the Curia Hostilia.

Ancus Marcius (642-617 B.C.) can also be accepted as an historical figure and not a mere reproduction of Numa.

While he did not build the Aqua Marcia or capture and colonise Ostia, there seems to be no doubt that he enlarged Rome and extended her territory southward to the sea at the mouth of the Tiber, where there were important salt pits.

The three remaining kings in our list, L. Tarquinius Priscus, Servius Tullius, and L. Tarquinius Superbus undoubtedly belong to a phase in the period of Roman history when Etruscan influence was strong.

L. Tarquinius Priscus (616-579 B.C.) and L. Tarquinius Superbus (534-510 B.C.) are certainly of Etruscan origin, although it is probable that the family came not from Tarquinii—a mere inference from the similarity of the name, but from Caere. Their arrival in Rome was the political consequence of the extension of Etruscan power and influence southward from Caere to Praeneste which, it is known, took place in the middle of the seventh century.

Although the details in the career of the first Tarquin seem to be duplications of what we are told of the second, there is no genuine reason why we should regard the first bearer of this name as a double of the second. For example, the foundation of the temple of the Capitoline Triad and other public works, and his wars against neighbouring tribes, may well be historical. In any case, tradition shows quite rightly that it was the Tarquins who brought the Etruscan arts to Rome.

The reigns of the two Tarquins are interrupted by that of Servius Tullius (578-535 B.C.), an undoubtedly historical figure, even though it can be argued that his servile birth is a punning explanation of his name, and scholars do not accept the tradition that makes him the son-in-law of his predecessor. What is important is that Servius is of Latin origin and therefore represents a reaction against the Etruscan influence which has been described in the previous paragraphs. His Latin birth is attested by the fact that the Aventine temple of Diana and the treaty with the Latins were both attributed to him. The treaty, preserved on a stele, was still in existence in the Augustan age.

On the other hand, many scholars reject not only the stories of his birth, but also of his building the fortifications of Rome, and his reorganisation of the army and the development of the comitia centuriata. Others, however, maintain that Servius was responsible for the fortification of the city and for constitutional reform, although they are willing to admit that his achievements may have been greatly elaborated by having included within them developments that belonged to the following two centuries.

Finally, the last of our seven kings, Tarquinius Superbus, is shown to have been an historical figure, first by the preservation of a treaty between Rome and Gabii which is ascribed to him, and secondly, and this is much more important, by the strength of tradition.

While the fact that the monarchy came to a sudden end is proved by the detestation in which the title ' rex ' was held in Rome during the subsequent centuries, we are told

by scholars that many details in Tarquin's career have to
be rejected and some of them have obviously been borrowed from the stories of wicked tyrants in Greek litera-
ture.[1] But we need not therefore doubt that Tarquinius
Superbus made himself odious by tyrannical behaviour
and that he was overthrown by a conspiracy of the nobles
under the leadership of L. Junius.

[1] E.g. Herodotus, v. 92, 24 ff. supplies the model for Tarquin's silent
lesson in kingcraft to his son. (Livy I, 54.)

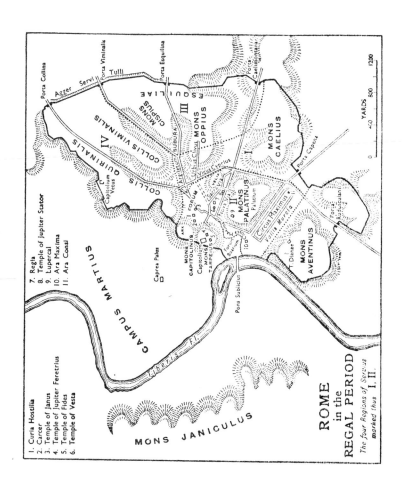

ROME
in the
REGAL PERIOD

The four Regions of Servius
marked thus I, II.

1. Curia Hostilia
2. Carcer
3. Temple of Janus
4. Temple of Jupiter Feretrius
5. Temple of Fides
6. Temple of Vesta

7. Regia
8. Temple of Jupiter Stator
9. Lupercal
10. Ara Maxima
11. Ara Consi

CAMPUS MARTIUS

MONS JANICULUS

Tiberis Fl.

Pons Sublicius

MONS AVENTINUS

MONS CAELIUS

MONS PALATINUS

Palatium

Circus Maximus

Villa Murcia

MONS CAPITOLINUS

MONS TARPEIUS

Capitolium

Capreæ Palus

COLLIS QUIRINALIS

COLLIS VIMINALIS

MONS CISPIUS

MONS OPPIUS

ESQUILIAE

SUBURA

FORUM

ARX

Porta Collina

Porta Viminalis

Porta Esquilina

Porta Capena

Tulli

Agger Servi

YARDS

0   400   800   1200

TITI LIVI AB URBE CONDITA

PRAEFATIO

Facturusne operae pretium sim, si a primordio
urbis res populi Romani perscripserim, nec satis scio,
2 nec, si sciam, dicere ausim, quippe qui cum veterem
tum vulgatam esse rem videam, dum novi semper
scriptores aut in rebus certius aliquid adlaturos se aut 5
scribendi arte rudem vetustatem superaturos credunt.
3 Utcumque erit, iuvabit tamen rerum gestarum
memoriae principis terrarum populi pro virili parte
et ipsum consuluisse, et si in tanta scriptorum turba
mea fama in obscuro sit, nobilitate ac magnitudine 10
4 eorum me, qui nomini officient meo, consoler. Res
est praeterea et immensi operis, ut quae supra sep-
tingentesimum annum repetatur et quae ab exiguis
profecta initiis eo creverit, ut iam magnitudine
laboret sua ; et legentium plerisque haud dubito quin 15
primae origines proximaque originibus minus prae-
bitura voluptatis sint, festinantibus ad haec nova,
quibus iam pridem praevalentis populi vires se ipsae
5 conficiunt. Ego contra hoc quoque laboris praemium petam, ut me a conspectu malorum, quae 20
nostra tot per annos vidit aetas, tantisper certe dum
prisca illa [tota] mente repeto, avertam, omnis expers

curae, quae scribentis animum, etsi non flectere a
vero, sollicitum tamen efficere posset.

6   Quae ante conditam condendamve urbem poeticis 25
magis decora fabulis quam incorruptis rerum gestarum monumentis traduntur, ea nec adfirmare nec
7 refellere in animo est. Datur haec venia antiquitati,
ut miscendo humana divinis primordia urbium
augustiora faciat ; et si cui populo licere oportet con- 30
secrare origines suas et ad deos referre auctores, ea
belli gloria est populo Romano, ut, cum suum con-
ditorisque sui parentem Martem potissimum ferat,
tam et hoc gentes humanae patiantur aequo animo
8 quam imperium patiuntur. Sed haec et his similia 35
utcumque animadversa aut existimata erunt, haud
in magno equidem ponam discrimine : ad illa mihi
9 pro se quisque acriter intendat animum, quae vita,
qui mores fuerint, per quos viros quibusque artibus
domi militiaeque et partum et auctum imperium sit ; 40
labente deinde paulatim disciplina velut desidentes
primo mores sequatur animo, deinde ut magis magis-
que lapsi sint, tum ire coeperint praecipites, donec
ad haec tempora, quibus nec vitia nostra nec remedia
10 pati possumus, perventum est. Hoc illud est praeci- 45
pue in cognitione rerum salubre ac frugiferum,
omnis te exempli documenta in illustri posita monu-
mento intueri ; inde tibi tuaeque rei publicae quod
imitere capias, inde foedum inceptu, foedum exitu,
11 quod vites. Ceterum aut me amor negotii suscepti 50
fallit, aut nulla unquam res publica nec maior nec

sanctior nec bonis exemplis ditior fuit, nec in quam
[civitatem] tam serae avaritia luxuriaque immi-
graverint, nec ubi tantus ac tam diu paupertati ac
parsimoniae honos fuerit.   Adeo quanto rerum 55
12 minus, tanto minus cupiditatis erat. Nuper divitiae
avaritiam et abundantes voluptates desiderium per
luxum atque libidinem pereundi perdendique omnia
invexere. Sed querellae, ne tum quidem gratae
futurae cum forsitan necessariae erunt, ab initio certe 60
13 tantae ordiendae rei absint : cum bonis potius omini-
bus votisque et precationibus deorum dearumque, si,
ut poetis, nobis quoque mos esset, libentius incipere-
mus, ut orsis tantum operis successus prosperos
darent.

TITI LIVI AB URBE CONDITA

LIBER I

Arrival of Aeneas and Antenor in Italy. Founding of Lavinium.

1. Iam primum omnium satis constat Troia capta in ceteros saevitum esse Troianos ; duobus, Aeneae Antenorique, et vetusti iure hospitii et quia pacis reddendaeque Helenae semper auctores fuerunt, 2 omne ius belli Achivos abstinuisse ; casibus deinde 5 variis Antenorem cum multitudine Enetum, qui seditione ex Paphlagonia pulsi et sedes et ducem rege Pylaemene ad Troiam amisso quaerebant, venisse in 3 intimum Hadriatici maris sinum, Euganeisque, qui inter mare Alpesque incolebant, pulsis Enetos Troi- 10 anosque eas tenuisse terras. Et in quem primo egressi sunt locum Troia vocatur, pagoque inde Troiano nomen est ; gens universa Veneti appellati. 4 Aeneam ab simili clade domo profugum, sed ad maiora rerum initia ducentibus fatis, primo in Macedon- 15 iam venisse, inde in Siciliam quaerentem sedes 5 delatum, ab Sicilia classe ad Laurentem agrum tenuisse. Troia et huic loco nomen est. Ibi egressi Troiani, ut quibus ab immenso prope errore nihil praeter arma et naves superesset, cum praedam ex 20 agris agerent, Latinus rex Aboriginesque, qui tum ea

4

tenebant loca, ad arcendam vim advenarum armati
ex urbe atque agris concurrunt.

6   Duplex inde fama est : alii proelio victum Latinum
pacem cum Aenea, deinde adfinitatem iunxisse 25
7 tradunt ; alii, cum instructae acies constitissent,
priusquam signa canerent, processisse Latinum inter
primores ducemque advenarum evocasse ad con-
8 loquium ; percontatum deinde qui mortales essent,
unde aut quo casu profecti domo quidve quaerentes 30
in agrum Laurentinum exissent, postquam audierit
multitudinem Troianos esse, ducem Aeneam filium
Anchisae et Veneris, cremata patria domo profugos,
sedem condendaeque urbi locum quaerere, et nobilitatem admiratum gentis virique et animum vel bello 35
vel paci paratum, dextra data fidem futurae ami-
9 citiae sanxisse. Inde foedus ictum inter duces, inter
exercitus salutationem factam.   Aeneam apud
Latinum fuisse in hospitio ; ibi Latinum apud
penates deos domesticum publico adiunxisse foedus 40
10 filia Aeneae in matrimonium data. Ea res utique
Troianis spem adfirmat tandem stabili certaque sede
finiendi erroris. Oppidum condunt : Aeneas ab
11 nomine uxoris Lavinium appellat. Brevi stirpis
quoque virilis ex novo matrimonio fuit, cui Ascanium 45
parentes dixere nomen.

Aeneas is involved in war with the Rutulians and
Etruscans. His apotheosis.

2. Bello deinde Aborigines Troianique simul petiti.

Turnus rex Rutulorum, cui pacta Lavinia ante adventum Aeneae fuerat, praelatum sibi advenam aegre
patiens, simul Aeneae Latinoque bellum intulerat.
2 Neutra acies laeta ex eo certamine abiit : victi 5
Rutuli ;   victores Aborigines Troianique ducem
3 Latinum amisere.   Inde Turnus Rutulique diffisi
rebus ad florentes opes Etruscorum Mezentiumque
regem eorum confugiunt, qui Caere opulento tum
oppido imperitans, iam inde ab initio minime laetus 10
novae origine urbis, et tum nimio plus quam satis
tutum esset accolis rem Troianam crescere ratus,
4 haud gravatim socia arma Rutulis iunxit.   Aeneas,
adversus tanti belli terrorem ut animos Aboriginum
sibi conciliaret nec sub eodem iure solum sed etiam 15
nomine omnes essent, Latinos utramque gentem
5 appellavit ; nec deinde Aborigines Troianis studio ac
fide erga regem Aeneam cessere.   Fretusque his
animis coalescentium in dies magis duorum populorum Aeneas, quamquam tanta opibus Etruria erat, ut 20
iam non terras solum sed mare etiam per totam Italiae
longitudinem ab Alpibus ad fretum Siculum fama
nominis sui implesset, tamen, cum moenibus bellum
6 propulsare posset, in aciem copias eduxit.   Secundum inde proelium Latinis, Aeneae etiam ultimum 25
operum mortalium fuit.   Situs est, quemcumque eum
dici ius fasque est, super Numicum fluvium :   Iovem
indigetem appellant.

The foundation of Alba Longa and the line of the Alban
kings down to Numitor and Amulius.

3. Nondum maturus imperio Ascanius Aeneae
filius erat ; tamen id imperium ei ad puberem
aetatem incolume mansit : tantisper tutela muliebri
—tanta indoles in Lavinia erat—res Latina et regnum
2 avitum paternumque puero stetit. Haud ambigam 5
—quis enim rem tam veterem pro certo adfirmet?—
hicine fuerit Ascanius an maior quam hic, Creusa
matre Ilio incolumi natus comesque inde paternae
fugae, quem Iulum eundem Iulia gens auctorem
3 nominis sui nuncupat. Is Ascanius, ubicumque et 10
quacumque matre genitus—certe natum Aenea constat—abundante Lavinii multitudine florentem iam,
ut tum res erant, atque opulentam urbem matri seu
novercae relinquit, novam ipse aliam sub Albano
monte condidit, quae ab situ porrectae in dorso urbis 15
4 Longa Alba appellata. Inter Lavinium et Albam
Longam coloniam deductam triginta ferme inter-
fuere anni. Tantum tamen opes creverant maxime
fusis Etruscis, ut ne morte quidem Aeneae nec deinde
inter muliebrem tutelam rudimentumque primum 20
5 puerilis regni movere arma aut Mezentius Etruscique
aut ulli alii accolae ausi sint. Pax ita convenerat ut
Etruscis Latinisque fluvius Albula, quem nunc
Tiberim vocant, finis esset.
6 Silvius deinde regnat, Ascani filius, casu quodam 25
7 in silvis natus. Is Aeneam Silvium creat ; is deinde
Latinum Silvium. Ab eo coloniae aliquot deductae,

Prisci Latini appellati. Mansit Silviis postea omni-
8 bus cognomen, qui Albae regnarunt. Latino Alba
ortus, Alba Atys, Atye Capys, Capye Capetus, Capeto 30
Tiberinus, qui in traiectu Albulae amnis submersus
9 celebre ad posteros nomen flumini dedit. Agrippa
inde Tiberini filius, post Agrippam Romulus Silvius
a patre accepto imperio regnat. Aventino fulmine
ipse ictus regnum per manus tradidit. Is sepultus in 35
eo colle, qui nunc pars Romanae est urbis, cognomen
10 colli fecit. Proca deinde regnat. Is Numitorem
atque Amulium procreat; Numitori, qui stirpis
maximus erat, regnum vetustum Silviae gentis legat.
Plus tamen vis potuit quam voluntas patris aut 40
verecundia aetatis. Pulso fratre Amulius regnat.
11 Addit sceleri scelus: stirpem fratris virilem interemit,
fratris filiae Reae Silviae per speciem honoris, cum
Vestalem eam legisset, perpetua virginitate spem
partus adimit.   45

The story of Romulus, Remus, and the she-wolf

4. Sed debebatur, ut opinor, fatis tantae origo
urbis maximique secundum deorum opes imperii
2 principium. Vi compressa Vestalis cum geminum
partum edidisset, seu ita rata seu quia deus auctor
culpae honestior erat, Martem incertae stirpis patrem 5
3 nuncupat. Sed nec di nec homines aut ipsam aut
stirpem a crudelitate regia vindicant : sacerdos
vincta in custodiam datur, pueros in profluentem
aquam mitti iubet. Forte quadam divinitus super

ripas Tiberis effusus lenibus stagnis nec adiri usquam 10
ad iusti cursum poterat amnis et posse quamvis
languida mergi aqua infantes spem ferentibus dabat.
5 Ita velut defuncti regis imperio in proxima alluvie,
ubi nunc ficus Ruminalis est—Romularem vocatam
6 ferunt—pueros exponunt.   Vastae tum in his locis 15
solitudines erant.   Tenet fama cum fluitantem
alveum, quo iam expositi erant pueri, tenuis in sicco
aqua destituisset, lupam sitientem ex montibus qui
circa sunt ad puerilem vagitum cursum flexisse : eam
submissas infantibus adeo mitem praebuisse mam- 20
mas ut lingua lambentem pueros magister regii
7 pecoris invenerit—Faustulo fuisse nomen ferunt—
ab eo ad stabula Larentiae uxori educandos datos.
Sunt qui Larentiam vulgato corpore lupam inter
pastores vocatam putent : inde locum fabulae ac 25
8 miraculo datum.   Ita geniti itaque educati, cum
primum adolevit aetas, nec in stabulis nec ad pecora
9 segnes venando peragrare saltus.   Hinc robore corporibus animisque sumpto iam non feras tantum
subsistere, sed in latrones praeda onustos impetus 36
facere, pastoribusque rapta dividere et (cum his)
crescente in dies grege iuvenum) seria ac iocos cele-
brare.

*The festival of Lupercalia.   The arrest of Remus leads to the
   discovery of the twins' parentage and to the slaying of
   Amulius.*

5. Iam tum in Palatio [monte] Lupercal hoc fuisse

ludicrum ferunt, et a Pallanteo, urbe Arcadica, Pal-
2 lantium, dein Palatium montem appellatum : ibi
Evandrum, qui ex eo genere Arcadum multis ante
tempestatibus tenuerit loca, sollemne adlatum ex 5
Arcadia instituisse, ut nudi iuvenes Lycaeum Pana
venerantes per lusum atque lasciviam currerent,
3 quem Romani deinde vocarunt Inuum. Huic deditis
ludicro, cum sollemne notum esset, insidiatos ob iram
praedae amissae latrones, cum Romulus vi se defend- 10
isset, Remum cepisse, captum regi Amulio tradidisse
4 ultro accusantes. Crimini maxime dabant in
Numitoris agros ab iis impetum fieri ; inde eos
collecta iuvenum manu hostilem in modum praedas
agere. Sic Numitori ad supplicium Remus deditur. 15
5 Iam inde ab initio Faustulo spes fuerat regiam stirpem apud se educari ; nam et expositos iussu regis
infantes sciebat et tempus quo ipse eos sustulisset
ad id ipsum congruere ; sed rem immaturam nisi aut
per occasionem aut per necessitatem aperiri noluerat. 20
6 Necessitas prior venit. Ita metu subactus Romulo
rem aperit. Forte et Numitori, cum in custodia
Remum haberet audissetque geminos esse fratres,
comparando et aetatem eorum et ipsam minime servilem indolem, tetigerat animum memoria nepotum ; 25
sciscitandoque eodem pervenit ut haud procul esset
quin Remum agnosceret. Ita undique regi dolus
7 nectitur. Romulus non cum globo iuvenum—nec
enim erat ad vim apertam par—sed aliis alio itinere
iussis certo tempore ad regiam venire pastoribus ad 30

regem impetum facit ; et a domo Numitoris alia
comparata manu adiuvat Remus. Ita regem obtruncat.

*Numitor is restored to his throne and Romulus and Remus
decide to found a new city.*

6. Numitor inter primum tumultum hostes invas-
isse urbem atque adortos regiam dictitans, cum
pubem Albanam in arcem praesidio armisque ob-
tinendam avocasset, postquam iuvenes perpetrata
caede pergere ad se gratulantes vidit, extemplo ad- 5
vocato concilio scelera in se fratris, originem nepotum,
ut geniti, ut educati, ut cogniti essent, caedem
deinceps tyranni seque eius auctorem ostendit.
2 Iuvenes per mediam contionem agmine ingressi cum
avum regem salutassent, secuta ex omni multitudine 10
consentiens vox ratum nomen imperiumque regi
efficit.
3   Ita Numitori Albana re permissa Romulum Re-
mumque cupido cepit in iis locis ubi expositi ubique
educati erant urbis condendae. Et supererat multi- 15
tudo Albanorum Latinorumque ; ad id pastores
quoque accesserant, qui omnes facile spem facerent
parvam Albam, parvum Lavinium prae ea urbe quae
4 conderetur fore. Intervenit deinde his cogitationibus
avitum malum, regni cupido, atque inde foedum 20
certamen coortum a satis miti principio. Quoniam
gemini essent nec aetatis verecundia discrimen facere
posset, ut di quorum tutelae ea loca essent auguriis

legerent qui nomen novae urbi daret, qui conditam
imperio regeret, Palatium Romulus, Remus Aven- 25
tinum ad inaugurandum templa capiunt.)

*Romulus slays Remus, and founds Rome. The story of
Hercules and Cacus, the arrival of Evander, and the institution of the cult of Hercules.*

7. Priori Remo augurium venisse fertur, sex vul-
tures ;(iamque nuntiato augurio cum duplex numerus
Romulo se ostendisset,(utrumque regem sua multitudo consalutaverat) : (tempore illi praecepto,) at hi
2 numero avium regnum trahebant. Inde cum alter- 5
catione congressi (certamine irarum) ad caedem
vertuntur ; ibi in turba ictus Remus cecidit. Vul-
gatior fama est ludibrio fratris Remum novos
transiluisse muros ; inde ab irato Romulo(cum verbis
quoque increpitans adiecisset, " Sic deinde quicum- 10
3 que alius transiliet moenia mea)," interfectum. Ita
solus potitus imperio Romulus ; condita urbs conditoris nomine appellata.

Palatium primum, in quo ipse erat educatus,
muniit. Sacra dis aliis Albano ritu, Graeco Herculi, 15
4 ut ab Evandro instituta erant, facit. Herculem in ea
loca Geryone interempto boves mira specie abegisse
memorant, ac prope Tiberim fluvium, qua prae se
armentum agens nando traiecerat, loco herbido, ut
quiete et pabulo laeto reficeret boves et ipsum fessum 20
5 via procubuisse. Ibi cum eum cibo vinoque grava-
tum sopor oppressisset, pastor accola eius loci, nomine

Cacus, ferox viribus, captus pulchritudine boum
cum avertere eam praedam vellet, quia si agendo
armentum in speluncam compulisset ipsa vestigia 25
quaerentem dominum eo deductura erant, aversos
boves eximium quemque pulchritudine caudis in
6 speluncam traxit. Hercules ad primam auroram
somno excitus cum gregem perlustrasset oculis et
partem abesse numero sensisset, pergit ad proximam 30
speluncam, si forte eo vestigia ferrent. Quae ubi
omnia foras versa vidit nec in partem aliam ferre,
confusus atque incertus animi ex loco infesto agere
7 porro armentum occepit. Inde cum actae boves
quaedam ad desiderium, ut fit, relictarum mugissent, 35
reddita inclusarum ex spelunca boum vox Herculem
convertit. Quem cum vadentem ad speluncam
Cacus vi prohibere conatus esset, ictus clava fidem
pastorum nequiquam invocans [morte] occubuit.
8 Evander tum ea, profugus ex Peloponneso, auctori- 40
tate magis quam imperio regebat loca, venerabilis vir
miraculo litterarum, rei novae inter rudes artium
homines, venerabilior divinitate credita Carmentae
matris, quam fatiloquam ante Sibyllae in Italiam
9 adventum miratae eae gentes fuerant. Is tum 45
Evander concursu pastorum trepidantium circa
advenam manifestae reum caedis excitus postquam
facinus facinorisque causam audivit, habitum for-
mamque viri aliquantum ampliorem augustioremque
10 humana intuens, rogitat qui vir esset. Ubi nomen 50
patremque ac patriam accepit, ' Iove nate, Hercules,

salve,' inquit. ' Te mihi mater, veridica interpres
deum. aucturum caelestium numerum cecinit tibique
aram hic dicatum iri quam opulentissima olim in
11 terris gens maximam vocet tuoque ritu colat.' Dex- 55
tra Hercules data accipere se omen impleturumque
12 fata ara condita ac dicata ait. Ibi tum primum bove
eximia capta de grege sacrum Herculi, adhibitis ad
ministerium dapemque Potitiis ac Pinariis, quae tum
familiae maxime inclitae ea loca incolebant, factum. 60
13 Forte ita evenit ut Potitii ad tempus praesto essent
iisque exta apponerentur, Pinarii extis adesis ad
ceteram venirent dapem. Inde institutum mansit
donec Pinarium genus fuit, ne extis eorum sollem-
14 nium vescerentur. Potitii ab Evandro edocti antis- 65
tites sacri eius per multas aetates fuerunt, donec
tradito servis publicis sollemni familiae ministerio
15 genus omne Potitiorum interiit. Haec tum sacra
Romulus una ex omnibus peregrina suscepit, iam tum
immortalitatis virtute partae ad quam eum sua fata 70
ducebant fautor.

*Romulus gives his people a code of law and himself the in-
signia of authority. He then opens a refuge and appoints
a hundred senators.*

8. Rebus divinis rite perpetratis vocataque ad
concilium multitudine, quae coalescere in populi
unius corpus nulla re praeter quam legibus poterat,
2 iura dedit ; quae ita sancta generi hominum agresti
fore ratus, si se ipse venerabilem insignibus imperii 5

facisset, cum cetero habitu se augustiorem, tum
3 maxime lictoribus duodecim sumptis fecit. Alii ab
numero avium quae augurio regnum portenderant
eum secutum numerum putant: me haud paenitet
eorum sententiae esse, quibus et apparitores hoc 10
genus ab Etruscis finitimis, unde sella curulis, unde
toga praetexta sumpta est, numerum quoque ipsum
ductum placet, et ita habuisse Etruscos quod ex
duodecim populis communiter creato rege singulos
singuli populi lictores dederint.   15
4 Crescebat interim urbs munitionibus alia atque alia
appetendo loca, cum in spem magis futurae multitudinis quam ad id quod tum hominum erat
5 munirent. Deinde ne vana urbis magnitudo esset,
adiciendae multitudinis causa vetere consilio con- 20
dentium urbes, qui obscuram atque humilem con-
ciendo ad se multitudinem natam e terra sibi prolem
ementiebantur, locum qui nunc saeptus escendenti-
6 bus inter duos lucos est asylum aperit. Eo ex
finitimis populis turba omnis sine discrimine, liber 25
an servus esset, avida novarum rerum perfugit,
idque primum ad coeptam magnitudinem roboris
7 fuit. Cum iam virium haud paeniteret consilium
deinde viribus parat. Centum creat senatores, sive
quia is numerus satis erat, sive quia soli centum erant 30
qui creari patres possent. Patres certe ab honore
patriciique progenies eorum appellati.

The rape of the Sabine women provides
wives for the Romans.

9. Iam res Romana adeo erat valida, ut cuilibet
finitimarum civitatum bello par esset ; sed penuria
mulierum hominis aetatem duratura magnitudo erat,
quippe quibus nec domi spes prolis nec cum finitimis
2 conubia essent. Tum ex consilio patrum Romulus 5
legatos circa vicinas gentes misit qui societatem
3 conubiumque novo populo peterent : urbes quoque
ut cetera, ex infimo nasci ; dein, quas sua virtus ac di
iuvent, magnas opes sibi magnumque nomen facere ;
4 satis scire origini Romanae et deos adfuisse et 10
non defuturam virtutem ; proinde ne gravarentur
homines cum hominibus sanguinem ac genus
5 miscere. Nusquam benigne legatio audita est ;
adeo simul spernebant, simul tantam in medio
crescentem molem sibi ac posteris suis metuebant. 15
Ac plerisque rogitantibus dimissi ecquod feminis
quoque asylum aperuissent : id enim demum compar
6 conubium fore. Aegre id Romana pubes passa et
haud dubie ad vim spectare res coepit. Cui tempus
locumque aptum ut daret Romulus, aegritudinem 20
animi dissimulans, ludos ex industria parat Neptuno
7 equestri sollemnes ; Consualia vocat. Indici deinde
finitimis spectaculum iubet ; quantoque apparatu
tum sciebant aut poterant, concelebrant ut rem
8 claram exspectatamque facerent. Multi mortales 25
convenere, studio etiam videndae novae urbis,
maxime proximi quique, Caeninenses, Crustumini,

9 Antemnates ; iam Sabinorum omnis multitudo cum
liberis ac coniugibus venit. Invitati hospitaliter per
domos cum situm moeniaque et frequentem tectis 30
urbem vidissent, mirantur tam brevi rem Romanam
10 crevisse. Ubi spectaculi tempus venit deditaeque eo
mentes cum oculis erant, tum ex composito orta vis
signoque dato iuventus Romana ad rapiendas virgines
11 discurrit. Magna pars forte in quem quaeque in- 35
ciderat raptae ; quasdam forma excellentes, primoribus patrum destinatas, ex plebe homines quibus
12 datum negotium erat domos deferebant. Unam
ante alias specie ac pulchritudine insignem a
globo Thalassii cuiusdam raptam ferunt multisque 40
sciscitantibus cuinam eam ferrent, identidem ne quis
violaret Thalassio ferri clamitatum ; inde nuptialem
hanc vocem factam.
13 Turbato per metum ludicro maesti parentes vir-
ginum profugiunt, incusantes violati hospitii foedus 45
deumque invocantes cuius ad sollemne ludosque per
14 fas ac fidem decepti venissent. Nec raptis aut spes
de se melior aut indignatio est minor. Sed ipse
Romulus circumibat docebatque patrum id superbia
factum qui conubium finitimis negassent ; illas 50
tamen in matrimonio, in societate fortunarum
omnium civitatisque et quo nihil carius humano
15 generi sit liberum fore ; mollirent modo iras et,
quibus fors corpora dedisset, darent animos ; saepe
ex iniuria postmodum gratiam ortam ; eoque meliori- 55
bus usuras viris quod adnisurus pro se quisque sit ut,

cum suam vicem functus officio sit, parentium etiam
16 patriaeque expleat desiderium. Accedebant blan-
ditiae virorum, factum purgantium cupiditate atque
amore, quae maxime ad muliebre ingenium efficaces 60
preces sunt.

In war against the Caeninenses, Romulus slays their king and
dedicates the Spolia Opima to Jupiter Feretrius.

10. Iam admodum mitigati animi raptis erant ;
At raptarum parentes tum maxime sordida veste
lacrimisque et querellis civitates concitabant. Nec
domi tantum indignationes continebant sed con-
gregabantur undique ad T. Tatium regem Sabinorum, 5
et legationes eo quod maximum Tati nomen in iis
2 regionibus erat conveniebant. Caeninenses Crus-
tuminique et Antemnates erant ad quod eius iniuriae
pars pertinebat. Lente agere his Tatius Sabinique
visi sunt : ipsi inter se tres populi communiter bellum 10
3 parant. Ne Crustumini quidem atque Antemnates
pro ardore iraque Caeninensium satis se impigre
movent ; ita per se ipsum nomen Caeninum in agrum
4 Romanum impetum facit. Sed effuse vastantibus fit
obvius cum exercitu Romulus levique certamine docet 15
vanam sine viribus iram esse. Exercitum fundit
fugatque, fusum persequitur : regem in proelio
obtruncat et spoliat : duce hostium occiso urbem
5 primo impetu capit. Inde exercitu victore reducto,
ipse cum factis vir magnificus tum factorum osten- 20

tator haud minor, spolia ducis hostium caesi suspensa
fabricato ad id apte ferculo gerens in Capitolium
escendit ; ibique ea cum ad quercum pastoribus
sacram deposuisset, simul cum dono designavit
6 templo Iovis fines cognomenque addidit deo : ' Iup- 25
piter Feretri ' inquit, ' haec tibi victor Romulus rex
regia arma fero, templumque his regionibus quas
modo animo metatus sum dedico, sedem opimis
spoliis, quae regibus ducibusque hostium caesis me
7 auctorem sequentes posteri ferent.' Haec templi est 30
origo quod primum omnium Romae sacratum est.
Ita deinde dis visum nec inritam conditoris templi
vocem esse qua laturos eo spolia posteros nuncupavit
nec multitudine compotum eius doni vulgari laudem.
Bina postea inter tot annos, tot bella, opima parta 35
sunt spolia : adeo rara eius fortuna decoris fuit.

*The first Roman colonies at Antemnae and Crustumerium. The
    Sabines capture the Roman citadel through the treachery
    of Tarpeia.*

11. Dum ea ibi Romani gerunt, Antemnatium exercitus per occasionem ac solitudinem hostiliter in fines
Romanos incursionem facit. Raptim et ad hos
2 Romana legio ducta palatos in agris oppressit. Fusi
igitur primo impetu et clamore hostes, oppidum cap- 5
tum ; duplicique victoria ovantem Romulum Hersilia
coniunx precibus raptarum fatigata orat ut parentibus earum det veniam et in civitatem accipiat ; ita
rem coalescere concordia posse. Facile impetratum.

3 Inde contra Crustuminos profectus bellum inferentes. 10
Ibi minus etiam quod alienis cladibus ceciderant
4 animi certaminis fuit. Utroque coloniae missae ;
plures inventi qui propter ubertatem terrae in Crus-
tuminum nomina darent. Et Romam inde frequenter migratum est, a parentibus maxime ac propinquis 15
raptarum.

5   Novissimum ab Sabinis bellum ortum multoque id
maximum fuit ; nihil enim per iram aut cupiditatem
actum est, nec ostenderunt bellum prius quam in-
6 tulerunt. Consilio etiam additus dolus. Sp. Tarpeius 20
Romanae praeerat arci. Huius filiam virginem auro
corrumpit Tatius ut armatos in arcem accipiat ;
aquam forte ea tum sacris extra moenia petitum ierat.
7 Accepti obrutam armis necavere, seu ut vi capta
potius arx videretur seu prodendi exempli causa, ne 25
8 quid usquam fidum proditori esset. Additur fabula,
quod vulgo Sabini aureas armillas magni ponderis
brachio laevo gemmatosque magna specie anulos
habuerint, pepigisse eam quod in sinistris manibus
haberent ; eo scuta illi pro aureis donis congesta. 30
9 Sunt qui eam ex pacto tradendi quod in sinistris
manibus esset derecto arma petisse dicant et
fraude visam agere sua ipsam peremptam mercede.

Romulus, hard-pressed by the Sabines, vows a temple to
Jupiter Stator and victory is vouchsafed to him.

12. Tenuere tamen arcem Sabini ; atque inde
postero die, cum Romanus exercitus instructus quod

inter Palatinum Capitolinumque collem campi est
complesset, non prius descenderunt in aequum quam
ira et cupiditate reciperandae arcis stimulante animos 5
2 in adversum Romani subiere. Principes utrimque
pugnam ciebant, ab Sabinis Mettius Curtius, ab
Romanis Hostius Hostilius. Hic rem Romanam
iniquo loco ad prima signa animo atque audacia
3 sustinebat. Ut Hostius cecidit, confestim Romana 10
inclinatur acies fusaque est. Ad veterem portam
Palati Romulus et ipse turba fugientium actus, arma
4 ad caelum tollens, ' Iuppiter, tuis ' inquit ' iussus
avibus hic in Palatio prima urbi fundamenta ieci.
Arcem iam scelere emptam Sabini habent ; inde huc 15
5 armati superata media valle tendunt ; at tu, pater
deum hominumque, hinc saltem arce hostes ; deme
6 terrorem Romanis fugamque foedam siste. Hic ego
tibi templum Statori Iovi, quod monumentum sit
posteris tua praesenti ope servatam urbem esse, 20
7 voveo.' Haec precatus, veluti sensisset auditas
preces, ' Hinc ' inquit, ' Romani, Iuppiter optimus
maximus resistere atque iterare pugnam iubet.'
Restitere Romani tamquam caelesti voce iussi : ipse
8 ad primores Romulus provolat. Mettius Curtius ab 25
Sabinis princeps ab arce decucurrerat et effusos
egerat Romanos toto quantum foro spatium est.
Nec procul iam a porta Palati erat, clamitans :
' Vicimus perfidos hospites, imbelles hostes : iam
sciunt longe aliud esse virgines rapere, aliud pugnare 30
9 cum viris.' In eum haec gloriantem cum globo

ferocissimorum iuvenum Romulus impetum facit.
Ex equo tum forte Mettius pugnabat : eo pelli facilius
fuit. Pulsum Romani persequuntur ; et alia Romana
10 acies, audacia regis accensa, fundit Sabinos. Mettius 35
in paludem sese strepitu sequentium trepidante equo
coniecit ; averteratque ea res etiam Sabinos tanti
periculo viri. Et ille quidem adnuentibus ac vocanti-
bus suis favore multorum addito animo evadit ;
Romani Sabinique in media convalle duorum mon- 40
tium redintegrant proelium ; sed res Romana erat
superior.

*The Sabine women intervene between the two armies. Origin
of the Quirites, the Thirty Curiae, and the Three Centuriae.*

13. Tum Sabinae mulieres, quarum ex iniuria
bellum ortum erat, crinibus passis scissaque veste,
victo malis muliebri pavore, ausae se inter tela volan-
2 tia inferre, ex transverso impetu facto dirimere
infestas acies, dirimere iras, hinc patres, hinc viros 5
orantes, ne sanguine se nefando soceri generique
respergerent, ne parricidio macularent partus suos,
3 nepotum illi, hi liberum progeniem. ' Si adfinitatis
inter vos, si conubii piget, in nos vertite iras ; nos 10
causa belli, nos vulnerum ac caedium viris ac parentibus sumus ; melius peribimus quam sine alteris
4 vestrum viduae aut orbae vivemus.' Movet res cum
multitudinem tum duces ; silentium et repentina fit
quies ; inde ad foedus faciendum duces prodeunt. 15
Nec pacem modo sed civitatem unam ex duabus faci-

unt. Regnum consociant ; imperium omne con-
5 ferunt Romam. Ita geminata urbe ut Sabinis tamen
aliquid daretur Quirites a Curibus appellati. Monumentum eius pugnae, ubi primum ex profunda 20
emersus palude equus Curtium in vado statuit, Curtium lacum appellarunt.
6 Ex bello tam tristi laeta repente pax cariores
Sabinas viris ac parentibus et ante omnes Romulo
ipsi fecit. Itaque cum populum in curias triginta 25
7 divideret, nomina earum curiis imposuit. Id non
traditur, cum haud dubie aliquanto numerus maior
hoc mulierum fuerit, aetate an dignitatibus suis viror-
umve an sorte lectae sint, quae nomina curiis darent.
8 Eodem tempore et centuriae tres equitum conscriptae 30
sunt. Ramnenses ab Romulo, ab T. Tatio Titienses
appellati ; Lucerum nominis et originis causa incerta
est. Inde non modo commune, sed concors etiam
regnum duobus regibus fuit.

Death of Tatius and war with the Fidenates.

14. Post aliquot annos propinqui regis Tati legatos
Laurentium pulsant ; cumque Laurentes iure gentium agerent, apud Tatium gratia suorum et preces
2 plus poterant. Igitur illorum poenam in se vertit :
nam Lavinii, cum ad sollemne sacrificium eo venisset, 5
3 concursu facto interficitur. Eam rem minus aegre
quam dignum erat tulisse Romulum ferunt, seu ob
infidam societatem regni seu quia haud iniuria caesum
credebat. Itaque bello quidem abstinuit ; ut tamen

expiarentur legatorum iniuriae regisque caedes, 10
foedus inter Romam Laviniumque urbes renovatum
est.

4 Et cum his quidem insperata pax erat : aliud
multo propius atque in ipsis prope portis bellum
ortum. Fidenates nimis vicinas prope se convales- 15
cere opes rati, priusquam tantum roboris esset
quantum futurum apparebat, occupant bellum facere.
Iuventute armata immissa vastatur agri quod inter
5 urbem ac Fidenas est : inde ad laevam versi, quia
dextra Tiberis arcebat, cum magna trepidatione 20
agrestium populantur, tumultusque repens ex agris
6 in urbem inlatus pro nuntio fuit. Excitus Romulus
—neque enim dilationem pati tam vicinum bellum
poterat—exercitum educit, castra a Fidenis mille
7 passuum locat. Ibi modico praesidio relicto, egressus 25
omnibus copiis partem militum locis circa densa
obsita virgulta obscuris subsidere in insidiis iussit :
cum parte maiore atque omni equitatu profectus, id
quod quaerebat, tumultuoso et minaci genere pugnae
adequitando ipsis prope portis hostem excivit. 30
Fugae quoque, quae simulanda erat, eadem equestris
8 pugna causam minus mirabilem dedit. Et cum, velut
inter pugnae fugaeque consilium trepidante equitatu,
pedes quoque referret gradum, plenis repente portis
effusi hostes impulsa Romana acie studio instandi 35
9 sequendique trahuntur ad locum insidiarum. Inde
subito exorti Romani transversam invadunt hostium
aciem : addunt pavorem mota e castris signa eorum

qui in praesidio relicti fuerant.   Ita multiplici terrore
perculsi Fidenates prius paene, quam Romulus qui- 40
que ⟨avehi⟩ cum eo visi erant circumagerent frenis
10 equos, terga vertunt ; multoque effusius, quippe vera
fuga, qui simulantes paulo ante secuti erant oppidum
11 repetebant.   Non tamen eripuere se hosti : haerens
in tergo Romanus, priusquam fores portarum 45
obicerentur, velut agmine uno inrumpit.

*Defeat of the Veientines.   Popularity of Romulus among
his soldiers.*

   15. Belli Fidenatis contagione inritati Veientium
animi et consanguinitate—nam Fidenates quoque
Etrusci fuerunt—et quod ipsa propinquitas loci, si
Romana arma omnibus infesta finitimis essent,
stimulabat.   In fines Romanos excucurrerunt popu- 5
2 labundi magis quam iusti more belli.   Itaque non
castris positis, non exspectato hostium exercitu,
raptam ex agris praedam portantes Veios rediere.
Romanus contra, postquam hostem in agris non
invenit, dimicationi ultimae instructus intentusque 10
3 Tiberim transit.   Quem postquam castra ponere et ad
urbem accessurum Veientes audivere, obviam egressi
ut potius acie decernerent quam inclusi de tectis
4 moenibusque dimicarent.   Ibi viribus nulla arte adiu-
tis, tantum veterani robore exercitus rex Romanus 15
vicit ; persecutusque fusos ad moenia hostes, urbe
valida muris ac situ ipso munita abstinuit, agros
rediens vastat, ulciscendi magis quam praedae

5 studio ; eaque clade haud minus quam adversa
pugna subacti Veientes pacem petitum oratores 20
Romam mittunt. Agri parte multatis in centum
annos indutiae datae.

6 Haec ferme Romulo regnante domi militiaeque
gesta, quorum nihil absonum fidei divinae originis
divinitatisque post mortem creditae fuit, non animus 25
in regno avito reciperando, non condendae urbis con-
7 silium, non bello ac pace firmandae. Ab illo enim
profecto viribus datis tantum valuit ut in quadra-
8 ginta deinde annos tutam pacem haberet. Multitudini tamen gratior fuit quam patribus, longe ante 30
alios acceptissimus militum animis ; trecentosque
armatos ad custodiam corporis, quos Celeres appellavit, non in bello solum sed etiam in pace habuit.

*Mysterious vanishing of Romulus, who is believed by some
to have joined the gods in Heaven.*

16. His immortalibus editis operibus cum ad exercitum recensendum contionem in campo ad Caprae
paludem haberet, subito coorta tempestas cum
magno fragore tonitribusque tam denso regem operuit
nimbo ut conspectum eius contioni abstulerit ; nec 5
2 deinde in terris Romulus fuit. Romana pubes,
sedato tandem pavore, postquam ex tam turbido die
serena et tranquilla lux rediit, ubi vacuam sedem
regiam vidit, etsi satis credebat patribus qui proximi
steterant sublimem raptum procella, tamen velut 10
orbitatis metu icta maestum aliquamdiu silentium

3 obtinuit. Deinde a paucis initio facto, deum deo
natum, regem parentemque urbis Romanae salvere
universi Romulum iubent ; pacem precibus exposcunt, uti volens propitius suam semper sospitet 15
4 progeniem. Fuisse credo tum quoque aliquos qui
discerptum regem patrum manibus taciti arguerent ;
manavit enim haec quoque sed perobscura fama ;
illam alteram admiratio viri et pavor praesens
5 nobilitavit. Et consilio etiam unius hominis addita 20
rei dicitur fides. Namque Proculus Iulius, sollicita
civitate desiderio regis et infensa patribus, gravis, ut
traditur, quamvis magnae rei auctor in contionem
6 prodit. ' Romulus,' inquit, ' Quirites, parens urbis
huius, prima hodierna luce caelo repente delapsus se 25
mihi obvium dedit. Cum perfusus horrore venera-
bundusque adstitissem petens precibus ut contra
7 intueri fas esset, " Abi, nuntia," inquit, " Romanis,
caelestes ita velle ut mea Roma caput orbis terrarum
sit ; proinde rem militarem colant sciantque et ita 30
posteris tradant nullas opes humanas armis Romanis
8 resistere posse." Haec ' inquit ' locutus sublimis
abiit.' Mirum quantum illi viro nuntianti haec fidei
fuerit, quamque desiderium Romuli apud plebem
exercitumque facta fide immortalitatis lenitum sit. 35

The Interregnum.

17. Patrum interim animos certamen regni ac
cupido versabat ; necdum ad singulos, quia nemo
magnopere eminebat in novo populo, pervenerat :

2 factionibus inter ordines certabatur. Oriundi ab
Sabinis, ne quia post Tati mortem ab sua parte non 5
erat regnatum, in societate aequa possessionem imperii amitterent, sui corporis creari regem volebant :
Romani veteres peregrinum regem aspernabantur.
3 In variis voluntatibus regnari tamen omnes volebant,
4 libertatis dulcedine nondum experta. Timor deinde 10
patres incessit ne civitatem sine imperio, exercitum
sine duce, multarum circa civitatium inritatis animis,
vis aliqua externa adoriretur. Et esse igitur aliquod
caput placebat, et nemo alteri concedere in animum
5 inducebat. Ita rem inter se centum patres, decem 15
decuriis factis singulisque in singulas decurias creatis
6 qui summae rerum praeessent consociant. Decem
imperitabant : unus cum insignibus imperii et lictoribus erat : quinque dierum spatio finiebatur imperium
ac per omnes in orbem ibat, annuumque intervallum 20
regni fuit. Id ab re quod nunc quoque tenet nomen
7 interregnum appellatum. Fremere deinde plebs multiplicatam servitutem, centum pro uno dominos
factos ; nec ultra nisi regem et ab ipsis creatum vide-
8 bantur passuri. Cum sensissent ea moveri patres, 25
offerendum ultro rati quod amissuri erant, ita gratiam
ineunt summa potestate populo permissa ut non plus
9 darent iuris quam detinerent. Decreverunt enim ut
cum populus regem iussisset, id sic ratum esset si
patres auctores fierent. Hodie quoque in legibus 30
magistratibusque rogandis usurpatur idem ius, vi
adempta : priusquam populus suffragium ineat, in

incertum comitiorum eventum patres auctores fiunt.
10 Tum interrex contione advocata, ' Quod bonum,
faustum felixque sit ' inquit, ' Quirites, regem create : 35
ita patribus visum est. Patres deinde si dignum qui
secundus ab Romulo numeretur crearitis, auctores
11 fient.' Adeo id gratum plebi fuit ut, ne victi beneficio
viderentur, id modo sciscerent iuberentque ut
senatus decerneret qui Romae regnaret.   40

Numa Pompilius, a Sabine, is elected king.

18. Inclita iustitia religioque ea tempestate Numae
Pompili erat. Curibus Sabinis habitabat, consultissimus vir, ut in illa quisquam esse aetate poterat,
2 omnis divini atque humani iuris. Auctorem doc-
trinae eius, quia non exstat alius, falso Samium 5
Pythagoram edunt, quem Servio Tullio regnante
Romae centum amplius post annos in ultima Italiae
ora circa Metapontum Heracleamque et Crotona
iuvenum aemulantium studia coetus habuisse con-
3 stat. Ex quibus locis, etsi eiusdem aetatis fuisset, 10
quae fama in Sabinos? Aut quo linguae commercio
quemquam ad cupiditatem discendi excivisset?
Quove praesidio unus per tot gentes dissonas sermone
4 moribusque pervenisset? Suopte igitur ingenio
temperatum animum virtutibus fuisse opinor magis 15
instructumque non tam peregrinis artibus quam
disciplina tetrica ac tristi veterum Sabinorum, quo
5 genere nullum quondam incorruptius fuit. Audito
nomine Numae patres Romani, quamquam inclinari

opes ad Sabinos rege inde sumpto videbantur, tamen 20
neque se quisquam nec factionis suae alium nec
denique patrum aut civium quemquam praeferre illi
viro ausi, ad unum omnes Numae Pompilio regnum
6 deferendum decernunt. Accitus, sicut Romulus
augurato urbe condenda regnum adeptus est, de se 25
quoque deos consuli iussit. Inde ab augure, cui
deinde honoris ergo publicum id perpetuumque
sacerdotium fuit, deductus in arcem, in lapide ad
7 meridiem versus consedit. Augur ad laevam eius
capite velato sedem cepit, dextra manu baculum sine 30
nodo aduncum tenens, quem lituum appellarunt.
Inde ubi prospectu in urbem agrumque capto deos
precatus regiones ab oriente ad occasum determin-
avit, dextras ad meridiem partes, laevas ad septen-
8 trionem esse dixit; signum contra, quoad longissime 35
conspectum oculi ferebant, animo finivit ; tum lituo
in laevam manum translato, dextra in caput Numae
9 imposita, ita precatus est : ' Iuppiter pater, si est fas
hunc Numam Pompilium cuius ego caput teneo
regem Romae esse, uti tu signa nobis certa adclarassis 40
10 inter eos fines quos feci.' Tum peregit verbis auspicia
quae mitti vellet. Quibus missis declaratus rex Numa
de templo descendit.

Numa builds a temple to Janus. He claims to be guided
by the goddess Egeria, and reforms the calendar.

19. Qui regno ita potitus urbem novam conditam
vi et armis, iure eam legibusque ac moribus de in-

2 tegro condere parat. Quibus cum inter bella ad-
suescere videret non posse—quippe efferari militia
animos—mitigandum ferocem populum armorum 5
desuetudine ratus, Ianum ad infimum Argiletum
indicem pacis bellique fecit, apertus ut in armis esse
civitatem, clausus pacatos circa omnes populos
3 significaret.—Bis deinde post Numae regnum clausus
fuit, semel T. Manlio consule post Punicum primum 10
perfectum bellum, iterum, quod nostrae aetati di
dederunt ut videremus, post bellum Actiacum ab im-
peratore Caesare Augusto pace terra marique parta.
4 —Clauso eo cum omnium circa finitimorum societate
ac foederibus iunxisset animos, positis externorum 15
periculorum curis, ne luxuriarent otio animi quos
metus hostium disciplinaque militaris continuerat,
omnium primum, rem ad multitudinem imperitam
et illis saeculis rudem efficacissimam, deorum metum
5 iniciendum ratus est. Qui cum descendere ad animos 20
sine aliquo commento miraculi non posset, simulat
sibi cum dea Egeria congressus nocturnos esse ; eius
se monitu quae acceptissima dis essent sacra institu-
6 ere, sacerdotes suos cuique deorum praeficere. Atque
omnium primum ad cursus lunae in duodecim menses 25
discribit annum ; quem quia tricenos dies singulis
mensibus luna non explet desuntque sex dies solido
anno qui solstitiali circumagitur orbe, intercalariis
mensibus interponendis ita dispensavit, ut vicesimo
anno ad metam eandem solis unde orsi essent, plenis 30
7 omnium annorum spatiis dies congruerent. Idem

nefastos dies fastosque fecit quia aliquando nihil
cum populo agi utile futurum erat.

Numa establishes new priesthoods, and the office of
Pontifex Maximus.

20. Tum sacerdotibus creandis animum adiecit,
quamquam ipse plurima sacra obibat, ea maxime
2 quae nunc ad Dialem flaminem pertinent. Sed quia
in civitate bellicosa plures Romuli quam Numae
similes reges putabat fore iturosque ipsos ad bella, ne 5
sacra regiae vicis desererentur, flaminem Iovi adsiduum sacerdotem creavit insignique eum veste et curuli
regia sella adornavit. Huic duos flamines adiecit,
3 Marti unum, alterum Quirino, virginesque Vestae
legit, Alba oriundum sacerdotium et genti conditoris 10
haud alienum. His ut adsiduae templi antistites
essent stipendium de publico statuit ; virginitate
aliisque caerimoniis venerabiles ac sanctas fecit.
4 Salios item duodecim Marti Gradivo legit, tunicaeque
pictae insigne dedit et super tunicam aeneum pectori 15
tegumen ; caelestiaque arma, quae ancilia appellan-
tur, ferre ac per urbem ire canentes carmina cum
5 tripudiis sollemnique saltatu iussit. Pontificem
deinde Numam Marcium, Marci filium, ex patribus
legit eique sacra omnia exscripta exsignataque attri- 20
buit, quibus hostiis, quibus diebus, ad quae templa
sacra fierent, atque unde in eos sumptus pecunia
6 erogaretur. Cetera quoque omnia publica privataque
sacra pontificis scitis subiecit, ut esset quo consultum

plebes veniret, ne quid divini iuris neglegendo patrios 25
7 ritus peregrinosque adsciscendo turbaretur ; nec
caelestes modo caerimonias, sed iusta quoque funebria
placandosque manes ut idem pontifex edoceret,
quaeque prodigia fulminibus aliove quo visu missa
susciperentur atque curarentur. Ad ea elicienda ex 30
mentibus divinis Iovi Elicio aram in Aventino dicavit
deumque consuluit auguriis, quae suscipienda essent.

Effect of Numa's reforms on Rome and her neighbours ;
success of his peaceful policy.

21. Ad haec consultanda procurandaque multitudine omni a vi et armis conversa, et animi aliquid agendo
occupati erant, et deorum adsidua insidens cura, cum
interesse rebus humanis caeleste numen videretur, ea
pietate omnium pectora imbuerat ut fides ac ius iur- 5
andum proximo legum ac poenarum metu civitatem
2 regerent. Et cum ipsi se homines in regis velut unici
exempli mores formarent, tum finitimi etiam populi,
qui antea castra non urbem positam in medio ad
sollicitandam omnium pacem crediderant, in eam 10
verecundiam adducti sunt, ut civitatem totam in
cultum versam deorum violari ducerent nefas.
3 Lucus erat quem medium ex opaco specu fons perenni
rigabat aqua. Quo quia se persaepe Numa sine
arbitris velut ad congressum deae inferebat, Camenis 15
eum lucum sacravit, quod earum ibi concilia cum
4 coniuge sua Egeria essent. Et [soli] Fidei sollemne
instituit. Ad id sacrarium flamines bigis curru arcu-

ato vehi iussit, manuque ad digitos usque involuta
rem divinam facere, significantes fidem tutandam 20
5 sedemque eius etiam in dexteris sacratam esse. Multa
alia sacrificia locaque sacris faciendis quae Argeos
pontifices vocant dedicavit. Omnium tamen maximum eius operum fuit tutela per omne regni tempus
6 haud minor pacis quam regni. Ita duo deinceps 25
reges, alius alia via, ille bello, hic pace, civitatem
auxerunt. Romulus septem et triginta regnavit
annos, Numa tres et quadriginta. Cum valida tum
temperata et belli et pacis artibus erat civitas.

The new king Tullus Hostilius hastens to
pick a quarrel with the Albans.

22. Numae morte ad interregnum res rediit. Inde
Tullum Hostilium, nepotem Hostili, cuius in infima
arce clara pugna adversus Sabinos fuerat, regem
2 populus iussit ; patres auctores facti. Hic non solum
proximo regi dissimilis, sed ferocior etiam quam 5
Romulus fuit. Cum aetas viresque tum avita
quoque gloria animum stimulabat. Senescere igitur
civitatem otio ratus undique materiam excitandi
3 belli quaerebat. Forte evenit ut agrestes Romani ex
Albano agro, Albani ex Romano praedas in vicem 10
4 agerent. Imperitabat tum Gaius Cluilius Albae.
Utrimque legati fere sub idem tempus ad res repeten-
das missi. Tullus praeceperat suis ne quid prius
quam mandata agerent ; satis sciebat negaturum
5 Albanum : ita pie bellum indici posse. Ab Albanis 15

socordius res acta ; excepti hospitio ab Tullo blande
ac benigne, comiter regis convivium celebrant.
Tantisper Romani et res repetiverant priores et
neganti Albano bellum in tricesimum diem indix-
6 erant. Haec renuntiant Tullo. Tum legatis Tullus ₂₀
dicendi potestatem quid petentes venerint facit. Illi
omnium ignari primum purgando terunt tempus : se
invitos quicquam quod minus placeat Tullo dicturos,
sed imperio subigi ; res repetitum se venisse ; ni
7 reddantur bellum indicere iussos. Ad haec Tullus ₂₅
' Nuntiate ' inquit ' regi vestro regem Romanum deos
facere testes, uter prius populus res repetentes legatos
aspernatus dimiserit, ut in eum omnes expetant
huiusce clades belli.'

*Death of Cluilius. His successor as Alban
leader confers with Tullus.*

23. Haec nuntiant domum Albani. Et bellum
utrimque summa ope parabatur, civili simillimum
bello, prope inter parentes natosque, Troianam
utramque prolem, cum Lavinium ab Troia, ab
Lavinio Alba, ab Albanorum stirpe regum oriundi ₅
2 Romani essent. Eventus tamen belli minus misera-
bilem dimicationem fecit, quod nec acie certatum est
et tectis modo dirutis alterius urbis duo populi in
3 unum confusi sunt. Albani priores ingenti exercitu
in agrum Romanum impetum fecere. Castra ab ₁₀
urbe haud plus quinque milia passuum locant, fossa
circumdant : fossa Cluilia ab nomine ducis per aliquot

saecula appellata est, donec cum re nomen quoque
4 vetustate abolevit. In his castris Cluilius Albanus
rex moritur ; dictatorem Albani Mettium Fufetium 15
creant. Interim Tullus ferox praecipue morte regis,
magnumque deorum numen ab ipso capite orsum in
omne nomen Albanum expetiturum poenas ob bellum
impium dictitans, nocte praeteritis hostium castris,
5 infesto exercitu in agrum Albanum pergit. Ea res 20
ab stativis excivit Mettium. Ducit quam proxime
ad hostem potest ; inde legatum praemissum nun-
tiare Tullo iubet, priusquam dimicent, opus esse con-
loquio : si secum congressus sit, satis scire ea se ad-
laturum, quae nihilo minus ad rem Romanam quam 25
6 ad Albanam pertineant. Haud aspernatus Tullus,
tamen si vana adferantur, in aciem educit. Exeunt
contra et Albani. Postquam instructi utrimque sta-
bant, cum paucis procerum in medium duces pro-
7 cedunt. Ibi infit Albanus : ' Iniurias et non redditas 30
res, ex foedere quae repetitae sint, et ego regem
nostrum Cluilium causam huiusce esse belli audisse
videor, nec te dubito, Tulle, eadem prae te ferre. Sed
si vera potius quam dictu speciosa dicenda sunt,
cupido imperii duos cognatos vicinosque populos ad 35
8 arma stimulat. Neque, recte an perperam, interpretor : fuerit ista eius deliberatio, qui bellum
suscepit. Me Albani gerendo bello ducem creavere.
Illud te, Tulle, monitum velim : Etrusca res quanta
circa nos teque maxime sit, quo propior es [Volscis] 40
hoc magis scis. Multum illi terra, plurimum mari

9 pollent. Memor esto, iam cum signum pugnae dabis, has duas acies spectaculo fore, ut fessos confectosque simul victorem ac victum adgrediantur. Itaque si nos di amant, quoniam non contenti liber- 45 tate certa in dubiam imperii servitiique aleam imus, ineamus aliquam viam qua utri utris imperent, sine magna clade, sine multo sanguine utriusque populi 10 decerni possit.' Haud displicet res Tullo, quamquam cum indole animi tum spe victoriae ferocior erat. 50 Quaerentibus utrimque ratio initur, cui et fortuna ipsa praebuit materiam.

The war is to be decided by a combat between the Horatii and the Curiatii.

24. Forte in duobus tum exercitibus erant trigemini fratres nec aetate nec viribus dispares. Horatios Curiatiosque fuisse satis constat, nec ferme res antiqua alia est nobilior ; tamen in re tam clara nominum error manet, utrius populi Horatii, utrius Curiatii 5 fuerint. Auctores utroque trahunt : plures tamen invenio qui Romanos Horatios vocent ; hos ut sequar 2 inclinat animus. Cum trigeminis agunt reges ut pro sua quisque patria dimicent ferro : ibi imperium fore unde victoria fuerit. Nihil recusatur ; tempus et 10 3 locus convenit. Priusquam dimicarent, foedus ictum inter Romanos et Albanos est his legibus, ut, cuiusque populi cives eo certamine vicissent, is alteri populo cum bona pace imperitaret. Foedera alia 4 aliis legibus, ceterum eodem modo omnia fiunt. Tum 15

ita factum accepimus, nec ullius vetustior foederis
memoria est. Fetialis regem Tullum ita rogavit :
' Iubesne me, rex, cum patre patrato populi Albani
foedus ferire? ' Iubente rege, ' Sagmina ' inquit ' te,
5 rex, posco.' Rex ait ' Pura tollito.' Fetialis ex arce 20
graminis herbam puram attulit. Postea regem ita
rogavit : ' Rex, facisne me tu regium nuntium
populi Romani Quiritium, vasa comitesque meos? '
Rex respondit : ' Quod sine fraude mea populique
6 Romani Quiritium fiat, facio.' Fetialis erat M. 25
Valerius. Is patrem patratum Sp. Fusium fecit,
verbena caput capillosque tangens. Pater patratus
ad ius iurandum patrandum, id est sanciendum fit
foedus ; multisque id verbis, quae longo effata car-
mine non operae est referre, peragit. Legibus deinde 30
7 recitatis, ' Audi,' inquit ' Iuppiter ; audi, pater
patrate populi Albani ; audi tu, populus Albanus.
Ut illa palam prima postrema ex illis tabulis cerave
recitata sunt sine dolo malo, utique ea hic hodie
rectissime intellecta sunt, illis legibus populus 35
8 Romanus prior non deficiet. Si prior defexit publico consilio dolo malo, tum tu ille Diespiter populum
Romanum sic ferito, ut ego hunc porcum hic hodie
feriam, tantoque magis ferito, quanto magis potes
9 pollesque.' Id ubi dixit, porcum saxo silice percus- 40
sit. Sua item carmina Albani suumque ius iurandum
per suum dictatorem suosque sacerdotes peregerunt.

The combat and its results.

25. Foedere icto trigemini, sicut convenerat, arma capiunt. Cum sui utrosque adhortarentur, deos patrios, patriam ac parentes, quidquid civium domi, quidquid in exercitu sit, illorum tunc arma, illorum intueri manus, feroces et suopte ingenio et pleni 5 adhortantium vocibus in medium inter duas acies 2 procedunt. Consederant utrimque pro castris duo exercitus periculi magis praesentis quam curae expertes : quippe imperium agebatur in tam paucorum virtute atque fortuna positum. Itaque ergo erecti 10 suspensique in minime gratum spectaculum animo 3 incenduntur. Datur signum infestisque armis velut acies terni iuvenes magnorum exercituum animos gerentes concurrunt. Nec his nec illis periculum suum, publicum imperium servitiumque obversatur animo 15 futuraque ea deinde patriae fortuna, quam ipsi 4 fecissent. Ut primo statim concursu increpuere arma micantesque fulsere gladii, horror ingens spectantes perstringit, et neutro inclinata spe torpebat vox 5 spiritusque. Consertis deinde manibus cum iam non 20 motus tantum corporum agitatioque anceps telorum armorumque sed vulnera quoque et sanguis spectaculo essent, duo Romani super alium alius, vulneratis 6 tribus Albanis, exspirantes corruerunt. Ad quorum casum cum conclamasset gaudio Albanus exercitus, 25 Romanas legiones iam spes tota, nondum tamen cura deseruerat, exanimes vice unius quem tres Curiatii

7 circumsteterant. Forte is integer fuit, ut universis
solus nequaquam par, sic adversus singulos ferox.
Ergo ut segregaret pugnam eorum capessit fugam, 30
ita ratus secuturos ut quemque vulnere adfectum
8 corpus sineret. Iam aliquantum spatii ex eo loco ubi
pugnatum est aufugerat, cum respiciens videt magnis
intervallis sequentes, unum haud procul ab sese
9 abesse. In eum magno impetu rediit ; et dum Al- 35
banus exercitus inclamat Curiatiis ut opem ferant
fratri, iam Horatius, caeso hoste victor, secundam
pugnam petebat. Tunc clamore, qualis ex insperato
faventium solet, Romani adiuvant militem suum ; et
10 ille defungi proelio festinat. Prius itaque quam alter, 40
qui nec procul aberat, consequi posset, et alterum
11 Curiatium conficit. Iamque aequato Marte singuli
supererant, sed nec spe nec viribus pares. Alterum
intactum ferro corpus et geminata victoria ferocem
in certamen tertium dabat ; alter, fessum vulnere, 45
fessum cursu trahens corpus victusque fratrum ante
se strage, victori obicitur hosti. Nec illud proelium
fuit. Romanus exsultans ' Duos ' inquit ' fratrum
manibus dedi ; tertium causae belli huiusce, ut
12 Romanus Albano imperet, dabo.' Male sustinenti 50
arma gladium superne iugulo defigit, iacentem
13 spoliat. Romani ovantes ac gratulantes Horatium
accipiunt, eo maiore cum gaudio, quo prope metum
res fuerat. Ad sepulturam inde suorum nequaquam
paribus animis vertuntur, quippe imperio alteri aucti, 55
14 alteri dicionis alienae facti. Sepulcra exstant quo

quisque loco cecidit, duo Romana uno loco propius
Albam, tria Albana Romam versus, sed distantia
locis ut et pugnatum est.

*Horatius slays his sister. He is condemned, but later
acquitted.*

26. Priusquam inde digrederentur, roganti Mettio
ex foedere icto quid imperaret, imperat Tullus uti
iuventutem in armis habeat : usurum se eorum
2 opera si bellum cum Veientibus foret. Ita exercitus
inde domos abducti. Princeps Horatius ibat, tri- 5
gemina spolia prae se gerens. Cui soror virgo, quae
desponsa uni ex Curiatiis fuerat, obvia ante portam
Capenam fuit, cognitoque super umeros fratris palu-
damento sponsi, quod ipsa confecerat, solvit crines et
3 flebiliter nomine sponsum mortuum appellat. Movet 10
feroci iuveni animum comploratio sororis in victoria
sua tantoque gaudio publico. Stricto itaque gladio
4 simul verbis increpans transfigit puellam. ' Abi hinc
cum immaturo amore ad sponsum,' inquit, ' oblita
fratrum mortuorum vivique, oblita patriae. Sic eat 15
5 quaecumque Romana lugebit hostem.' Atrox visum
id facinus patribus plebique : sed recens meritum
facto obstabat. Tamen raptus in ius ad regem. Rex,
ne ipse tam tristis ingratique ad vulgus iudicii ac
secundum iudicium supplicii auctor esset, concilio 20
populi advocato, ' Duumviros ' inquit ' qui Horatio
6 perduellionem iudicent, secundum legem facio.' Lex
horrendi carminis erat : ' Duumviri perduellionem

iudicent : si a duumviris provocarit, provocatione
certato : si vincent, caput obnubito, infelici arbori 25
reste suspendito ; verberato vel intra pomerium vel
7 extra pomerium.' Hac lege duumviri creati, qui se
absolvere non rebantur ea lege ne innoxium quidem
posse, cum condemnassent, tum alter ex eis ' Publi
Horati, tibi perduellionem iudico ' inquit. ' I, lictor 30
8 colliga manus.' Accesserat lictor iniciebatque la-
queum. Tum Horatius auctore Tullo, clemente
legis interprete, ' Provoco ' inquit. Ita provocatione
9 certatum ad populum est. Moti homines sunt in eo
iudicio maxime P. Horatio patre proclamante se 35
filiam iure caesam iudicare : ni ita esset, patrio iure
in filium animadversurum fuisse. Orabat deinde ne
se, quem paulo ante cum egregia stirpe conspexissent,
10 orbum liberis facerent. Inter haec senex iuvenem
amplexus, spolia Curiatiorum fixa eo loco qui nunc 40
Pila Horatia appellatur ostentans, ' Huncine ' aiebat,
' quem modo decoratum ovantemque victoria incedentem vidistis, Quirites, eum sub furca vinctum
inter verbera et cruciatus videre potestis? quod vix
Albanorum oculi tam deforme spectaculum ferre 45
11 possent. I, lictor, colliga manus, quae paulo ante
armatae imperium populo Romano pepererunt. I,
caput obnube liberatoris urbis huius ; arbore infelici
suspende ; verbera vel intra pomerium, modo inter
illa pila et spolia hostium, vel extra pomerium, modo 50
inter sepulcra Curiatiorum ; quo enim ducere hunc
invenem potestis ubi non sua decora eum a tanta

12 foeditate supplicii vindicent? ' Non tulit populus
nec patris lacrimas nec ipsius parem in omni periculo
animum, absolveruntque admiratione magis virtutis 55
quam iure causae. Itaque ut caedes manifesta aliquo
tamen piaculo lueretur, (imperatum) patri ut filium
13 expiaret pecunia publica.) Is quibusdam piacularibus
sacrificiis factis, quae deinde genti Horatiae tradita
sunt, (transmisso per viam tigillo,) capite adoperto 60
velut sub iugum misit iuvenem. Id hodie quoque
publice semper refectum)manet; sororium tigillum
14 vocant. Horatiae sepulcrum, (quo loco corruerat icta,
constructum est saxo quadrato.

War with Veii and Fidenae. The treachery of Mettius
Fufetius.

27. Nec diu pax Albana mansit. Invidia vulgi,
quod tribus militibus fortuna publica commissa
fuerit, vanum ingenium dictatoris corrupit et, quoniam recta consilia haud bene evenerant, pravis re-
2 conciliare popularium animos coepit. Igitur ut prius 5
in bello pacem, sic in pace bellum quaerens, quia suae
civitati animorum plus quam virium cernebat esse,
ad bellum palam atque ex edicto gerundum alios
concitat populos, suis per speciem societatis prodi-
3 tionem reservat. Fidenates, colonia Romana, Veien- 10
tibus sociis consilii adsumptis, pacto transitionis
4 Albanorum ad bellum atque arma incitantur. Cum
Fidenae aperte descissent, Tullus Mettio exercituque
eius ab Alba accito contra hostes ducit. Ubi Anie-

nem transiit, ad confluentes conlocat castra. Inter 15
eum locum et Fidenas Veientium exercitus Tiberim
5 transierat. Hi et in acie prope flumen tenuere dex-
trum cornu ; in sinistro Fidenates propius montes
consistunt. Tullus adversus Veientem hostem derigit
suos, Albanos contra legionem Fidenatium conlocat. 20
Albano non plus animi erat quam fidei. Nec manere
ergo nec transire aperte ausus sensim ad montes
6 succedit. Inde ubi satis subisse sese ratus est, erigit
totam aciem, fluctuansque animo, ut tereret tempus,
ordines explicat. Consilium erat qua fortuna rem 25
7 daret, ea inclinare vires. Miraculo primo esse
Romanis qui proximi steterant, ut nudari latera sua
sociorum digressu senserunt : inde eques citato equo
nuntiat regi abire Albanos. Tullus in re trepida duo-
8 decim vovit Salios fanaque Pallori ac Pavori. Equi- 30
tem clara increpans voce ut hostes exaudirent, redire
in proelium iubet : nihil trepidatione opus esse :
suo iussu circumduci Albanum exercitum, ut Fidenatium nuda terga invadant. Idem imperat ut
9 hastas equites erigerent. Id factum magnae 35
parti peditum Romanorum conspectum abeuntis
Albani exercitus intersaepsit : qui viderant, id quod
ab rege auditum erat rati, eo acrius pugnant. Terror
ad hostes transit : et audiverant clara voce dictum,
et magna pars Fidenatium, ut quibus coloni additi 40
10 Romani essent, Latine sciebant. Itaque, ne subito
ex collibus decursu Albanorum intercluderentur ab
oppido, terga vertunt. Instat Tullus fusoque Fide-

natium cornu in Veientem alieno pavore perculsum
ferocior redit. Nec illi tulere impetum, sed ab effusa 45
11 fuga flumen obiectum ab tergo arcebat. Quo postquam fuga inclinavit, alii arma foede iactantes in
aquam caeci ruebant, alii, dum cunctantur in ripis,
inter fugae pugnaeque consilium oppressi. Non alia
ante Romana pugna atrocior fuit. 50

Mettius, is punished for his treachery.

28. Tum Albanus exercitus, spectator certaminis,
deductus in campos. Mettius Tullo devictos hostes
gratulatur; contra Tullus Mettium benigne adloquitur. Quod bene vertat, castra Albanos Romanis
castris iungere iubet; sacrificium lustrale in diem 5
2 posterum parat. Ubi inluxit, paratis omnibus ut
adsolet, vocari ad contionem utrumque exercitum
iubet. Praecones ab extremo orsi primos excivere
Albanos. Hi novitate etiam rei moti, ut regem
Romanum contionantem audirent, proximi consti- 10
3 tere. Ex composito armata circumdatur Romana
legio; centurionibus datum negotium erat ut sine
4 mora imperia exsequerentur. Tum ita Tullus infit:
' Romani, si unquam ante alias ullo in bello fuit quod
primum dis immortalibus gratias ageretis, deinde 15
vestrae ipsorum virtuti, hesternum id proelium fuit.
Dimicatum est enim non magis cum hostibus quam,
quae dimicatio maior atque periculosior est, cum pro-
5 ditione ac perfidia sociorum. Nam, ne vos falsa
opinio teneat, iniussu meo Albani subiere ad montes, 20

nec imperium illud meum, sed consilium et imperii
simulatio fuit, ut nec vobis, ignorantibus deseri vos,
averteretur a certamine animus, et hostibus, circum-
6 veniri se ab tergo ratis, terror ac fuga iniceretur. Nec
ea culpa quam arguo omnium Albanorum est : ducem 25
secuti sunt, ut et vos, si quo ego inde agmen declinare
voluissem, fecissetis. Mettius ille est ductor itineris
huius, Mettius idem huius machinator belli, Mettius
foederis Romani Albanique ruptor. Audeat deinde
talia alius, nisi in hunc insigne iam documentum 30
7 mortalibus dedero.' Centuriones armati Mettium
circumsistunt ; rex cetera ut orsus erat peragit :
' Quod bonum faustum felixque sit populo Romano
ac mihi vobisque, Albani, populum omnem Albanum
Romam traducere in animo est, civitatem dare plebi, 35
primores in patres legere, unam urbem, unam rem
publicam facere ; ut ex uno quondam in duos populos divisa Albana res est, sic nunc in unum redeat.'
8 Ad haec Albana pubes, inermis ab armatis saepta, in
variis voluntatibus communi tamen metu cogente, 40
9 silentium tenet. Tum Tullus ' Metti Fufeti,' inquit,
' si ipse discere posses fidem ac foedera servare, vivo
tibi ea disciplina a me adhibita esset ; nunc, quoniam
tuum insanabile ingenium est, at tu tuo supplicio
doce humanum genus ea sancta credere quae a te 45
violata sunt. Ut igitur paulo ante animum inter
Fidenatem Romanamque rem ancipitem gessisti, ita
10 iam corpus passim distrahendum dabis.' Exinde
duabus admotis quadrigis, in currus earum disten-

tum inligat Mettium; deinde in diversum iter equi 50
concitati, lacerum in utroque curru corpus, qua in-
11 haeserant vinculis membra, portantes. Avertere
omnes ab tanta foeditate spectaculi oculos. Primum
ultimumque illud supplicium apud Romanos exempli
parum memoris legum humanarum fuit ; in aliis 55
gloriari licet nulli gentium mitiores placuisse poenas.

*Alba Longa is destroyed and the inhabitants
removed to Rome.*

29. Inter haec iam praemissi Albam erant equites
qui multitudinem traducerent Romam. Legiones
2 deinde ductae ad diruendam urbem. Quae ubi
intravere portas, non quidem fuit tumultus ille nec
pavor qualis captarum esse urbium solet, cum 5
effractis portis stratisve ariete muris aut arce vi capta
clamor hostilis et cursus per urbem armatorum
3 omnia ferro flammaque miscet ; sed silentium triste
ac tacita maestitia ita defixit omnium animos, ut
prae metu obliti, quid relinquerent, quid secum 10
ferrent, deficiente consilio rogitantesque alii alios,
nunc in liminibus starent, nunc errabundi domos
4 suas ultimum illud visuri pervagarentur. Ut vero
iam equitum clamor exire iubentium instabat, iam
fragor tectorum quae diruebantur ultimis urbis 15
partibus audiebatur, pulvisque ex distantibus locis
ortus velut nube inducta omnia impleverat, raptim
quibus quisque poterat elatis, cum larem ac penates
tectaque, in quibus natus quisque educatusque esset.

relinquentes exirent, iam continens agmen migran- 20
5 tium impleverat vias, et conspectus aliorum mutua
miseratione integrabat lacrimas, vocesque etiam
miserabiles exaudiebantur, mulierum praecipue. cum
obsessa ab armatis templa augusta praeterirent ac
6 velut captos relinquerent deos. Egressis urbe Albanis 25
Romanus passim publica privataque omnia tecta
adaequat solo, unaque hora quadringentorum annorum opus, quibus Alba steterat, excidio ac ruinis
dedit. Templis tamen deum—ita enim edictum ab
rege fuerat—temperatum est.   30

*Rome increases in size. War is declared
on the Sabines.*

30. Roma interim crescit Albae ruinis. Duplicatur
civium numerus ; Caelius additur urbi mons, et, quo
frequentius habitaretur, eam sedem Tullus regiae
2 capit ibique habitavit.   Principes Albanorum in
patres, ut ea quoque pars rei publicae cresceret, legit, 5
Iulios, Servilios, Quinctios, Geganios, Curiatios,
Cloelios ; templumque ordini ab se aucto curiam
fecit, quae Hostilia usque ad patrum nostrorum
3 aetatem appellata est.   Et, ut omnium ordinum viribus aliquid ex novo populo adiceretur, equitum 10
decem turmas ex Albanis legit, legiones et veteres
eodem supplemento explevit et novas scripsit.
4   Hac fiducia virium Tullus Sabinis bellum indicit,
genti ea tempestate secundum Etruscos opulentis-
simae viris armisque.   Utrimque iniuriae factae ac 15

5 res nequiquam erant repetitae. Tullus ad Feroniae
fanum mercatu frequenti negotiatores Romanos
comprehensos querebatur, Sabini suos prius in lucum
confugisse ac Romae retentos. Hae causae belli
6 ferebantur. Sabini, haud parum memores et suarum 20
virium partem Romae ab Tatio locatam et Romanam
rem nuper etiam adiectione populi Albani auctam,
7 circumspicere et ipsi externa auxilia. Etruria erat
vicina, proximi Etruscorum Veientes. Inde ob
residuas bellorum iras maxime sollicitatis ad defec- 25
tionem animis voluntarios traxere, et apud vagos
quosdam ex inopi plebe etiam merces valuit : publico auxilio nullo adiuti sunt valuitque apud Veientes
—nam de ceteris minus mirum est—pacta cum
8 Romulo indutiarum fides. Cum bellum utrimque 30
summa ope pararent vertique in eo res videretur, utri
prius arma inferrent, occupat Tullus in agrum
9 Sabinum transire. Pugna atrox ad silvam Malitios-
am fuit, ubi et peditum quidem robore, ceterum
equitatu aucto nuper plurimum Romana acies valuit. 35
10 Ab equitibus repente invectis turbati ordines sunt
Sabinorum, nec pugna deinde illis constare nec fuga
explicari sine magna caede potuit.

*A miraculous portent is followed by a plague and a renewed
interest on the part of the people in religious matters.*

31. Devictis Sabinis cum in magna gloria magnis-
que opibus regnum Tulli ac tota res Romana esset,
nuntiatum regi patribusque est in monte Albano

2 lapidibus pluvisse. Quod cum credi vix posset,
missis ad id visendum prodigium in conspectu haud 5
aliter quam cum grandinem venti glomeratam in
3 terras agunt crebri cecidere caelo lapides. Visi etiam
audire vocem ingentem ex summi cacuminis luco, ut
patrio ritu sacra Albani facerent, quae, velut dis
quoque simul cum patria relictis, oblivioni dederant, 10
et aut Romana sacra susceperant aut fortunae, ut fit,
4 obirati cultum reliquerant deum. Romanis quoque
ab eodem prodigio novendiale sacrum publice sus-
ceptum est, seu voce caelesti ex Albano monte missa
—nam id quoque traditur—seu haruspicum monitu ; 15
mansit certe sollemne ut quandoque idem prodigium
nuntiaretur feriae per novem dies agerentur.
5   Haud ita multo post pestilentia laboratum est.
Unde cum pigritia militandi oreretur, nulla tamen ab
armis quies dabatur a bellicoso rege, salubriora etiam 20
credente militiae quam domi iuvenum corpora esse,
donec ipse quoque longinquo morbo est implicitus.
6 Tunc adeo fracti simul cum corpore sunt spiritus illi
feroces ut qui nihil ante ratus esset minus regium quam
sacris dedere animum, repente omnibus magnis 25
parvisque superstitionibus obnoxius degeret religion-
7 ibusque etiam populum impleret. Vulgo iam homines
eum statum rerum qui sub Numa rege fuerat re-
quirentes, unam opem aegris corporibus relictam si
8 pax veniaque ab dis impetrata esset credebant. Ip- 30
sum regem tradunt volventem commentarios Numae,
cum ibi quaedam occulta sollemnia sacrificia Iovi

Elicio facta invenisset, operatum his sacris se abdi-
disse ; sed non rite initum aut curatum id sacrum
esse, nec solum nullam ei oblatam caelestium speciem 35
sed ira Iovis sollicitati prava religione fulmine ictum
cum domo conflagrasse. Tullus magna gloria belli
regnavit annos duos et triginta.

*On the death of Tullus, Ancus Martius becomes king ; he
restores religious observances and introduces certain formalities
in the declaration of war.*

32. Mortuo Tullo res, ut institutum iam inde ab
initio erat, ad patres redierat hique interregem
nominaverant. Quo comitia habente Ancum Marcium regem populus creavit ; patres fuere auctores.
Numae Pompili regis nepos filia ortus Ancus Marcius 5
2 erat. Qui ut regnare coepit et avitae gloriae memor
et quia proximum regnum, cetera egregium, ab una
parte haud satis prosperum fuerat aut neglectis
religionibus aut prave cultis, longe antiquissimum
ratus sacra publica ut ab Numa instituta erant facere, 10
omnia ea ex commentariis regiis pontificem in album
elata proponere in publico iubet. Inde et civibus
otii cupidis et finitimis civitatibus facta spes in avi
3 mores atque instituta regem abiturum. Igitur
Latini cum quibus Tullo regnante ictum foedus 15
erat sustulerant animos, et cum incursionem in
agrum Romanum fecissent repetentibus res Romanis
superbe responsum reddunt, desidem Romanum
regem inter sacella et aras acturum esse regnum rati.

4 Medium erat in Anco ingenium, et Numae et Romuli 20
memor ; et praeterquam quod avi regno magis
necessariam fuisse pacem credebat cum in novo tum
feroci populo, etiam quod illi contigisset otium sine
iniuria id se haud facile habiturum ; temptari
patientiam et temptatam contemni, temporaque esse 25
5 Tullo regi aptiora quam Numae. Ut tamen, quoniam
Numa in pace religiones instituisset, a se bellicae
caerimoniae proderentur, nec gererentur solum sed
etiam indicerentur bella aliquo ritu, ius ab antiqua
gente Aequicolis quod nunc fetiales habent descripsit, 30
6 quo res repetuntur. Legatus ubi ad fines eorum venit
unde res repetuntur, capite velato filo—lanae velamen est—' Audi, Iuppiter ' inquit ; ' audite, fines '—
cuiuscumque gentis sunt, nominat ; ' audiat fas!
Ego sum publicus nuntius populi Romani ; iuste 35
pieque legatus venio, verbisque meis fides sit.'
Peragit deinde postulata. Inde Iovem testem facit :
7 ' Si ego iniuste impieque illos homines illasque res
dedier mihi exposco, tum patriae compotem me num-
8 quam siris esse.' Haec, cum fines suprascandit, haec, 40
quicumque ei primus vir obvius fuerit, haec portam
ingrediens, haec forum ingressus, paucis verbis
carminis concipiendique iuris iurandi mutatis, pera-
9 git. Si non deduntur quos exposcit diebus tribus et
triginta—tot enim sollemnes sunt—peractis bellum 45
ita indicit : ' Audi, Iuppiter, et tu, Iane Quirine,
dique omnes caelestes, vosque terrestres vosque
10 inferni. audite ; ego vos testor populum illum '—

quicumque est, nominat—' iniustum esse neque ius
persolvere ; sed de istis rebus in patria maiores natu 50
consulemus, quo pacto ius nostrum adipiscamur.'
11 Tum nuntius Romam ad consulendum redit. Confestim rex his ferme verbis patres consulebat : ' Quarum rerum litium causarum condixit pater patratus
populi Romani Quiritium patri patrato Priscorum 55
Latinorum hominibusque Priscis Latinis, quas res nec
dederunt [nec solverunt] nec fecerunt,quas res dari fieri
[solvi] oportuit,dic,'inquit ei quem primum sententiam
12 rogabat, ' quid censes? ' Tum ille : ' Puro pioque
duello quaerendas censeo, itaque consentio con- 60
sciscoque.' Inde ordine alii rogabantur ; quandoque
pars maior eorum qui aderant in eandem sententiam
ibat, bellum erat consensum. Fieri solitum ut fetialis
hastam ferratam aut praeustam sanguineam ad fines
eorum ferret et non minus tribus puberibus praesenti- 65
13 bus diceret : ' Quod populi Priscorum Latinorum
hominesque Prisci Latini adversus populum Romanum Quiritium fecerunt deliquerunt, quod populus
Romanus Quiritium bellum cum Priscis Latinis iussit
esse senatusque populi Romani Quiritium censuit 70
consensit conscivit ut bellum cum Priscis Latinis
fieret, ob eam rem ego populusque Romanus populis
Priscorum Latinorum hominibusque Priscis Latinis
14 bellum indico facioque,' Id ubi dixisset, hastam in
fines eorum emittebat. Hoc tum modo ab Latinis 75
repetitae res ac bellum indictum, moremque eum
posteri acceperunt.

Ancus at war with the Latins.   The Aventine and Janiculum
added to the city.

33. Ancus demandata cura sacrorum flaminibus
sacerdotibusque aliis, exercitu novo conscripto profectus, Politorium, urbem Latinorum, vi cepit ;
secutusque morem regum priorum, qui rem Romanam auxerant hostibus in civitatem accipiendis, mul- 5
2 titudinem omnem Romam traduxit.   Et, cum circa
Palatium, sedem veterum Romanorum, Sabini
Capitolium atque arcem, Caelium montem Albani
implessent, Aventinum novae multitudini datum.
Additi eodem haud ita multo post, Tellenis Ficanaque 10
3 captis, novi cives.   Politorium inde rursus bello
repetitum quod vacuum occupaverant Prisci Latini,
eaque causa diruendae urbis eius fuit Romanis ne
4 hostium semper receptaculum esset.   Postremo omni
bello Latino Medulliam compulso, aliquamdiu ibi 15
Marte incerto, varia victoria pugnatum est ; nam et
urbs tuta munitionibus praesidioque firmata valido
erat, et castris in aperto positis aliquoticns exercitus
Latinus comminus cum Romanis signa contulerat.
5 Ad ultimum omnibus copiis conisus Ancus acie 20
primum vincit ; inde ingenti praeda potens Romam
redit, tum quoque multis milibus Latinorum in
civitatem acceptis, quibus, ut iungeretur Palatio
6 Aventinum, ad Murciae datae sedes.   Ianiculum
quoque adiectum, non inopia loci sed ne quando 25
ea arx hostium esset.   Id non muro solum sed
etiam ob commoditatem itineris ponte sublicio,

tum primum in Tiberi facto, coniungi urbi placuit.
7 Quiritium quoque fossa, haud parvum munimentum
8 a planioribus aditu locis, Anci regis opus est. In- 30
genti incremento rebus auctis, cum in tanta multitudine hominum, discrimine recte an perperam facti
confuso, facinora clandestina fierent, carcer ad
terrorem increscentis audaciae media urbe imminens
9 foro aedificatur. Nec urbs tantum hoc rege crevit 35
sed etiam ager finesque. Silva Maesia Veientibus
adempta usque ad mare imperium prolatum et in ore
Tiberis Ostia urbs condita, salinae circa factae,
egregieque rebus bello gestis aedis Iovis Feretri
amplificata.   40

Tarquinius Priscus comes to Rome and becomes very popular.

34. Anco regnante Lucumo, vir impiger ac divitiis
potens, Romam commigravit cupidine maxime ac
spe magni honoris, cuius adipiscendi Tarquiniis—
nam ibi quoque peregrina stirpe oriundus erat—
2 facultas non fuerat. Demarati Corinthii filius erat, 5
qui ob seditiones domo profugus cum Tarquiniis
forte consedisset, uxore ibi ducta duos filios genuit.
Nomina his Lucumo atque Arruns fuerunt. Lucumo
superfuit patri bonorum omnium heres : Arruns
prior quam pater moritur, uxore gravida relicta. 10
3 Nec diu manet superstes filio pater ; qui cum, ig-
norans nurum ventrem ferre, immemor in testando
nepotis decessisset, puero post avi mortem in nullam
sortem bonorum nato ab inopia Egerio inditum

4 nomen. Lucumoni contra, omnium heredi bonorum, 15
cum divitiae iam animos facerent, auxit ducta in
matrimonium Tanaquil, summo loco nata et quae
haud facile iis in quibus nata erat humiliora sineret
5 ea quo innupsisset. Spernentibus Etruscis Lucu-
monem, exsule advena ortum, ferre indignitatem non 20
potuit, oblitaque ingenitae erga patriam caritatis
dummodo virum honoratum videret, consilium
6 migrandi ab Tarquiniis cepit. Roma est ad id
potissima visa : in novo populo, ubi omnis repentina
atque ex virtute nobilitas sit, futurum locum forti ac 25
strenuo viro ; regnasse Tatium Sabinum, arcessitum
in regnum Numam a Curibus, et Ancum Sabina
matre ortum nobilemque una imagine Numae esse.
7 Facile persuadet ut cupido honorum et cui Tarquinii
materna tantum patria esset. Sublatis itaque rebus 30
8 amigrant Romam. Ad Ianiculum forte ventum erat :
ibi ei carpento sedenti cum uxore aquila suspensis
demissa leviter alis pilleum aufert, superque carpentum cum magno clangore volitans rursus velut
ministerio divinitus missa capiti apte reponit ; inde 35
9 sublimis abiit. Accepisse id augurium laeta dicitur
Tanaquil, perita, ut vulgo Etrusci, caelestium
prodigiorum mulier. Excelsa et alta sperare complexa virum iubet : eam alitem ea regione caeli et
eius dei nuntiam venisse ; circa summum culmen 40
hominis auspicium fecisse ; levasse humano super-
positum capiti decus ut divinitus eidem redderet.
10 Has spes cogitationesque secum portantes urbem

ingressi sunt, domicilioque ibi comparato **L.** Tar-
11 quinium Priscum edidere nomen. Romanis con- 45
spicuum eum novitas divitiaeque faciebant ; et ipse
fortunam benigno adloquio, comitate invitandi
beneficiisque quos poterat sibi conciliando adiuvabat,
donec in regiam quoque de eo fama perlata est.
12 Notitiamque eam brevi apud regem liberaliter 50
dextereque obeundo officia in familiaris amicitiae
adduxerat iura, ut publicis pariter ac privatis consiliis bello domique interesset et per omnia expertus
postremo tutor etiam liberis regis testamento
institueretur. 55

*Tarquin becomes king. War with the Latins ; the Circus
Maximus and the Ludi Romani.*

35. Regnavit Ancus annos quattuor et viginti,
cuilibet superiorum regum belli pacisque et artibus et
gloria par. Iam filii prope puberem aetatem erant.
Eo magis Tarquinius instare ut quam primum
2 comitia regi creando fierent. Quibus indictis sub 5
tempus pueros venatum ablegavit. Isque primus et
petisse ambitiose regnum et orationem dicitur
habuisse ad conciliandos plebis animos compositam :
3 se non rem novam petere, quippe qui non primus,
quod quisquam indignari mirarive posset, sed tertius 10
Romae peregrinus regnum adfectet ; et Tatium non
ex peregrino solum, sed etiam ex hoste regem factum,
et Numam ignarum urbis, non petentem, in regnum
4 ultro accitum : se, ex quo sui potens fuerit Romam

cum coniuge ac fortunis omnibus commigrasse ; 15
maiorem partem aetatis eius qua civilibus officiis
fungantur homines, Romae se quam in vetere patria
5 vixisse ; domi militiaeque sub haud paenitendo
magistro, ipso Anco rege, Romana se iura, Romanos
ritus didicisse ; obsequio et observantia in regem 20
cum omnibus, benignitate erga alios cum rege ipso
6 certasse.   Haec eum haud falsa memorantem ingenti
consensu populus Romanus regnare iussit.   Ergo
virum cetera egregium secuta, quam in petendo
habuerat, etiam regnantem ambitio est ; nec minus 25
regni sui firmandi quam augendae rei publicae memor
centum in patres legit, qui deinde minorum gentium
sunt appellati, factio haud dubia regis cuius beneficio
in curiam venerant.
7   Bellum primum cum Latinis gessit et oppidum ibi 30
Apiolas vi cepit ; praedaque inde maiore quam
quanta belli fama fuerat revecta ludos opulentius
8 instructiusque quam priores reges fecit.   Tum
primum circo qui nunc Maximus dicitur designatus
locus est.   Loca divisa patribus equitibusque, ubi 35
spectacula sibi quisque facerent ; fori appellati ;
9 spectavere furcis duodenos ab terra spectacula alta
sustinentibus pedes.   Ludicrum fuit equi pugilesque
ex Etruria maxime acciti.   Sollemnes deinde annui
10 mansere ludi, Romani magnique varie appellati.   Ab 40
eodem rege et circa forum privatis aedificanda divisa
sunt loca ; porticus tabernaeque factae.

For the war with the Sabines, Tarquinius proposes to increase the cavalry but is opposed by the augur Attus Navius.

36. Muro quoque lapideo circumdare urbem parabat, cum Sabinum bellum coeptis intervenit. Adeoque ea subita res fuit ut prius Anienem transirent hostes quam obviam ire ac prohibere exercitus 2 Romanus posset. Itaque trepidatum Romae est ; 5 et primo dubia victoria, magna utrimque caede pugnatum est. Reductis deinde in castra hostium copiis datoque spatio Romanis ad comparandum de integro bellum, Tarquinius equitem maxime suis deesse viribus ratus ad Ramnes, Titienses, Luceres, quas 10 centurias Romulus scripserat, addere alias constituit 3 suoque insignes relinquere nomine. Id quia inaugurato Romulus fecerat, negare Attus Navius, inclitus ea tempestate augur, neque mutari neque 4 novum constitui nisi aves addixissent posse. Ex eo 15 ira regi mota ; eludensque artem ut ferunt, ' Age dum ' inquit, ' divine tu, inaugura fierine possit quod nunc ego mente concipio.' Cum ille augurio rem expertus profecto futuram dixisset, ' Atqui hoc animo agitavi ' inquit, ' te novacula cotem discis- 20 surum. Cape haec et perage, quod aves tuae fieri posse portendunt.' Tum illum haud cunctanter dis-5 cidisse cotem ferunt. Statua Atti capite velato, quo in loco res acta est, in comitio in gradibus ipsis ad laevam curiae fuit ; cotem quoque eodem loco sitam 25 fuisse memorant, ut esset ad posteros miraculi eius 6 monumentum. Auguriis certe sacerdotioque augur-

um tantus honos accessit ut nihil belli domique postea nisi auspicato gereretur, concilia populi, exercitus
vocati, summa rerum, ubi aves non admisissent, 30
7 dirimerentur. Neque tum Tarquinius de equitum
centuriis quicquam mutavit ; numero alterum tantum adiecit, ut mille et octingenti equites in tribus
8 centuriis essent. Posteriores modo sub iisdem
nominibus qui additi erant appellati sunt ; quas 35
nunc, quia geminatae sunt, sex vocant centurias.

The Roman cavalry rout the Sabines.

37. Hac parte copiarum aucta iterum cum Sabinis
confligitur. Sed praeterquam quod viribus creverat
Romanus exercitus, ex occulto etiam additur dolus,
missis qui magnam vim lignorum in Anienis ripa
iacentem, ardentem in flumen conicerent ; ventoque 5
iuvante accensa ligna, et pleraque in ratibus impacta
2 sublicis ⟨que⟩ cum haererent, pontem incendunt. Ea
quoque res in pugna terrorem attulit Sabinis, et fusis
eadem fugam impedit ; multique mortales, cum
hostem effugissent, in flumine ipso periere ; quorum 10
fluitantia arma ad urbem cognita in Tiberi, prius
paene quam nuntiari posset, insignem victoriam
3 fecere. Eo proelio praecipua equitum gloria fuit ;
utrimque ab cornibus positos, cum iam pelleretur
media peditum suorum acies, ita incurrisse ab lateri- 15
bus ferunt, ut non sisterent modo Sabinas legiones
ferociter instantes cedentibus, sed subito in fugam
4 averterent. Montes effuso cursu Sabini petebant, et

pauci tenuere ; maxima pars, ut ante dictum est, ab
5 equitibus in flumen acti sunt.   Tarquinius instandum 20
perterritis ratus, praeda captivisque Romam missis,
spoliis hostium—id votum Vulcano erat—ingenti
cumulo accensis, pergit porro in agrum Sabinum
6 exercitum inducere ; et quamquam male gesta res
erat nec gesturos melius sperare poterant, tamen, 25
quia consulendi res non dabat spatium, ire obviam
Sabini tumultuario milite ; iterumque ibi fusi,
perditis iam prope rebus, pacem petiere.

*The surrender of Collatia is followed by the capture of
Latin towns.*

38. Collatia et quidquid citra Collatiam agri erat
Sabinis ademptum ; Egerius—fratris hic filius erat
regis—Collatiae in praesidio relictus.   Deditosque
Collatinos ita accipio eamque deditionis formulam
2 esse : rex interrogavit : ' Estisne vos legati oratores- 5
que missi a populo Collatino, ut vos populumque
Collatinum dederetis? '—' Sumus.'—' Estne populus Collatinus in sua potestate? '—' Est.'—' Dedit-
isne vos populumque Collatinum, urbem, agros,
aquam, terminos, delubra, utensilia, divina humana- 10
que omnia, in meam populique Romani dicionem? '
—' Dedimus.'—' At ego recipio.'
3   Bello Sabino perfecto Tarquinius triumphans
4 Romam redit.   Inde Priscis Latinis bellum fecit ; ubi
nusquam ad universae rei dimicationem ventum est, 15
ad singula oppida circumferendo arma omne nomen

Latinum domuit. Corniculum, Ficulea vetus, Cameria, Crustumerium, Ameriola, Medullia, Nomentum, haec de Priscis Latinis aut qui ad Latinos
defecerant capta oppida. Pax deinde est facta. 20
5 Maiore inde animo pacis opera inchoata quam
quanta mole gesserat bella, ut non quietior populus
6 domi esset quam militiae fuisset. Nam et muro
lapideo, cuius exordium operis Sabino bello turbatum
erat, urbem qua nondum munierat cingere parat, et 25
infima urbis loca circa forum aliasque interiectas
collibus convalles, quia ex planis locis haud facile
evehebant aquas, cloacis fastigio in Tiberim ductis
7 siccat, et aream ad aedem in Capitolio Iovis, quam
voverat bello Sabino, iam praesagiente animo 30
futuram olim amplitudinem loci, occupat fundamentis.

The birth and early life of Servius Tullius.

39. Eo tempore in regia prodigium visu eventuque
mirabile fuit. Puero dormienti, cui Servio Tullio fuit
nomen, caput arsisse ferunt multorum in conspectu ;
2 plurimo igitur clamore inde ad tantae rei miraculum
orto excitos reges, et, cum quidam familiarium 5
aquam ad restinguendum ferret, ab regina retentum,
sedatoque eam tumultu moveri vetuisse puerum,
donec sua sponte experrectus esset ; mox cum somno
3 et flammam abisse. Tum abducto in secretum viro
Tanaquil ' Viden tu puerum hunc ' inquit, ' quem tam 10
humili cultu educamus? Scire licet hunc lumen

quondam rebus nostris dubiis futurum praesidium-
que regiae adflictae; proinde materiam ingentis
publice privatimque decoris omni indulgentia nostra
4 nutriamus.' Inde puerum liberum loco coeptum 15
haberi erudirique artibus, quibus ingenia ad magnae
fortunae cultum excitantur. Evenit facile quod dis
cordi esset; iuvenis evasit vere indolis regiae, nec,
cum quaereretur gener Tarquinio, quisquam Romanae iuventutis ulla arte conferri potuit, filiamque 20
5 ei suam rex despondit. Hic quacumque de causa
tantus illi honos habitus credere prohibet serva
natum eum parvumque ipsum servisse. Eorum
magis sententiae sum qui Corniculo capto Ser. Tulli,
qui princeps in illa urbe fuerat, gravidam viro occiso 25
uxorem, cum inter reliquas captivas cognita esset, ob
unicam nobilitatem ab regina Romana prohibitam
ferunt servitio partum Romae edidisse Prisci Tar-
6 quini ⟨in⟩ domo; inde tanto beneficio et inter
mulieres familiaritatem auctam, et puerum, ut in 30
domo a parvo eductum, in caritate atque honore
fuisse ; fortunam matris, quod capta patria in hostium manus venerit, ut serva natus crederetur fecisse.

Tarquinius is assassinated at the instigation
of the sons of Ancus.

40. Duodequadragesimo ferme anno ex quo regnare coeperat Tarquinius, non apud regem modo sed
apud patres plebemque longe maximo honore Ser.
2 Tullius erat. Tum Anci filii duo, etsi antea semper

pro indignissimo habuerant se patrio regno tutoris 5
fraude pulsos, regnare Romae advenam non modo
vicinae sed ne Italicae quidem stirpis, tum impensius
iis indignitas crescere, si ne ab Tarquinio quidem ad
3 se rediret regnum, sed praeceps inde porro ad servitia
caderet, ut in eadem civitate post centesimum fere 10
annum quam Romulus, deo prognatus deus ipse,
tenuerit regnum donec in terris fuerit, id servus serva
natus possideat. Cum commune Romani nominis,
tum praecipue id domus suae dedecus fore, si Anci
regis virili stirpe salva non modo advenis sed servis 15
4 etiam regnum Romae pateret. Ferro igitur eam
arcere contumeliam statuunt ; sed et iniuriae dolor
in Tarquinium ipsum magis quam in Servium eos
stimulabat, et, quia gravior ultor caedis, si superesset, rex futurus erat quam privatus ; tum Servio 20
occiso, quemcumque alium generum delegisset,
eundem regni heredem facturus videbatur ;   ob haec
5 ipsi regi insidiae parantur. Ex pastoribus duo
ferocissimi delecti ad facinus, quibus consueti erant
uterque agrestibus ferramentis, in vestibulo regiae 25
quam potuere tumultuosissime specie rixae in se
omnes apparitores regios convertunt ; inde, cum
ambo regem appellarent clamorque eorum penitus in
6 regiam pervenisset, vocati ad regem pergunt. Primo
uterque vociferari et certatim alter alteri obstrepere ; 30
coerciti ab lictore et iussi in vicem dicere tandem
obloqui desistunt ; unus rem ex composito orditur.
7 Cum intentus in eum se rex totus averteret, alter

elatam securim in caput deiecit, relictoque in vulnere
telo ambo se foras eiciunt. 35

Tanaquil secures the throne for Servius.

41. Tarquinium moribundum cum qui circa erant
excepissent, illos fugientes lictores comprehendunt.
Clamor inde concursusque populi, mirantium quid rei
esset. Tanaquil inter tumultum claudi regiam iubet,
arbitros eiecit. Simul, quae curando vulneri opus 5
sunt, tamquam spes subesset, sedulo comparat, simul,
2 si destituat spes, alia praesidia molitur. Servio
propere accito cum paene exsanguem virum ostendisset, dextram tenens orat ne inultam mortem soceri,
3 ne socrum inimicis ludibrio esse sinat. 'Tuum est' 10
inquit, 'Servi, si vir es, regnum, non eorum qui
alienis manibus pessinum facinus fecere. Erige te
deosque duces sequere, qui clarum hoc fore caput
divino quondam circumfuso igni portenderunt.
Nunc te illa caelestis excitet flamma ; nunc exper- 15
giscere vere. Et nos peregrini regnavimus : qui sis,
non unde natus sis, reputa. Si tua re subita consilia
4 torpent, at tu mea consilia sequere.' Cum clamor
impetusque multitudinis vix sustineri posset, ex
superiore parte aedium per fenestras in Novam viam 20
versas—habitabat enim rex ad Iovis Statoris—
5 populum Tanaquil adloquitur. Iubet bono animo
esse : sopitum fuisse regem subito ictu ; ferrum haud
alte in corpus descendisse : iam ad se redisse : in-
spectum vulnus absterso cruore ; omnia salubria 25

esse ; confidere propediem ipsum eos visuros. Interim Ser. Tullio iubere populum dicto audientem
esse : eum iura redditurum obiturumque alia regis
6 munia esse. Servius cum trabea et lictoribus prodit,
ac sede regia sedens alia decernit, de aliis consul- 30
turum se regem esse simulat. Itaque per aliquot dies,
cum iam exspirasset Tarquinius, celata morte per
speciem alienae fungendae vicis suas opes firmavit ;
tum demum palam factum est comploratione in regia
orta. Servius praesidio firmo munitus, primus 35
7 iniussu populi, voluntate patrum regnavit. Anci
liberi iam tum comprensis sceleris ministris ut vivere
regem et tantas esse opes Servi nuntiatum est,
Suessam Pometiam exsulatum ierant.

*Tullius secures his power by matrimonial, military,
and political measures.*

42. Nec iam publicis magis consiliis Servius quam
privatis munire opes, et ne, qualis Anci liberum
animus adversus Tarquinium fuerat, talis adversus
se Tarquini liberum esset, duas filias iuvenibus regiis,
2 Lucio atque Arrunti Tarquiniis iungit ; nec rupit 5
tamen fati necessitatem humanis consiliis, quin
invidia regni etiam inter domesticos infida omnia
atque infesta faceret.

Peropportune ad praesentis quietem status bellum
cum Veientibus—iam enim indutiae exierant— 10
3 aliisque Etruscis sumptum. In eo bello et virtus et
fortuna enituit Tulli ; fusoque ingenti hostium

exercitu haud dubius rex, seu patrum seu plebis
4 animos periclitaretur, Romam rediit. Adgrediturque
inde ad pacis longe maximum opus, ut, quemad- 15
modum Numa divini auctor iuris fuisset, ita Servium
conditorem omnis in civitate discriminis ordinum-
que, quibus inter gradus dignitatis fortunaeque
5 aliquid interlucet, posteri fama ferrent. Censum
enim instituit, rem saluberrimam tanto futuro im- 20
perio, ex quo belli pacisque munia non viritim, ut
ante, sed pro habitu pecuniarum fierent ; tum classes
centuriasque et hunc ordinem ex censu discripsit, vel
paci decorum vel bello.

The census of Servius Tullius.

43. Ex iis qui centum milium aeris aut maiorem
censum haberent octoginta confecit centurias,
2 quadragenas seniorum ac iuniorum ; prima classis
omnes appellati ; seniores ad urbis custodiam ut
praesto essent, iuvenes ut foris bella gererent ; arma 5
his imperata galea, clipeum, ocreae, lorica, omnia ex
aere ; haec ut tegumenta corporis essent ; tela in
3 hostem hastaque et gladius. Additae huic classi duae
fabrum centuriae, quae sine armis stipendia facerent ;
4 datum munus ut machinas in bello facerent. Secun- 10
da classis intra centum usque ad quinque et septuaginta milium censum instituta, et ex iis, senioribus
iunioribusque, viginti conscriptae centuriae ; arma
imperata scutum pro clipeo et praeter loricam omnia
5 eadem. Tertiae classis [in] quinquaginta milium 15

censum esse voluit ; totidem centuriae et hae
eodemque discrimine aetatium factae ; nec de armis
6 quicquam mutatum, ocreae tantum ademptae. In
quarta classe census quinque et viginti milium, totidem centuriae factae, arma mutata : nihil praeter 20
7 hastam et verutum datum. Quinta classis aucta,
centuriae triginta factae ; fundas lapidesque missiles
hi secum gerebant ; [in] his accensi, cornicines
tubicinesque, in duas centurias distributi ; undecim
8 milibus haec classis censebatur. Hoc minor census 25
reliquam multitudinem habuit : inde una centuria
facta est, immunis militia. Ita pedestri exercitu
ornato distributoque, equitum ex primoribus civitatis
9 duodecim scripsit centurias ; sex item alias centurias,
tribus ab Romulo institutis, sub iisdem quibus 30
inauguratae erant nominibus fecit. Ad equos
emendos dena milia aeris ex publico data, et quibus
equos alerent, viduae attributae, quae bina milia
aeris in annos singulos penderent. Haec omnia in
10 dites a pauperibus inclinata onera. Deinde est honos 35
additus. Non enim, ut ab Romulo traditum ceteri
servaverant reges, viritim suffragium eadem vi
eodemque iure promisce omnibus datum est ; sed
gradus facti, ut neque exclusus quisquam suffragio
videretur et vis omnis penes primores civitatis esset ; 40
11 equites enim vocabantur primi, octoginta inde primae
classis centuriae ; ibi si variaret, quod raro incidebat,
secundae classis ; nec fere umquam infra ita de-
12 scenderunt, ut ad infimos pervenirent. Nec mirari

oportet hunc ordinem, qui nunc est post expletas 45
quinque et triginta tribus, duplicato earum numero
centuriis iuniorum seniorumque, ad institutam ab
13 Servio Tullio summam non convenire. Quadrifariam
enim urbe divisa [regionibus] collibus, qui habitabantur, partes eas tribus appellavit, ut ego arbitror a 50
tributo ; nam eius quoque aequaliter ex censu con-
ferendi ab eodem inita ratio est : neque eae tribus
ad centuriarum distributionem numerumque quicquam pertinuere.

*Purification of the army and the enclosure of the city
by a wall.*

44. Censu perfecto, quem maturaverat metu legis
de incensis latae cum vinculorum minis mortisque,
edixit ut omnes cives Romani, equites peditesque, in
suis quisque centuriis, in campo Martio prima luce
2 adessent. Ibi instructum exercitum omnem suo- 5
vetaurilibus lustravit, idque conditum lustrum
appellatum, quia in censendo finis factus est. Milia
octoginta eo lustro civium censa dicuntur ; adicit
scriptorum antiquissimus Fabius Pictor, eorum qui
3 arma ferre possent eum numerum fuisse. Ad eam 10
multitudinem urbs quoque amplificanda visa est.
Addit duos colles, Quirinalem Viminalemque : Viminalem inde deinceps auget Esquiliis, ibique ipse,
ut loco dignitas fieret, habitat ; aggere et fossis et
muro circumdat urbem : ita pomerium profert. 15
4 Pomerium verbi vim solam intuentes postmoerium

interpretantur esse ; est autem magis circamoerium,
locus, quem in condendis urbibus quondam Etrusci,
qua murum ducturi erant, certis circa terminis
inaugurato consecrabant, ut neque interiore parte 20
aedificia moenibus continuarentur, quae nunc vulgo
etiam coniungunt, et extrinsecus puri aliquid ab
5 humano cultu pateret soli. Hoc spatium, quod
neque habitari neque arari fas erat, non magis quod
post murum esset quam quod murus post id, pomer- 25
ium Romani appellarunt ; et in urbis incremento
semper, quantum moenia processura erant, tantum
termini hi consecrati proferebantur.

A temple to Diana is erected on the
Aventine Hill.

45. Aucta civitate magnitudine urbis, formatis
omnibus domi et ad belli et ad pacis usus, ne semper
armis opes adquirerentur, consilio augere imperium
2 conatus est, simul et aliquod addere urbi decus. Iam
tum erat inclitum Dianae Ephesiae fanum ; id com- 5
muniter a civitatibus Asiae factum fama ferebat.
Eum consensum deosque consociatos laudare mire
Servius inter proceres Latinorum, cum quibus publice privatimque hospitia amicitiasque de industria
iunxerat. Saepe iterando eadem perpulit tandem, ut 10
Romae fanum Dianae populi Latini cum populo
3 Romano facerent. Ea erat confessio caput rerum
Romam esse, de quo totiens armis certatum fuerat.
Id quamquam omissum iam ex omnium cura Latin-

orum ob rem totiens infeliciter temptatam armis 15
videbatur, uni se ex Sabinis fors dare visa est privato
4 consilio imperii reciperandi. Bos in Sabinis nata
cuidam patri familiae dicitur miranda magnitudine
ac specie ; fixa per multas aetates cornua in vestibulo
5 templi Dianae monumentum ei fuere miraculo. Ha- 20
bita, ut erat, res prodigii loco est, et cecinere vates,
cuius civitatis eam civis Dianae immolasset, ibi fore
6 imperium ; idque carmen pervenerat ad antistitem
fani Dianae Sabinusque ut prima apta dies sacrificio
visa est, bovem Romam actam deducit ad fanum 25
Dianae et ante aram statuit. Ibi antistes Romanus,
cum eum magnitudo victimae celebrata fama movis-
set, memor responsi Sabinum ita adloquitur :
' Quidnam tu, hospes, paras? ' inquit ; ' inceste
sacrificium Dianae facere? Quin tu ante vivo per- 30
funderis flumine? Infima valle praefluit Tiberis.'
7 Religione tactus hospes, qui omnia, ut prodigio
responderet eventus, cuperet rite facta, extemplo
descendit ad Tiberim ; interea Romanus immolat
Dianae bovem. Id mire gratum regi atque civitati 35
fuit.

The crimes of Tullia and of Lucius Tarquinius ;
their plot against Servius.

46. Servius quamquam iam usu haud dubie regnum possederat, tamen quia interdum iactari voces a
iuvene Tarquinio audiebat se iniussu populi regnare,
conciliata prius voluntate plebis agro capto ex

hostibus viritim diviso, ausus est ferre ad populum, 5
vellent iuberentne se regnare ; tantoque consensu,
quanto haud quisquam alius ante, rex est declaratus.
2 Neque ea res Tarquinio spem adfectandi regni
minuit ; immo eo impensius, quia de agro plebis
adversa patrum voluntate senserat agi, criminandi 10
Servi apud patres crescendique in curia sibi occasionem datam ratus est, et ipse iuvenis ardentis animi
et domi uxore Tullia inquietum animum stimulante.
3 Tulit enim et Romana regia sceleris tragici exemplum
ut taedio regum maturior veniret libertas ultimum- 15
4 que regnum esset quod scelere partum foret. Hic
L. Tarquinius—Prisci Tarquini regis filius neposne
fuerit, parum liquet ; pluribus tamen auctoribus
filium ediderim—fratrem habuerat Arruntem Tar-
5 quinium mitis ingenii iuvenem. His duobus, ut ante 20
dictum est, duae Tulliae regis filiae nupserant, et ipsae
longe dispares moribus. Forte ita inciderat ne duo
violenta ingenia matrimonio iungerentur fortuna,
credo, populi Romani, quo diuturnius Servi regnum
6 esset constituique civitatis mores possent. Ange- 25
batur ferox Tullia, nihil materiae in viro neque ad
cupiditatem neque ad audaciam esse ; tota in
alterum aversa Tarquinium eum mirari, eum virum
dicere ac regio sanguine ortum ; spernere sororem,
7 quod virum nacta muliebri cessaret audacia. Con- 30
trahit celeriter similitudo eos, ut fere fit ; malum
malo aptissimum ; sed initium turbandi omnia a
femina ortum est. Ea secretis viri alieni adsuefacta

sermonibus nullis verborum contumeliis parcere de
viro ad fratrem, de sorore ad virum ; et se rectius 35
viduam et illum caelibem futurum fuisse contendere,
quam cum impari iungi, ut elanguescendum aliena
8 ignavia esset ; si sibi eum quo digna esset di dedissent virum, domi se propediem visuram regnum
9 fuisse, quod apud patrem videat. Celeriter adule- 40
scentem suae temeritatis implet ; Arruns Tarquinius et Tullia minor prope continuatis funeribus
cum domos vacuas novo matrimonio fecissent,
iunguntur nuptiis, magis non prohibente Servio
quam approbante. 45

At the instigation of Tullia, Tarquinius seizes the throne.

47. Tum vero in dies infestior Tulli senectus, in-
festius coepit regnum esse ; iam enim ab scelere ad aliud
spectare mulier scelus. Nec nocte nec interdiu virum
conquiescere pati, ne gratuita praeterita parricidia
2 essent : non sibi defuisse cui nupta diceretur, nec 5
cum quo tacita serviret ; defuisse qui se regno dignum putaret, qui meminisset se esse Prisci Tarquini
filium, qui habere quam sperare regnum mallet.
3 ' Si tu is es cui nuptam esse me arbitror, et virum et
regem appello ; sin minus, eo nunc peius mutata res 10
4 est quod istic cum ignavia est scelus. Quin accingeris? Non tibi ab Corintho nec ab Tarquiniis, ut
patri tuo, peregrina regna moliri necesse est ; di te
penates patriique et patris imago et domus regia et in
domo regale solium et nomen Tarquinium creat 15

5 vocatque regem. Aut si ad haec parum est animi,
quid frustraris civitatem? Quid te ut regium
iuvenem conspici sinis? Facesse hinc Tarquinios aut
Corinthum; devolvere retro ad stirpem, fratri
6 similior quam patri.' His aliisque increpando 20
iuvenem instigat, nec conquiescere ipsa potest si, cum
Tanaquil, peregrina mulier, tantum moliri potuisset
animo ut duo continua regna viro ac deinceps genero
dedisset, ipsa regio semine orta nullum momentum
7 in dando adimendoque regno faceret. His muliebri- 25
bus instinctus furiis Tarquinius circumire et prensare
minorum maxime gentium patres ; admonere paterni
beneficii ac pro eo gratiam repetere ; allicere donis
iuvenes ; cum de se ingentia pollicendo tum regis
8 criminibus omnibus locis crescere. Postremo ut iam 30
agendae rei tempus visum est, stipatus agmine
armatorum in forum inrupit. Inde omnibus perculsis
pavore, in regia sede pro curia sedens, patres in curiam per praeconem ad regem Tarquinium citari iussit.
9 Convenere extemplo, alii iam ante ad hoc praeparati, 35
alii metu, ne non venisse fraudi esset, novitate ac
10 miraculo attoniti et iam de Servio actum rati. Ibi
Tarquinius maledicta ab stirpe ultima orsus ; servum
servaque natum post mortem indignam parentis sui,
non interregno, ut antea, inito, non comitiis habitis, 40
non per suffragium populi, non auctoribus patribus,
11 muliebri dono regnum occupasse. Ita natum, ita
creatum regem, fautorem infimi generis hominum, ex
quo ipse sit, odio alienae honestatis ereptum primori-

12 pus agrum sordidissimo cuique divisisse ; omnia 45
onera, quae communia quondam fuerint inclinasse in
primores civitatis ; instituisse censum ut insignis ad
invidiam locupletiorum fortuna esset et parata unde,
ubi vellet, egentissimis largiretur.

*The brutal murder of Servius and the inhuman conduct of
his daughter Tullia.*

48. Huic orationi Servius cum intervenisset trepido nuntio excitatus, extemplo a vestibulo curiae
magna voce ' Quid hoc ' inquit, ' Tarquini, rei est?
qua tu audacia me vivo vocare ausus es patres aut
2 in sede considere mea? ' Cum ille ferociter ad haec, 5
—se patris sui tenere sedem ; multo quam servum
potiorem filium regis regni heredem ; satis illum diu
per licentiam eludentem insultasse dominis—clamor ab utriusque fautoribus oritur et concursus
populi fiebat in curiam, apparebatque regnaturum 10
3 qui vicisset. Tum Tarquinius, necessitate iam et
ipsa cogente ultima audere, multo et aetate et viribus
validior, medium arripit Servium elatumque e curia
in inferiorem partem per gradus deiecit ; inde ad
4 cogendum senatum in curiam rediit. Fit fuga regis 15
apparitorum atque comitum ; ipse prope exsanguis
cum sine regio comitatu domum se reciperet, ab iis
qui missi ab Tarquinio fugientem consecuti erant
5 interficitur. Creditur, quia non abhorret a cetero
scelere, admonitu Tulliae id factum. Carpento certe, 20

id quod satis constat, in forum invecta nec reverita
coetum virorum, evocavit virum e curia regemque
6 prima appellavit. A quo facessere iussa ex tanto
tumultu cum se domum reciperet pervenissetque ad
summum Cyprium vicum, ubi Dianium nuper fuit, 25
flectenti carpentum dextra in Urbium clivum, ut in
collem Esquiliarum eveheretur, restitit pavidus atque
inhibuit frenos is qui iumenta agebat, iacentemque
7 dominae Servium trucidatum ostendit. Foedum
inhumanumque inde traditur scelus monumentoque 30
locus est—Sceleratum vicum vocant—quo amens,
agitantibus furiis sororis ac viri, Tullia per patris
corpus carpentum egisse fertur, partemque sanguinis
ac caedis paternae cruento vehiculo, contaminata
ipsa respersaque, tulisse ad penates suos virique sui, 35
quibus iratis malo regni principio similes propediem
exitus sequerentur.
8   Ser. Tullius regnavit annos quattuor et quadraginta ita ut bono etiam moderatoque succedenti regi
difficilis aemulatio esset ; ceterum id quoque ad 40
gloriam accessit, quod cum illo simul iusta ac legitima
9 regna occiderunt. Id ipsum tam mite ac tam moder-
atum imperium tamen, quia unius esset, deponere
eum in animo habuisse quidam auctores sunt, ni
scelus intestinum liberandae patriae consilia agitanti 45
intervenisset.

Tarquinius Superbus begins to reign.

49. Inde L. Tarquinius regnare occepit, cui

Superbo cognomen facta indiderunt, quia socerum
gener sepultura prohibuit, Romulum quoque insepul-
2 tum perisse dictitans, primoresque patrum, quos
Servi rebus favisse credebat, interfecit ; conscius 5
deinde male quaerendi regni ab se ipso adversus se
exemplum capi posse, armatis corpus circumsaepsit ;
3 neque enim ad ius regni quicquam praeter vim
habebat, ut qui neque populi iussu neque auctoribus
4 patribus regnaret.   Eo accedebat ut in caritate 10
civium nihil spei reponenti metu regnum tutandum
esset.   Quem ut pluribus incuteret, cognitiones
capitalium rerum sine consiliis per se solus exercebat,
5 perque eam causam occidere, in exsilium agere, bonis
multare poterat non suspectos modo aut invisos, sed 15
unde nihil aliud quam praedam sperare posset.
6 Praecipue ita patrum numero imminuto statuit
nullos in patres legere, quo contemptior paucitate
ipsa ordo esset, minusque per se nihil agi indignaren-
7 tur.   Hic enim regum primus traditum a prioribus 20
morem de omnibus senatum consulendi solvit ;
domesticis consiliis rem publicam administravit ;
bellum, pacem, foedera, societates per se ipse, cum
quibus voluit, iniussu populi ac senatus fecit diremit-
8 que.   Latinorum sibi maxime gentem conciliabat, ut 25
peregrinis quoque opibus tutior inter cives esset,
neque hospitia modo cum primoribus eorum sed
9 adfinitates quoque iungebat.   Octavio Mamilio
Tusculano—is longe princeps Latini nominis erat,
si famae credimus, ab Ulixe deaque Circa oriundus,— 30

ei Mamilio filiam nuptum dat, perque eas nuptias
multos sibi cognatos amicosque eius conciliat.

*Dissatisfaction with the rule of Tarquinius is expressed by
Turnus of Aricia.*

50. Iam magna Tarquini auctoritas inter Latinorum proceres erat, cum in diem certam ut ad lucum
Ferentinae conveniant indicit : esse quae agere de
2 rebus communibus velit. Conveniunt frequentes
prima luce : ipse Tarquinius diem quidem servavit 5
sed paulo ante quam sol occideret venit. Multa ibi
toto die in concilio variis iactata sermonibus erant.
3 Turnus Herdonius ab Aricia ferociter in absentem
Tarquinium erat invectus : haud mirum esse,
Superbo inditum Romae cognomen :—iam enim 10
ita clam quidem mussitantes, vulgo tamen eum
appellabant :—an quicquam superbius esse quam
4 ludificari sic omne nomen Latinum? longe ab domo
excitis, ipsum, qui concilium indixerit, non adesse :
temptari profecto patientiam, ut, si iugum acceperint, 15
obnoxios premat. Cui enim non apparere, adfectare
5 eum imperium in Latinos? Quod si sui bene crediderint cives, aut si creditum illud et non raptum
parricidio sit, credere et Latinos quamquam ne sic
6 quidem alienigenae debere ; sin suos eius paeniteat, 20
quippe qui alii super alios trucidentur, exsulatum
eant, bona amittant, quid spei melioris Latinis portendi? si se audiant, domum suam quemque inde
abituros neque magis observaturos diem concilii

7 quam ipse qui indixerit observet. Haec atque alia 25
eodem pertinentia seditiosus facinorosusque homo
hisque artibus opes domi nactus cum maxime disser-
8 eret, intervenit Tarquinius. Is finis orationi fuit ;
aversi omnes ad Tarquinium salutandum. Qui
silentio facto monitus a proximis ut purgaret se quod 30
id temporis venisset, disceptatorem ait se sumptum
inter patrem et filium cura reconciliandi eos in gratiam moratum esse, et quia ea res exemisset illum diem,
9 postero die acturum quae constituisset. Ne id
quidem ab Turno tulisse tacitum ferunt ; dixisse 35
enim nullam breviorem esse cognitionem quam inter
patrem et filium paucisque transigi verbis posse : ni
pareat patri, habiturum infortunium esse.

Tarquinius secures the death of Turnus.

51. Haec Aricinus in regem Romanum increpans
ex concilio abiit. Quam rem Tarquinius aliquanto
quam videbatur aegrius ferens confestim Turno
necem machinatur, ut eundem terrorem, quo civium
2 animos domi oppresserat, Latinis iniceret. Et quia 5
pro imperio palam interfici non poterat, oblato falso
crimine insontem oppressit. Per adversae factionis
quosdam Aricinos servum Turni auro corrupit, ut in
deversorium eius vim magnam gladiorum inferri
3 clam sineret. Ea cum una nocte perfecta essent, 10
Tarquinius paulo ante lucem accitis ad se principibus
Latinorum quasi re nova perturbatus, moram suam
hesternam, velut deorum quadam providentia in-

4 latam, ait saluti sibi atque illis fuisse. Ab Turno dici
sibi et primoribus populorum parari necem, ut 15
Latinorum solus imperium teneat. Adgressurum
fuisse hesterno die in concilio ; dilatam rem esse,
quod auctor concilii afuerit quem maxime peteret.
5 Inde illam absentis insectationem esse natam, quod
morando spem destituerit. Non dubitare, si vera 20
deferantur quin prima luce, ubi ventum in concilium
sit, instructus cum coniuratorum manu armatusque
6 venturus sit. Dici gladiorum ingentem esse numerum ad eum convectum. Id vanum necne sit, extemplo sciri posse. Rogare eos, ut inde secum ad 25
7 Turnum veniant. Suspectam fecit rem et ingenium
Turni ferox et oratio hesterna et mora Tarquini, quod
videbatur ob eam differri caedes potuisse. Eunt
inclinatis quidem ad credendum animis, tamen, nisi
8 gladiis deprehensis, cetera vana existimaturi. Ubi est 30
eo ventum, Turnum ex somno excitatum circumsistunt custodes ; comprehensisque servis, qui caritate domini vim parabant, cum gladii abditi ex
omnibus locis deverticuli protraherentur, enimvero
manifesta res visa iniectaeque Turno catenae ; 35
et confestim Latinorum concilium magno cum
9 tumultu advocatur. Ibi tam atrox invidia orta est
gladiis in medio positis, ut indicta causa, novo genere
leti, deiectus ad caput aquae Ferentinae crate superne
iniecta saxisque congestis mergeretur.	40

*Tarquinius persuades the Latins to renew the treaty
with Rome.*

52. Revocatis deinde ad concilium Latinis Tarquinius conlaudatisque, qui Turnum novantem res
pro manifesto parricidio merita poena adfecissent, ita
2 verba fecit : posse quidem se vetusto iure agere,
quod, cum omnes Latini ab Alba oriundi sint, [in] eo 5
foedere teneantur, quo sub Tullo res omnis Albana
cum colonis suis in Romanum cesserit imperium ;
3 ceterum se utilitatis id magis omnium causa censere
ut renovetur id foedus, secundaque potius fortuna
populi Romani ut participes Latini fruantur, quam 10
urbium excidia vastationesque agrorum, quas Anco
prius, patre deinde suo regnante perpessi sint, semper
4 aut exspectent aut patiantur.   Haud difficulter
persuasum Latinis quamquam in eo foedere superior
Romana res erat ; ceterum et capita nominis Latini 15
stare ac sentire cum rege videbant, et [Turnus] sui
cuique periculi, si adversatus esset, recens erat docu-
5 mentum.   Ita   renovatum   foedus,   indictumque
iunioribus Latinorum ut ex foedere die certa ad
6 lucum Ferentinae armati frequentes adessent. Qui 20
ubi ad edictum Romani regis ex omnibus populis
convenere, ne ducem suum neve secretum imperium
propriave signa haberent, miscuit manipulos ex
Latinis Romanisque ut ex binis singulos faceret
binosque ex singulis ; ita geminatis manipulis 25
centuriones imposuit.

War with the Volscians.   Sextus Tarquinius, feigning to be a
deserter, presents himself at Gabii.

53. Nec, ut iniustus in pace rex, ita dux belli
pravus fuit ; quin ea arte aequasset superiores reges,
ni degeneratum in aliis huic quoque decori offecisset.
2 Is primus Volscis bellum in ducentos amplius post
suam aetatem annos movit, Suessamque Pometiam 5
3 ex iis vi cepit.   Ubi cum divendita praeda quadraginta talenta argenti refecisset, concepit animo eam
amplitudinem Iovis templi, quae digna deum
hominumque rege, quae Romano imperio, quae
ipsius etiam loci maiestate esset ; captivam pecun- 10
iam in aedificationem eius templi seposuit.
4   Excepit deinde lentius spe bellum, quo Gabios, pro-
pinquam urbem, nequiquam vi adortus, cum obsi-
dendi quoque urbem spes pulso a moenibus adempta
esset, postremo minime arte Romana, fraude ac dolo, 15
5 adgressus est.   Nam cum, velut posito bello, fundamentis templi iaciendis aliisque urbanis operibus
intentum se esse simularet, Sextus filius eius, qui
minimus ex tribus erat, transfugit ex composito
Gabios, patris in se saevitiam intolerabilem con- 20
6 querens ; iam ab alienis in suos vertisse superbiam
et liberorum quoque eum frequentiae taedere, ut
quam in curia solitudinem fecerit, domi quoque faciat
ne quam stirpem, ne quem heredem regni relinquat.
7 Se quidem inter tela et gladios patris elapsum nihil 25
usquam sibi tutum nisi apud hostes L. Tarquini
credidisse.   Nam, ne errarent, manere iis bellum

quod positum simuletur, et per occasionem eum in-
8 cautos invasurum.   Quod si apud eos supplicibus
locus non sit, pererraturum se omne Latium, Volscos- 30
que se inde et Aequos et Hernicos petiturum, donec
ad eos perveniat, qui a patrum crudelibus atque im-
9 piis suppliciis tegere liberos sciant.   Forsitan etiam
ardoris aliquid ad bellum armaque se adversus super-
bissimum regem ac ferocissimum populum inven- 35
10 turum.   Cum, si nihil morarentur, infensus ira porro
inde abiturus videretur, benigne ab Gabinis excipitur :
vetant mirari si, qualis in cives, qualis in socios, talis
11 ad ultimum in liberos esset ; in se ipsum postremo
saeviturum, si alia desint.   Sibi vero gratum adven- 40
tum eius esse, futurumque credere brevi, ut illo
adiuvante a portis Gabinis sub Romana moenia
bellum transferatur.

Sextus Tarquinius treacherously hands over Gabii to his
father.

54. Inde in consilia publica adhiberi.   Ubi cum
de aliis rebus adsentire se veteribus Gabinis diceret
quibus eae notiores essent, ipse identidem belli auctor
esse et in eo sibi praecipuam prudentiam adsumere,
quod utriusque populi vires nosset, sciretque invisam 5
profecto superbiam regiam civibus esse, quam ferre
2 ne liberi quidem potuissent.   Ita cum sensim ad
rebellandum primores Gabinorum incitaret, ipse cum
promptissimis iuvenum praedatum atque in expedi-
tiones iret, et dictis factisque omnibus ad fallendum 10

instructis vana adcresceret fides, dux ad ultimum
3 belli legitur. Ibi cum, inscia multitudine quid ageretur, proelia parva inter Romam Gabiosque fierent,
quibus plerumque Gabina res superior esset, tum
certatim summi infimique Gabinorum Sex. Tar- 15
quinium dono deum sibi missum ducem credere.
4 Apud milites vero obeundo pericula ac labores pariter,
praedam munifice largiendo tanta caritate esse ut
non pater Tarquinius potentior Romae quam filius
5 Gabiis esset. Itaque postquam satis virium conlec- 20
tum ad omnes conatus videbat, tum ex suis unum
sciscitatum Romam ad patrem mittit, quidnam se
facere vellet, quando quidem ut omnia unus publice
6 Gabiis posset ei di dedissent. Huic nuntio, quia,
credo, dubiae fidei videbatur, nihil voce responsum 25
est ; rex velut deliberabundus in hortum aedium
transit sequente nuntio filii ; ibi inambulans tacitus
summa papaverum capita dicitur baculo decussisse.
7 Interrogando exspectandoque responsum nuntius
fessus, ut re imperfecta, redit Gabios ; quae dixerit 30
ipse quaeque viderit refert ; seu ira seu odio seu
superbia insita ingenio nullam eum vocem emisisse.
8 Sexto ubi quid vellet parens quidve praeciperet
tacitis ambagibus patuit, primores civitatis criminando alios apud populum, alios sua ipsos invidia 35
opportunos interemit. Multi palam, quidam in quibus minus speciosa criminatio erat futura, clam
9 interfecti. Patuit quibusdam volentibus fuga, aut
in exsilium acti sunt, absentiumque bona iuxta atque

10 interemptorum divisui fuere. Largitiones inde 40
praedaeque ; et dulcedine privati commodi sensus
malorum publicorum adimi, donec orba consilio
auxilioque Gabina res regi Romano sine ulla dimi-
catione in manum traditur.

*Tarquinius builds the temple of Jupiter as a monument to
his name and reign.*

55. Gabiis receptis Tarquinius pacem cum Aequo-
rum gente fecit, foedus cum Tuscis renovavit. Inde
ad negotia urbana animum convertit ; quorum erat
primum ut Iovis templum in monte Tarpeio monumentum regni sui nominisque relinqueret : Tar- 5
quinios reges ambos patrem vovisse, filium perfecisse.
2 Et ut libera a ceteris religionibus area esset tota Iovis
templique eius quod inaedificaretur, exaugurare fana
sacellaque statuit, quae aliquot ibi a Tatio rege
primum in ipso discrimine adversus Romulum 10
pugnae vota, consecrata inaugurataque postea
3 fuerant. Inter principia condendi huius operis
movisse numen ad indicandam tanti imperii molem
traditur deos ; nam cum omnium sacellorum ex-
augurationes admitterent aves, in Termini fano non 15
4 addixere ; idque omen auguriumque ita acceptum
est non motam Termini sedem unumque eum deorum
non evocatum sacratis sibi finibus firma stabiliaque
5 cuncta portendere. Hoc perpetuitatis auspicio
accepto, secutum aliud magnitudinem imperii por- 20
tendens prodigium est : caput humanum integra

facie aperientibus fundamenta templi dicitur ap-
6 paruisse. Quae visa species haud per ambages arcem
eam imperii caputque rerum fore portendebat ; idque
ita cecinere vates quique in urbe erant quosque ad 25
eam rem consultandam ex Etruria acciverant.
7 Augebatur ad impensas regis animus ; itaque
Pometinae manubiae, quae perducendo ad culmen
operi destinatae erant, vix in fundamenta suppedit-
8 avere. Eo magis Fabio, praeterquam quod antiquior 30
est, crediderim quadraginta ea sola talenta fuisse,
9 quam Pisoni, qui quadraginta milia pondo argenti
seposita in eam rem scribit, summam pecuniae neque
ex unius tum urbis praeda sperandam et nullius ne
horum quidem operum fundamenta non exsupera- 35
turam.

*The construction of the Cloaca Maxima. The two sons of
Tarquinius, accompanied by Brutus, consult the oracle at
Delphi.*

56. Intentus perficiendo templo, fabris undique ex
Etruria accitis, non pecunia solum ad id publica est
usus sed operis etiam ex plebe. Qui cum haud parvus
et ipse militiae adderetur labor, minus tamen plebs
gravabatur se templa deum exaedificare manibus 5
2 suis, quam postquam et ad alia, ut specie minora, sic
laboris aliquanto maioris traducebantur opera, foros
in circo faciendos cloacamque maximam, receptaculum omnium purgamentorum urbis, sub terram
agendam ; quibus duobus operibus vix nova haec 10

3 magnificentia quicquam adaequare potuit. His
laboribus exercita plebe, quia et urbi multitudinem,
ubi usus non esset, oneri rebatur esse, et colonis
mittendis occupari latius imperii fines volebat,
Signiam Circeiosque colonos misit, praesidia urbi 15
futura terra marique.

4   Haec agenti portentum terribile visum : anguis ex
columna lignea elapsus cum terrorem fugamque in
regia fecisset, ipsius regis non tam subito pavore
5 perculit pectus quam anxiis implevit curis. Itaque 20
cum ad publica prodigia Etrusci tantum vates ad-
hiberentur, hoc velut domestico exterritus visu
Delphos ad maxime inclitum in terris oraculum
6 mittere statuit. Neque responsa sortium ulli alii
committere ausus, duos filios per ignotas ea tempes- 25
7 tate terras, ignotiora maria in Graeciam misit. Titus
et Arruns profecti ; comes iis additus L. Iunius
Brutus, Tarquinia, sorore regis, natus, iuvenis longe
alius ingenii quam cuius simulationem induerat. Is
cum primores civitatis, in quibus fratrem suum, ab 30
avunculo interfectum audisset, neque in animo suo
quicquam regi timendum neque in fortuna concupiscendum relinquere statuit, contemptuque tutus
8 esse ubi in iure parum praesidii esset. Ergo ex
industria factus ad imitationem stultitiae, cum se 35
suaque praedae esse regi sineret, Bruti quoque haud
abnuit cognomen ut sub eius obtentu cognominis
liberator ille populi Romani animus latens opperir-
9 etur tempora sua. Is tum ab Tarquiniis ductus

Delphos, ludibrium verius quam comes, aureum 40
baculum inclusum corneo cavato ad id baculo tulisse
donum Apollini dicitur, per ambages effigiem ingenii
10 sui. Quo postquam ventum est, perfectis patris
mandatis, cupido incessit animos iuvenum sciscitandi
ad quem eorum regnum Romanum esset venturum. 45
Ex infimo specu vocem redditam ferunt : ‘ Imperium summum Romae habebit qui vestrum primus,
11 o iuvenes, osculum matri tulerit.’ Tarquinii ut
Sextus, qui Romae relictus fuerat, ignarus responsi
expersque imperii esset, rem summa ope taceri 50
iubent ; ipsi inter se uter prior, cum Romam
redisset, matri osculum daret, sorti permittunt.
12 Brutus alio ratus spectare Pythicam vocem, velut
si prolapsus cecidisset, terram osculo contigit, scilicet
13 quod ea communis mater omnium mortalium esset. 55
Reditum inde Romam, ubi adversus Rutulos bellum
summa vi parabatur.

The siege of Ardea ; and a contest in
womanly virtue.

57. Ardeam Rutuli habebant, gens, ut in ea
regione atque in ea aetate, divitiis praepollens ;
eaque ipsa causa belli fuit, quod rex Romanus cum
ipse ditari, exhaustus magnificentia publicorum
operum, tum praeda delenire popularium animos 5
2 studebat, praeter aliam superbiam regno infestos
etiam quod se in fabrorum ministeriis ac servili tam
3 diu habitos opere ab rege indignabantur. Temptata

res est, si primo impetu capi Ardea posset ; ubi id
parum processit, obsidione munitionibusque coepti 10
4 premi hostes.   In his stativis, ut fit longo magis
quam acri bello, satis liberi commeatus erant, pri-
5 moribus tamen magis quam militibus ; regii quidem
iuvenes interdum otium conviviis comisationibusque
6 inter se terebant.   Forte potantibus his apud Sex. 15
Tarquinium, ubi et Collatinus cenabat Tarquinius,
Egeri filius, incidit de uxoribus mentio.   Suam quis-
7 que laudare miris modis ;   inde certamine accenso
Collatinus negat verbis opus esse ;   paucis id quidem
horis posse sciri quantum ceteris praestet Lucretia 20
sua.   'Quin, si vigor iuventae inest, conscendimus
equos invisimusque praesentes nostrarum ingenia?
id cuique spectatissimum sit quod nec opinato viri
8 adventu occurrerit oculis.'   Incaluerant vino ; ' Age
sane ' omnes ;   citatis equis avolant Romam.   Quo 25
cum primis se intendentibus tenebris pervenissent,
9 pergunt inde Collatiam, ubi Lucretiam haudquaquam ut regias nurus, quas in convivio luxuque
cum aequalibus viderant tempus terentes, sed nocte
sera deditam lanae inter lucubrantes ancillas in 30
medio aedium sedentem inveniunt.   Muliebris certa-
10 minis laus penes Lucretiam fuit.   Adveniens vir
Tarquiniique excepti benigne ;   victor maritus comiter invitat regios iuvenes.   Ibi Sex. Tarquinium mala
libido Lucretiae per vim stuprandae capit ;   cum 35
11 forma tum spectata castitas incitat.   Et tum quidem
ab nocturno iuvenali ludo in castra redeunt.

The foul deed of Sextus Tarquinius.

58. Paucis interiectis diebus Sex. Tarquinius inscio
2 Collatino cum comite uno Collatiam venit. Ubi
exceptus benigne ab ignaris consilii cum post cenam
in hospitale cubiculum deductus esset, amore ardens,
postquam satis tuta circa sopitique omnes videban- 5
tur, stricto gladio ad dormientem Lucretiam venit,
sinistraque manu mulieris pectore oppresso ‘ Tace,
Lucretia ’ inquit ; ‘ Sex. Tarquinius sum ; ferrum
3 in manu est ; moriere, si emiseris vocem.’ Cum
pavida ex somno mulier nullam opem, prope mortem 10
imminentem videret, tum Tarquinius fateri amorem,
orare, miscere precibus minas, versare in omnes
4 partes muliebrem animum. Ubi obstinatam videbat
et ne mortis quidem metu inclinari, addit ad metum
dedecus : cum mortua iugulatum servum nudum 15
positurum ait, ut in sordido adulterio necata dicatur.
5 Quo terrore cum vicisset obstinatam pudicitiam velut
⟨vi⟩ victrix libido, profectusque inde Tarquinius ferox
expugnato decore muliebri esset, Lucretia maesta
tanto malo nuntium Romam eundem ad patrem 20
Ardeamque ad virum mittit, ut cum singulis fidelibus
amicis veniant ; ita facto maturatoque opus esse ;
6 rem atrocem incidisse./ Sp. Lucretius cum P. Valerio
Volesi filio, Collatinus cum L. Iunio Bruto venit, cum
quo forte Romam rediens ab nuntio uxoris erat con- 25
ventus. Lucretiam sedentem maestam in cubiculo
7 inveniunt. Adventu suorum lacrimae obortae,
quaerentique viro ‘ Satin’ salve? ’ ‘ Minime ’ inquit ;

' quid enim salvi est mulieri amissa pudicitia? Vestigia viri alieni, Collatine, in lecto sunt tuo ; ceterum 30
corpus est tantum violatum, animus insons ; mors
testis erit. Sed date dexteras fidemque haud impune
8 adultero fore. Sex. est Tarquinius, qui hostis pro
hospite priore nocte vi armatus mihi sibique, si vos
9 viri estis, pestiferum hinc abstulit gaudium.' Dant 35
ordine omnes fidem ; consolantur aegram animi
avertendo noxam ab coacta in auctorem delicti :
mentem peccare, non corpus et, unde consilium
10 afuerit culpam abesse. ' Vos ' inquit ' videritis quid
illi debeatur ; ego me etsi peccato absolvo, supplicio 40
non libero ; nec ulla deinde impudica Lucretiae
11 exemplo vivet.' Cultrum, quem sub veste abditum
habebat, eum in corde defigit, prolapsaque in vulnus
12 moribunda cecidit. Conclamat vir paterque.

Brutus leads the Romans against the reigning house of
the Tarquins.

59. Brutus illis luctu occupatis cultrum ex vulnere
Lucretiae extractum, manantem cruore prae se
tenens, ' Per hunc ' inquit ' castissimum ante regiam
iniuriam sanguinem iuro, vosque, di, testes facio me
L. Tarquinium Superbum cum scelerata coniuge et 5
omni liberorum stirpe ferro, igni, quacumque dehinc
vi possim, exsecuturum, nec illos nec alium quem-
2 quam regnare Romae passurum.' Cultrum deinde
Collatino tradit, inde Lucretio ac Valerio, stupentibus
miraculo rei, unde novum in Bruti pectore ingenium. 10

Ut praeceptum erat iurant ; totique ab luctu versi in
iram, Brutum iam inde ad expugnandum regnum
vocantem sequuntur ducem.

3 Elatum domo Lucretiae corpus in forum deferunt,
concientque miraculo, ut fit, rei novae atque indigni- 1
tate homines. Pro se quisque scelus regium ac vim
4 queruntur. Movet cum patris maestitia, tum Brutus
castigator lacrimarum atque inertium querellarum
auctorque quod viros, quod Romanos deceret, arma
5 capiendi adversus hostilia ausos. Ferocissimus quis- 20
que iuvenum cum armis voluntarius adest ; sequitur
et cetera iuventus. Inde patre praeside relicto Collatiae [ad portas] custodibusque datis, ne quis eum
motum regibus nuntiaret, ceteri armati duce Bruto
6 Romam profecti. Ubi eo ventum est, quacumque 25
incedit armata multitudo, pavorem ac tumultum
facit : rursus ubi anteire primores civitatis vident,
7 quidquid sit, haud temere esse rentur. Nec minorem
motum animorum Romae tam atrox res facit quam
Collatiae fecerat ; ergo ex omnibus locis urbis in 30
forum curritur. Quo simul ventum est, praeco ad
tribunum Celerum, in quo tum magistratu forte
8 Brutus erat, populum advocavit. Ibi oratio habita
nequaquam eius pectoris ingeniique quod simu-
latum ad eam diem fuerat, de vi ac libidine Sex. 35
Tarquini, de stupro infando Lucretiae et miserabili
caede, de orbitate Tricipitini, cui morte filiae causa
9 mortis indignior ac miserabilior esset. Addita superbia ipsius regis miseriaeque et labores plebis in fossas

cloacasque exhauriendas demersae ; Romanos 40
homines, victores omnium circa populorum, opifices
10 ac lapicidas pro bellatoribus factos. Indigna Ser.
Tulli regis memorata caedes et invecta corpori patris
nefandoque vehiculo filia, invocatique ultores paren-
11 tum di. His atrocioribusque, credo, aliis, quae 45
praesens rerum indignitas haudquaquam relatu
scriptoribus facilia subicit, memoratis incensam
multitudinem perpulit ut imperium regi abrogaret
exsulesque esse iuberet L. Tarquinium cum coniuge
12 ac liberis. Ipse iunioribus qui ultro nomina dabant 50
lectis armatisque, ad concitandum inde adversus
regem exercitum Ardeam in castra est profectus :
imperium in urbe Lucretio, praefecto urbis iam ante
13 ab rege instituto, relinquit. Inter hunc tumultum
Tullia domo profugit exsecrantibus quacumque 55
incedebat invocantibusque parentum furias viris
mulieribusque.

*The banishment of the Tarquinii and the election of the
first Consuls.*

60. Harum rerum nuntiis in castra perlatis cum re
nova trepidus rex pergeret Romam ad comprimendos
motus, flexit viam Brutus—senserat enim adventum
—ne obvius fieret ; eodemque fere tempore diversis
itineribus Brutus Ardeam, Tarquinius Romam 5
2 venerunt. Tarquinio clausae portae exsiliumque
indictum : liberatorem urbis laeta castra accepere
exactique inde liberi regis. Duo patrem secuti sunt,

qui exsulatum Caere in Etruscos ierunt. Sex. Tarquinius Gabios tamquam in suum regnum profectus, 10
ab ultoribus veterum simultatium, quas sibi ipse
caedibus rapinisque concierat, est interfectus.

3   L. Tarquinius Superbus regnavit annos quinque et
viginti.   Regnatum Romae ab condita urbe ad liber-
4 atam annos ducentos quadraginta quattuor.   Duo 15
consules inde comitiis centuriatis a praefecto urbis ex
commentariis Ser. Tulli creati sunt, L. Iunius Brutus
et L. Tarquinius Collatinus.

NOTES

The preface was written to introduce the whole work, not the first book of it. Nevertheless, it is useful and interesting to read how Livy approached his task, and a translation is given below which keeps as close to the original Latin as the great differences of idiom permit.

Whether I shall achieve anything worth while, if I record the history of the Roman people from the foundation of the city, I neither know, nor would I dare to say so if I did, for I perceive that the subject is both old and hackneyed, since writers constantly succeeding one another believe either that they will in their facts introduce something more authentic, or that by their skill in writing they will surpass crude antiquity. However it shall be, it will none the less give me pleasure to have fostered, in my own person, and to the very best of my ability, the immortality of the achievements of the world's foremost race ; and if among so great a host of writers my own fame should be dimmed, I should console myself with the renown and the greatness of those who will obscure my name. Besides, the subject is one that requires enormous labour, seeing that it goes back more than 700 years and that, setting out from small beginnings, it has grown to such an extent that it is now suffering from its own immensity ; and I do not doubt that the earliest beginnings and the ages nearest to them will afford less pleasure to the majority of readers, in haste to read of these recent times in which the strength of a people long pre-eminent is actually destroying itself : I, on the other hand, shall be seeking this additional reward of my toil, that of distracting myself from the contemplation of the miseries which our age has witnessed over so many years—so long at least as I am recalling those ancient days in my thoughts, free from every care such as could render the mind of a writer anxious, even if it could not divert it from the truth.

Those tales which are handed down, dating from the period before the city was founded, or indeed before its foundation was planned—

tales glorified more in the fictions of poets than in the unadulterated records of history—it is not my intention either to support or reject. To antiquity this licence is conceded, that, by mingling with human affairs touches of the supernatural, it makes the origins of cities more imposing. And if any people should be permitted to claim divinity for its origins and to attribute them to the work of gods, such military glory belongs to the Roman people that when they put forward no less a god than Mars as their own and their founder's father, the races of mankind resignedly acquiesce in this claim too, as they do in their supremacy. But these tales and others like them, however they are considered and assessed, I shall not for my own part regard as of great importance. I would have each reader apply his mind acutely to these questions, what their life was, and what their customs were, through what men, and by what means, dominion was secured and extended. Next let him, in thought, follow what was at first, with the gradual collapse of discipline, a subsidence as it were of morals, then mark how they slipped more and more, and then began to move with headlong impetus, until we have reached the present times, in which we can endure neither our vices nor their cure. This is the particularly salutary and profitable feature in the study of history, that you contemplate instructive instances of every kind as though displayed upon a conspicuous memorial, to choose from them, for your own good and that of your country, what to imitate, and also what other things, shameful in their origin and shameful in their result, to avoid. Now either love of the task I have undertaken deceives me, or else no community has ever been greater, purer, or richer in good examples, nor has there been any into which greed and luxury have entered so late, nor in which frugality and thrift have enjoyed such great and such lasting respect. So true it is, that the less their property, the less also was their covetousness : latterly riches have introduced avarice, and a superfluity of pleasures an itch to ruin ourselves and everything else with unrestrained self-indulgence. But let not complaining, which is unlikely to be welcome even when it will perhaps be necessary, attend the commencement of so vast an undertaking : rather would we begin with good omens, and, if it were the custom for us historians too, as it is for the poets, with vows and prayers to gods and goddesses to grant us, embarking upon so great a task, the blessing of success.

CHAPTER I

Line 1. **Troia capta.** The ablative absolute precedes the indirect statement which depends on **constat** : ' it is established that, after the taking of Troy . . .'

l. 2. **saevitum esse.** The construction is acc. and infin., but no accusative subject *appears*, because **saevitum esse** is the infinitive of the subjectless impersonal passive **saevitum est,** ' rage was vented '.

l. 2. **duobus,** etc. At this point begins a second acc. and infin.— **Achivos abstinuisse**—also dependent on **constat.** **duobus** is a dative of advantage, ' in favour of two '.

l. 3. **iure** is an ablative of cause : ' both in consequence of an old tie of hospitality, and . . .' In the ancient world those who stood to one another in the relationship of host and guest were bound together by special ties, which often continued to be valid for their descendants. Aeneas and Antenor were protected by having a relationship of this kind with one or more of the Greek leaders. Vergil's account makes no mention of any special favour shown to Aeneas, and the poet represents Antenor also as ' *escaping* from the midst of the Greeks ' before founding in Italy the city of Patavium (Padua).

l. 5. **omne ius belli.** **ius** is the object of **abstinuisse.**

l. 5. **casibus variis,** abl. absolute, ' their destinies diverging ', *lit.* ' (being) different '. The Latin language has no present participle of **sum** and this deficiency is responsible for many difficulties in translation.

l. 6. **Antenorem,** subject to **venisse** in the acc. and infin. construction, also dependent on **constat** earlier.

l. 7. **Paphlagonia,** a country bordering on the southern shore of the Euxine (Black Sea).

l. 7. **rege Pylaemene ad Troiam amisso.** It would seem that the Eneti who joined forces with Antenor had accompanied their king to aid the Trojans in the war, and, when he was slain, were prevented from returning by political changes that had occurred in their home-land during their absence. **ad Troiam :** not locative, because the fighting took place ' near ' or ' by ', not ' in ', the city.

l. 10. **Enetos Troianosque tenuisse,** still dependent on **constat.**

l. 11. **Et in quem primo egressi sunt locum Troia vocatur,** i.e. **et locus, in quem primo egressi sunt, vocatur Troia.** The Romans tended to put their relative clauses early, and in consequence the antecedent is often, as here, incorporated into the relative clause and attracted into the case of the relative pronoun.

l. 12. **Troiano.** This is a somewhat similar case of attraction. The literal translation is ' and to the district the name is Trojan ', or as we should say ' the district is called Trojan '. But **Troiano** has been made to agree with **pago** rather than with the logical subject **nomen.**

l. 13. **appellati.** The third instance of attraction in the one sentence. **appellati (sunt),** agreeing with the complement **Veneti,** appears instead of the logical **appellata est.** Observe in **Veneti** the name Venice.

l. 14. **Aeneam.** The acc. and infin. construction, still dependent on **constat** in l. 1., is resumed here after the short digression. **Aeneam** is subject to three infinitives, **venisse, delatum (esse),** and **tenuisse.**

l. 14. **ab,** ' in consequence of '. **simili,** i.e. like that suffered by Antenor.

l. 14. **ad maiora rerum initia,** i.e. ' to the commencement of a greater destiny ', **maiora** going in grammar with **initia,** in sense with **rerum.** This is an instance of *hypallage*—transferred epithet.

l. 15. **ducentibus fatis,** abl. absolute. But proceed as if you had **fatis ductum,** which amounts almost to the same thing and runs more easily after the co-ordinate phrase ending with **profugum.**

l. 15. **Macedoniam.** Vergil makes Aeneas settle first on the coast of Thrace, where he founded Aenos.

l. 16. **quaerentem** is masculine, and governs **sedes.**

l. 17. **Laurentem agrum,** a coastal district of Italy, bounded to the north by the Tiber.

NOTES 99

l. 18. **tenuisse**, ' steered ', ' sailed '. The full expression, which Livy abridges, is **cursum tenere**, ' hold one's course '.

l. 18. **Ibi egressi**, etc. Begin this sentence with **cum** (='when '), and proceed thus : **cum Troiani, egressi ibi, agerent praedam ex agris, ut quibus** . . .

l. 19. **ut quibus**. **Ut** (or **quippe**) often precedes relative clauses which are in effect adverbial clauses of reason, and the accompanying verb is in the subjunctive. The construction is **ut quibus nihil superesset**, ' as (men) to whom nothing was left '. But the presence of the **ut** and the mood of the verb should be noticed in the translation by some such rendering as ' since they had nothing left '.

l. 19. **ab** has the same sense as in **ab simili clade** above, l. **14**.

l. 19. **prope** is an adverb here, and modifies **immenso**.

l. 20. **praedam**, consisting doubtless of cattle.

l. 24. **inde**, ' from that point '.

l. 25. **iunxisse**. **iungo** is a common word for ' make ' when such direct objects follow as are the product of union, e.g. **foedus, amicitia, societas**.

l. 26. **alii** is subject to a second **tradunt** understood.

l. 27. **canerent**, ' they sounded ', the ' they ' being the trumpeters. **signa** is acc., and means the signals (on the respective sides) to commence battle. **canerent** is subjunctive because the clause in which it occurs is a subordinate clause in indirect speech.

l. 27. **processisse Latinum**. Reverse the order to see the construction.

l. 28. **evocasse** =**evocavisse** ; such forms, occurring through the falling out of a v, with or without a following vowel, are called syncopated.

l. 29. **percontatum**. It will simplify this long sentence to proceed as if you had **percontatum esse**, with **eum** (=**Latinum**) as subject, in which case it will be necessary also to insert the conjunction **et** before **postquam** l. 31.

l. 30. **unde aut quo casu**, etc. Lit. ' whence, or through what chance having set out from home, or seeking what, they had landed on Laurentine soil '. I.e. ' where they came from, what chance had caused them to leave home, and what they sought in landing . . .'. Notice (i) **quo casu,** ablative of cause, (ii) *enclitic* **-ve,** meaning ' or ', (iii) **quaerentes,** the participle, not the main verb, carrying the chief weight of the indirect question.

l. 31. **audierit.** Observe how the sequence changes at this point. Livy frequently reproduces the tenses of **oratio recta** in the middle of a passage of **oratio obliqua,** even after clauses in which he has followed the strict usage and used historic tenses.

l. 32. **Aeneam filium.** Esse must be supplied between these words.

l. 33. **patria,** ' native *city* ' here.

l. 33. **profugos** is the complement of another **esse** to be supplied, the subject (eos = **Troianos et Aeneam**) being easily understood.

l. 34. **condendae urbi,** dative of purpose.

l. 34. **et nobilitatem : et** = ' both '.

l. 35. **admiratum** agrees with the **eum** mentioned above as the understood subject of **percontatum** (esse).

l. 36. **dextra data,** abl. absolute. Translate as if you had **dextram dedisse et.**

l. 37. **inde foedus,** etc. This sentence and the next are in the acc. and infin. construction, dependent on **tradunt** above.

l. 37. **inter exercitus salutationem factam,** ' the two armies exchanged greetings '.

l. 39. **fuisse in hospitio,** ' was entertained '.

l. 40. **publico,** ' to the public (one) '.

l. 41. **filia data,** ' by giving his daughter '.

l. 42. **Troianis** is dative. But English puts it differently, and we should say ' strengthened the Trojans' hope '.

l. 42. **sede,** an abl. of means in the Latin, but we should say ' *in* a . . . home '.

l. 43. **finiendi erroris.** The genitive depends on **spem,** and should be translated immediately after it.

l. 4 4. **uxoris.** Her name was Lavinia.

l. 44. **Brevi,** often used without any noun for ' in a short time '.

l. 46. **dixere.** The English idiom is ' gave '.

CHAPTER 2

l. 1. **petiti = petiti sunt.** Cf. **victi** below. Such omissions of parts of **sum** are common.

l. 2. **pacta fuerat = pacta erat,** 3 sg. pluperf. indic. pass. of **pacisco.**

l. 3. **praelatum,** i.e. **praelatum esse,** agreeing with its subject **advenam** in the acc. and infin. construction, dependent on **aegre patiens,** which together form one idea, ' resenting ', (*lit.,* ' enduring ill ').

l. 8. **rebus,** ' their situation ', dative after **diffisi.**

l. 8. **Etruscorum.** These people, of uncertain but probably Near-Eastern origin, lived to the northward of the river Tiber. Long the chief foe of the young Roman community, Etruria was eventually conquered but not before leaving indelible traces of her influence upon many features of the life of her conquerors. The Etruscan language, still a profound philological puzzle, continued to be used as late as the 2nd century A.D.

l. 9. **Caere,** ' at Caere '. The word is indeclinable.

l. 10. **iam inde ab initio.** The first two words intensify **initio,** ' from the very outset '.

l. 10. **minime laetus,** ' very little glad ' i.e. ' by no means pleased '.

l. 11. **origine,** abl. of cause with **laetus :** ' at the foundation ' .

l. 11. **et tum,** etc. The order for English translation is : **et tum ratus rem Troianam crescere nimio plus quam esset satis tutum accolis.** nimio is abl. of the measure of difference modifying **plus,** ' more by too much '. We should say ' far more than . . .'

l. 13. **socia arma Rutulis iunxit,** *lit.,* ' joined allied arms to the R.' i.e. ' joined forces with the R. as their ally '.

l. 15. **nec sub eodem,** etc., i.e. **et (ut) omnes essent, non solum sub eodem iure, sed (sub eodem) nomine.** The negative contained in **nec** goes closely with **solum.**

l. 17. **studio ac fide,** ablatives of respect, ' in . . .'

l. 19. **in dies,** ' daily '.

l. 19. **populorum** depends on **his animis,** and we should say 'on this spirit *in* . . .'.

l. 20. **opibus,** abl. of respect again.   See the note on **studio ac fide** above.

l. 23. **implesset,** i.e. **implevisset.**   Cf. note on **evocasse,** Ch. 1, l. 28. The subjunctive is consecutive.

l. 23. **cum,** ' although '.

l. 23. **bellum** =' invasion ' here.

l. 23. **moenibus,** i.e. could have thwarted his foes by successfully standing a siege.

l. 24. **posset,** ' was able '.   But in such a case English says ' could have . . .'.

l. 24. **secundum** is *predicative* adjective, ' was victorious '.

l. 26. **quemcumque** . . . **ius fasque est,** ' whatever it is lawful and right that he be called,' i.e. whether god or man, for Aeneas partook by birth of both natures.

l. 27. **Iovem indigetem.**   The words are complementary to **eum,** the understood object of **appellant.** ' Iupiter Indiges ' means something like ' local Jove ' as opposed to ' universal Jove ', the king of the gods, the word **indiges** being derived from **indu,** an old form of **in,** and the root of the verb **gigno,** ' beget ' or ' bear '.

CHAPTER 3

Line 3. **tutela muliebri,** abl. of cause, modifying **stetit,** ' stood firm under a woman's regency '.

l. 6. **adfirmet,** potential subjunctive, ' could affirm '.

l. 7. **hicine** =**hicne,** ' whether this.' The reference is to the **puer** of the preceding sentence.

l. 7. **maior,** used as a noun, ' an elder (brother) '.

l. 7. **Creusa matre,** etc.   Take **natus** first : ' born while Troy was intact, his mother being Creusa '.   Notice again how the absence of a Latin word for ' being ' makes for obscurity.   Creusa was the first wife of Aeneas, described by Vergil as having disappeared in the course of the flight from Troy. The poet follows the second of the two traditions mentioned by Livy, and calls Creusa's son now Ascanius, now Iulus.

l. 9. **quem Iulum,** etc. Begin with **eundem** : 'the same (one), whom . . .'

l. 9. **Iulia gens,** the family to which Julius Caesar and, through his grandmother, Augustus belonged.

l. 10. **ubicumque . . . genitus,** 'wherever born and of whatever mother ', **matre** being ablative of origin.

l. 11. **natum** is a noun here, and the full construction is **eum natum esse. Aenea** likewise is abl. of origin.

l. 12. **abundante Lavinii multitudine.** The abl. absolute is best turned by a clause of reason : ' as the population of L. was over-flowing.' It modifies **florentem.**

l. 13. **ut tum res erant,** ' as things were then ', i.e. considering that the times spoken of were primitive.

l. 15. **quae ab situ,** etc. The sentence is awkwardly constructed, for **quae** refers to **novam aliam** (**urbem**) in the preceding clause, and it would have been simpler and shorter for Livy to have written **porrecta** alone, in agreement with **quae.**

l. 16. **Inter Lavinium,** etc. After **Lavinium** must be supplied (readily enough in view of the following **deductam,** a word of meaning not greatly dissimilar) **conditum.** Then the literal translation is ' between Lavinium (founded) and the colony Alba Longa planted . . .'. Observe how the notions expressed by the perfect participles are conveyed in English by verbal nouns : ' between the *founding* of Lavinium and the *planting* of the colony of Alba Longa.'

l. 18. **Tantum,** acc. sg. neut. used as adverb, ' so much ', ' so greatly '.

l. 18. **maxime fusis Etruscis,** ' particularly after the rout of the Etruscans '.

l. 19. **morte,** temporal ablative, ' on the death '.

l. 20. **inter,** ' during '.

l. 20. **rudimentumque primum. Primum** is pleonastic, for **rudimentum** means ' first attempt '. Pleonasm is so common in

Livy that Suetonius [1] quotes a criticism by Caligula that he was **verbosum in historia neglegentemque.** This characteristic may, however, be regarded as due to the exuberant richness of his style.

l. 22. **ausi sint.** The perfect subj. in a consecutive (result) clause is used to emphasise the actual consequence or result, or to denote a single, instantaneous action.

l. 22. **ita ut,** ' on these terms, that . . .'.

l. 26. **creat.** Livy often uses the simple verb—a poetic practice— where classical writers prefer the compound ; here **creat** for **procreat,** ' was the father of '.

l. 28. **Prisci Latini.** Although Livy here gives the name ' ancient Latins ' to several colonies only, in Chap. 52 he speaks of all the Latins being derived from Alba, and in Chap. 32 he seems to make no difference between the **Prisci Latini** and the **Latini.**

It is probable either that the **Prisci Latini** were those Latins who lived before the foundation of Rome or that they were members of the Latin League before Rome became mistress of it.

l. 28. **Silviis,** should logically be in agreement with **cognomen,** ' the clan name Silvius ', but is attracted into the case of **omnibus.**

l. 29. **cognomen.** This word =' family name ' and is used for the more correct **nomen** =' clan name '. Thus in Gaius Julius Caesar, we have **praenomen** (individual name), **nomen** (clan name), and **cognomen** (family name).

l. 30. **ortus,** supply **est.**

l. 31. **amnis** is a poetical word, but often used by Livy along with **fluvius** and **flumen** of the same river—a good instance of his attempt to add variety to his narrative.

l. 32. **ad** = **apud. celebre . . . nomen,** ' the name in vogue with later generations '.

l. 35. **ipse,** ' the latter ', i.e. **Romulus Silvius. regnum . . . tradidit,** ' bequeathed the kingship in immediate succession '.

The phrase **per manus tradere** is commonly used for ' to hand down from father to son '.

l. 37. **is,** i.e. **Aventinus.**

l. 39. **maximus,** sc. **natu,** ' the eldest '.

---

[1] Calig. 34

l. 41. **verecundia aetatis,** ' respect due to seniority '. **Aetatis is** an excellent example of the objective genitive.

l. 42. **stirpem virilem,** i.e. ' son ' or ' sons '.

l. 43. **filiae Reae Silviae,** dative of disadvantage, with **ademit,** ' from his brother's daughter . . .'.

l. 43. **per speciem honoris,** ' on the pretext of doing her honour '.

l. 44. **perpetua virginitate,** ' by (imposing on her) perpetual virginity '.

Chapter 4

Line 1. **Sed debebatur . . . principium.** The verb **debebatur** has two subjects, **origo** and **principium ;** on the latter depends the phrase, **maximi . . . imperii,** i.e. ' the beginning of an empire greatest next to the power of the gods '.

debebatur fatis, *lit.,* ' was owed to destiny ', i.e. ' was predestined '.

l. 4. **seu . . . erat.** Notice again how Livy obtains variety, by using (1) **rata,** perf. partic. of a deponent verb, causally, and (ii) a causal clause introduced by **quia.** Translate this part of the sentence after **Martem . . . nuncupat.**

l. 9. **iubet.** The subject is **Amulius.** Note the asyndeton (lack of a connecting particle or conjunction) between the two clauses ending with **datur** and **iubet.** Asyndeton is used to suggest a quick succession of events (as here) or a contrast.

l. 9. **forte quadam divinitus,** *lit.,* ' by some chance providentially ', an expression which seems to be a contradiction in terms but one to which we can find parallels in Greek and English.

l. 10. **Tiberis effusus lenibus stagnis,** *lit.,* ' the Tiber having been poured forth in stagnant pools ', i.e. ' having overflowed its banks . . .'.

l. 10. **nec . . . dabat,** *lit.,* ' not only could not anywhere be approached to the course of the regular stream but gave hope to those carrying (the children) that they could be drowned in water however still '.

Note : (i) **nec . . . et,** ' not only not . . . but ', (ii) **iusti,** for **iustum** in agreement with **cursum** (hypallage) : cf. Chap. 1, l. 14. (iii) **quamvis,** used by Livy chiefly as an adverb to modify adjs. and advs.

l. 14. **ficus Ruminalis.** **Rumina** was a goddess of suckling or nursing. The fig-tree was on the north-west slope of the Palatine opposite the Capitoline hill.

l. 15. **ferunt** = ' they say ', as often. It was natural for many to see in the name **Ruminalis** a corruption of the hero's name **Romulus** : hence the name **Romularis. vocatam** ; supply **esse** and **eam** (i.e. the fig-tree).

ll. 16-23. **Tenet fama . . . datos.** In this sentence, note the following points : (i) **tenet** used intransitively, ' prevails '. (ii) **quo,** local abl., ' in which ' without a prep.—a poetical construction. (iii) **tenuis aqua,** ' the shallow water '. (iv) **in sicco,** ' on dry ground '. Livy often uses adjectives as nouns even in the oblique cases. (v) The use of the indicative in the clauses **quo . . . erant pueri, qui circa sunt,** the usual construction when the subordinate clauses are an addition by the author and not part of the original story or statement. (vi) **mitem,** adj. for adv. ' gently '. (vii) **eam submissas . . . praebuisse mammas,** ' that she offered her lowered dugs ', i.e. ' she lowered and offered her dugs '.

l. 24. **vulgato corpore,** ' in consequence of prostituting her person ', abl. of cause.

l. 25. **vocatam :** supply **esse.**

l. 25. **inde,** ' accordingly '. **locum,** ' occasion ', ' reason '.

l. 25. **fabulae ac miraculo,** hendiadys, ' for the wonderful story '. Hendiadys (frequent in Vergil) is a construction in which Latin uses two nouns when in English we prefer adjective and noun in one phrase or one noun depending upon the other.

l. 27. **nec in stabulis . . . segnes,** ' (though) not inactive in the folds and about the cattle '.

l. 28. **venando.** In Livy, the abl. of the gerund, (an abl. of manner), has often the force of an English present participle : ' hunting '. **peragrare,** historic infin. So also **subsistere, facere,** etc. in the next sentence.

l. 28. **Hinc . . . sumpto,** ' having gained strength for (=having strengthened) their bodies and spirits in-this-exercise (**hinc**) '.

l. 31. **cum his,** ' together with them ' (i.e. the shepherds).

l. 32. **crescente . . . iuvenum,** ' the number of their young companions daily increasing '.

CHAPTER 5

Line 1. **Iam tum . . . ferunt,** ' they say that this festival (of) the Lupercal (as now known) was (celebrated) even in those days (**tum**) on the hill Palatium.'

hoc is emphatic and refers to the time of Livy.

The festival of the **Lupercalia** was held in Rome on Feb. 15th. It was customary for young men, naked except for girdles made from the skins of the sacrificed victims (goats and a dog), to run about the bounds of the Palatine city and strike those whom they met, especially women (to induce fertility) with the goat-skins. The festival seems to have combined purificatory and fertility rites, and beating of the bounds.

l. 2. **et a Pallanteo . . . appellatum,** ' and that the hill was called Pallantium from Pallanteum, a city in Arcadia, and then the Palatium '.

The derivation of the word is much disputed, and we cannot definitely accept Livy's explanation.

l. 4. **Evandrum.** Evander was originally a minor deity, associated with Pan and worshipped in Arcadia. According to legend, however, he had also a more human descent and is said to have left Arcadia, and to have arrived in Italy, making a settlement on the hill which he called after his native city Pallantium and on which he instituted the worship of Faunus (Pan Lycaeus) and established the Lupercalia. Cf. Ovid, *Fasti,* v. 91 :

> **Exsul ab Arcadia Latios Evander in agros**
> **Venerat, impositos attuleratque deos.**

l. 4. **genere** = **gente.**

l. 4. **multis ante tempestabibus,** ' many seasons before '. Note the abl. of the measure of difference.

l. 5. **tenuerit.** Note the primary sequence, which is often found in the historians, sometimes side by side with the more regular historic sequence.

l. 5. sollemne adlatum . . . instituisse ut . . . , The **ut** clause **is** explanatory of **sollemne**; 'introduced the rite imported . . . namely that . . .'.

l 6. **Lycaeum Pana. Pana** has a Greek accusative ending. **Pan,** called **Lycaeus** from Mt. Lycaeus near Pallanteum in Arcadia, was a god of the herdsmen and flocks (his name is interpreted 'the Feeder ') and was later identified with the Italian Faunus (' kindly one '), a deity of the forests and of herdsmen. As the latter, Faunus was also identified with Inuus whose name was associated with the verb **inire,** ' to enter in ' (i.e. sexually), because he was regarded as the fertilizer of cattle.

l 7 **per lusum atque lasciviam,** hendiadys, ' in wanton sport '. Note (in the Latin) the alliteration, of which Livy is particularly fond.

ll. 8-12. **huic deditis . . . accusantes.** The acc. and infin. construction is continued. Order for translation : **latrones, ob iram amissae praedae insidiatos deditis huic ludicro, cum** (since) **. . . esset, cum . . . defendisset, cepisse Remum, (et) captum** (having captured him) **tradidisse regi Amulio ultro accusantes.**

ob iram . . . praedae, ' in anger at the loss of their booty '. Cf. Chap. 3, l. 16.

deditis, ' engrossed in ' ; *lit.*, ' surrendered to '. It is dative, governed by **insidiatos,** and agrees with **eis** (= Romulus and Remus) understood.

cepisse, captum. The repetition of the verb links the two sentences and expresses immediate sequence of events, ' seized R. and immediately handed him over '.

ultro is always used where an action goes beyond what is normally expected. Here we might translate, ' impudently '.

l. 12. **crimini maxime dabant,** *lit.*, ' they particularly offered (it) for a charge (predicative dative) that . . .'.

l. 13. **inde = ex eis,** ' from these ', i.e. the lands of Numitor.

l. 16. **inde ab initio,** ' right from the first '.

Faustulo spes fuerat, ' hope had been to F.' = ' Faustulus had hoped '.

l. 16. **regiam ... educari.** The emphasis falls on **regiam**, ' that the boys being brought up in his home were of royal birth '.

l. 18. **et.** The first **et** means ' both ' and can be ignored in translation.

l. 18. **quo,** ' at which '.

l. 19. **ad id ipsum,** ' with that event '.

l. 19. **nisi ... necessitatem,** ' unless either an opportunity arose or necessity compelled him '. **per occasionem** = occasione data.

l. 22. **Numitori,** dat. of the person interested, to be translated as a gen. with **animum,** l. 25.

l. 24. **comparando ... servilem.** For the abl. of the gerund, cf. Chap. 4, l. 28. Translate here by a clause, ' as he compared ...'.

l. 26. **eodem,** *adv.*, ' the same result '.

l. 26. **esset** = abesset (impersonal) (cf. Chap. 3, l. 26). **ut haud abesset ... agnosceret,** ' so that he practically recognised R.'

l. 29. **aliis alio itinere iussis ... pastoribus,** ' having told the shepherds ... by different routes '; *lit.*, ' some by one route, (others by another route)'.

CHAPTER 6

Lines 1-8. **Numitor ... ostendit.** Note this period and how it is composed. The nom. **Numitor** (which is the subject throughout) is followed by nom. pres. part. **dictitans, cum** + pluperf. subj., **postquam** + perf. indic., abl. absol. **advocato concilio,** and finally by the main verb **ostendit.** To obtain a good translation, we must split such a period into shorter sentences. In this case, we might make **dictitans** and **avocasset** main verbs linked by ' and ', begin a fresh sentence with **postquam** and make **advocato** a main verb: ' he summoned an assembly and revealed ...'.

l. 3. **praesidio armisque,** hendiadys, ' with an armed garrison '.

l. 5. **gratulantes.** The pres. part. seems here to be used almost as a fut. part. to express purpose, ' to congratulate him '.

l. 7. **ut,** ' how '.

i. 8. **deinceps.** Livy occasionally uses an adverb as an attribute of a noun, as here, where **deinceps** goes with **caedem,** ' the subsequent murder of the tyrant '.

l. 9. **agmine,** abl. of manner, ' in a troop '.

l. 11. **vox,** ' shout '.

l. 11. **ratum . . . efficit,** ' ratified '.

l. 13. **re =re publica** ' the government '.

l. 13. **Romulum . . . cepit.** This sentence would be better in English in the passive ; ' R. and R. were seized with a desire . . . .,

l. 16. **ad id pastores quoque accesserant,** *lit.,* ' the shepherds also had been added to this '. **ad id,** i.e. to the overflowing population.

l. 17. **qui omnes . . . facerent,** ' so that they all easily gave rise to the hope that . . .'. **facerent,** consecutive subj.

l. 22. **aetatis verecundia.** See Chap. 3, l. 41.

l. 22. **discrimen facere,** ' make (any) distinction (between them).'

ll. 23-26. **ut di . . . capiunt.** Note the following : (i) **ut di . . .** **legerent** depends on **capiunt** and should be translated after the main clause. (ii) **quorum tutelae . . . essent,** ' under whose protection (**tutelae,** gen. of possession) that country was '. (iii) **qui = uter.** (iv) **templa,** ' quarters (of the sky) ', is in loose apposition with **Palatium, Aventinum.** (v) **conditam,** ' (it when) founded '.

In the taking of auspices, it was customary to divide the heavens into four quarters by the intersection of two imaginary lines, the one from east to west, the other from north to south. In this case, Romulus chose the quarter above the Palatine for taking his observations, Remus that above the Aventine.

CHAPTER 7

Line 2. **iamque . . . augurio.** Make this abl. absol. a main verb and insert ' and ' before **utrumque regem.**

l. 3. **utrumque . . . consalutaverat.** This sentence would be better in the passive in English, ' each had been hailed . . .'.

l. 4. **tempore praecepto,** i.e. ' on the ground of priority of time '. **trahebant,** ' claimed '.

l. 6. **certamine irarum,** ' owing to the conflict of their passions '.

ll. 9-11. **cum . . . moenia mea.** Translate this clause after **ab irato Romulo interfectum esse. cum . . . adiecisset,** ' when he had added, chiding (him) also with words ', i.e. ' who added these words also in chiding him '.

l. 10. **Sic,** supply **pereat.**

l. 15. **Graeco.** Supply **ritu,** ' after the Greek custom '.

l. 17. **Geryone interempto,** ' after slaying Geryon '. The latter was a triple-headed monster who lived near Gades (Cadiz). His destruction constituted the tenth labour of Hercules.

l. 17. **mira specie,** abl. of quality *or* description, with **boves.**

ll. 18-21. **ac prope . . . procubuisse.** Keep the order of the Latin as far as **traiecerat,** then translate **procubuisse loco herbido** (local abl.), and finally **ut . . . via.**

Note that **ipsum fessum via** is a second object of **reficeret.**

nando traiecerat, ' he had crossed by swimming ', i.e. ' he had swum across '.

l. 21. **ibi cum . . . oppressisset.** This would be better in the passive in English.

l. 23. **Cacus.** Vergil calls him a son of Vulcan. Popular etymology connected his name (erroneously) with κακός, ' the bad man '.

l. 23. **ferox viribus,** ' insolent because of his strength '.

l. 23. **captus . . . vellet.** Make **captus** a main verb, drop the **cum,** insert ' and ' and translate **vellet** as an indicative. Begin a fresh sentence with **quia.**

l. 24. **si . . . compulisset, vestigia . . . deductura erant.** Note that this conditional clause (unreal in past time) has in the apodosis the future participle with the indicative instead of the more usual pluperfect subjunct. This variant which occurs several times in Livy is more graphic than the subj. ' If he had driven . . . , the tracks were likely to guide . . .'.

l. 26. **quaerentem,** in agreement with **dominum,** 'in his search '.

l. 27. **boves eximium quemque pulchritudine. Quemque** is in apposition with **boves** and used with **eximium** as with superlatives, *lit.,* ' the cattle, each choice one in beauty ', **i.e.** ' the choicest of the cattle in point of beauty.'

l. 30. **numero,** dat. with **abesse,** 'was missing from the number'.

l. 31. **si forte,** ' (to see) if perchance the tracks led there '. **Si is** regularly used in this meaning after verbs of trying and similar meaning, or where such a verb can easily be supplied.

l. 32. **nec in partem aliam ferre,** ' and did not lead in (any) other direction '. Notice **ferre** used intransitively.

l. 33. **animi,** locative case.

l. 34. **actae boves,** ' the cattle which were being driven off '. Owing to the absence of a pres. part. pass. in Latin, the perf. part. pass. had to be used instead.

l. 35. **ad desiderium ... relictarum,** ' in longing for (=missing) those left behind '. **relictarum** is an excellent example of the objective gen.

l. 35. **ut fit,** ' as usually happens '.

l. 40. **tum,** ' in those days '. **ea** agrees with **loca.**

l. 41. **venerabilis.** Begin a fresh sentence here and supply ' he was '.

l. 42. **miraculo litterarum,** ' for the wonderful invention of the alphabet '. Evander was said to have invented the Roman alphabet. While it has generally been held, however, that it was derived, along with the Italic alphabets in general, from a primitive version of a variety (the Chalcidian) of the Greek alphabet, the opinion of modern scholars suggests that Latin owes its alphabet directly to the Etruscans, who in turn derived their alphabet from a Greek one current on the Greek mainland north of the Corinthian Gulf.

l. 43. **venerabilior.** Supply ' but ' before this word. For the asyndeton, see Chap. 4, l. 9.

l. 43. **divinitate credita,** ' by reason of the supposed divinity.'

l. 44. **fatiloquam,** ' (as) a prophetess '.

l. 44. **Sibyllae.** For the Sibyl, see Vergil *Aeneid*, vi. 35 f. **miratae** with **fuerant** (the latter is sometimes put for **erant**).

l. 45. **is tum ... excitus postquam.** Make **excitus** a main verb and insert ' and ' before **postquam.**

l. 46. circa ... caedis, *lit.*, 'around the stranger accused (by them) of murder detected-on-the-spot (manifestae) '; i.e. ' around the stranger whom they accused as a murderer caught in the act '.

l. 49. aliquantum ... humana, ' somewhat grander and more august than a mortal's '. Note aliquantum, adv. acc. used instead of aliquanto, the abl. of the measure of difference.
With humana, supply forma.

l. 51. Hercules, voc.

l. 53. aucturum (esse) ... , ' that you would increase the number of the gods ', =' that you would be added to . . .'.

l. 54. opulentissima olim in terris, ' (destined) one day (to be) the most powerful on earth '.

l. 55. maximam. The ara maxima was not far from the Circus Maximus. For the origin of the Ara Maxima, see Vergil, *Aeneid*, viii. 182-277, Prop., iv. 9 ; Ovid, *Fasti*, i. 543-586.

l. 57. fata, ' the prophecy '.

l. 57. ara ... dicata, abl. absol., ' by the building and . . .'.

l. 58. sacrum is the subject to factum (est).

l. 58. adhibitis. adhibeo is commonly used in the meaning, ' use ', ' employ '. This abl. absol. might be made a main verb, ' the Potitii and Pinarii, families which . . . were used . . .'.

l. 61. ad tempus, ' at the right time'.

l. 62. Pinarii. Insert ' while ' before this word. The name Pinarii was popularly derived from πεῖνα, ' hunger ', ' fast '. According to Servius (*ad Aen.*, v. 26), Hercules had said to them, πεινάσετε.

l. 62. extis adesis, ' after the vitals had been eaten '.

It was the custom in Homeric times for the officiating priests to eat the vitals. Cf. Hom., *Od.*, iii. 461. The Roman practice was to burn the *exta* on the altar, or throw them into the sea, if the sacrifice was being made to a sea-god.

l. 64. eorum sollemnium. The gen. depends upon extis, but we should prefer to say, ' *at* those sacrifices '.

l. 67. sollemni is here an adj. in agreement with ministerio.

l. 67. **tradito.** .... This handing over to public slaves what was the solemn duty of the family was regarded by the Romans as an act of impiety which resulted in the extinction of the entire family. This incident occurred in 312 B.C. in the censorship of Appius Claudius Caecus, Cf. Livy, ix. 29, 9.

l. 68. **haec tum . . . suscepit.** The emphasis falls on **haec sacra,** on **una,** and **tum.** Thus we get : ' this, out of all, was the only foreign rite that Romulus adopted at this time".

l. 69. **iam tum . . . fautor.** Order for translation : **fautor immortalitatis partae virtute ad quam . . .**

CHAPTER 8

Line 1. **ad concilium,** ' to a meeting '.

l. 3. **nulla re . . . legibus,** *lit.,* ' by nothing except by law '.

l. 4. **quae.** The antecedent is **iura,**

l. 4. **iura,** ' a code of law '.

l. 4. **ita = ea tantum condicione,** ' only on this condition '.

l. 6. **cum cetero . . . fecit,** *lit.,* ' he made himself more august not only in the rest of his condition but also especially by the assumption of twelve lictors '.

The bodyguard of twelve lictors carried axes bound in rods as symbols of the king's (and later the consul's) right to flog and to execute.

For the translation of **lictoribus sumptis,** see note on Chap. 3, l. 16.

l. 9. **me haud paenitet . . . sententiae,** *lit.,* ' it does not repent me to be of the opinion of those '.

ll. 10-13. **quibus . . . placet,** *lit.,* ' to whom it pleases that attendants of this kind and the number itself were taken from the neighbouring Etruscans from whom . . .'. Perhaps we might say : ' who accept the derivation of . . '.

Notice : **hoc genus,** adv. acc.

The curule chair (i.e. inlaid with ivory) and the **toga praetexta** (i.e. edged with a broad purple stripe) were insignia of the two most important Roman magistrates, consuls and praetors (who alone of the magistrates had imperium) and of the censors and curule aediles

l. 13. et ita habuisse Etruscos ..., acc. and infin. construction continued, ' and (believe) that ...'.

l. 14. singulos ... dederint, ' the several tribes contributed the lictors, one each '.

l. 16. alia ... appetendo loca, *lit.*, ' by encroaching on some and other parts with its walls ', i.e. ' as it encroached on different parts ...'.

l. 18. ad id ... erat, *lit.*, ' with regard to that which was of the population then ', ' with regard to the existing population '.

l. 20. vetere ... urbes, ' following a plan long used by founders of cities '. **condentium.** Livy is fond of using the present participle as a noun.

l. 22. natam ... prolem, ' that sons have been born to them from the earth '.

l. 23. escendentibus, *lit.*, ' (to you) going up ' =' as you go up (the hill) '.
The hill is the Capitoline and the asylum was established in a depression between its two peaks.

l. 24. asylum, in apposition with **locum,** ' (as) a refuge '.

l. 25. liber ... esset, supply **utrum** before **liber.** The subjunctive is due to the fact that the clause is an indirect question, dependent on the verbal idea contained in **discrimine ;** ' without distinction as to whether they were ...'.

ll. 27-28. idque ... fuit. roboris (partit. gen.) depends on **primum ;** *lit.*, ' and that was the first (of) strength towards the greatness he had begun '. Add to the translation ' accession ' before ' strength ' and ' to plan ' after ' begun '

l. 28. cum ... paeniteret, ' since he was not dissatisfied with his strength '.

l. 28. consilium, ' an advisory body '. **viribus,** dat. of advantage, ' for the (directing of that) strength '.

ll. 31-32. patres ... appellati. patres is the complement ; then **appellati** has a second subject **progenies** with a second complement **patricii.**

The **patres** were probably the family heads of the original settlers, as opposed to the migrants that Romulus attracted to his city. Livy seems to suggest that it was the members of the first senate that formed the Patrician Order.

CHAPTER 9

Line 1. **res Romana,** ' Rome '.

l. 2. **penuria,** abl.

l. 3. **hominis aetatem,** ' for only one generation ', *lit.*, ' for the lifetime of a man '.

l. 4. **quibus ;** the antecedent is implied in **res Romana** : ' inasmuch as to them (*lit.*, whom) there were . . .'.

l. 5. **ex consilio,** ' in accordance with the advice '.

l. 7. **urbes quoque** . . . The construction becomes acc. and infin. as Livy is reporting the argument used by the envoys.

l. 8. **ut cetera,** ' like all other things '.

l. 8. **virtus,** ' worth ' *or* ' merit '.

l. 10. **satis scire.** Supply **se.** Such an omission of the personal pronoun is common in Livy.

l. 11. **ne gravarentur,** indirect command, ' let them not be reluctant '.

l. 12. **homines cum hominibus,** ' (being) human . . . with (their fellow) humans '.

l. 14. **simul** . . . **simul,** ' both . . . and '.

l. 16. **dimissi.** Supply **sunt.** The subject is the **legati. plerisque rogitantibus,** abl. absol.

l. 16. **ecquod,** ' if any ', in agreement with **asylum.**

l. 17. **id enim demum** . . . **fore,** *lit.*, ' for only that would be a suitable marriage ' = ' for only in that way would they get suitable wives '.

l. 19. **ad vim spectare,** ' to look to violence ' = ' to foreshadow hostilities '.

l. 19. **Cui,** ' for this ', i.e. ' for the use of force '.

l. 21. **Neptuno equestri.** Neptune (Poseidon) was said to have produced the horse in Thessaly or Attica by a blow of his trident. (Cf. Vergil, *Georg.*, I. 12.) A Roman god of agriculture Consus (from **condere,** ' to store ' (in barns)) had horse-races held in his honour as Neptune did, and therefore the Roman god was identified with the Greek one.

The festival of the Consualia was celebrated on the 21st Aug. and the 15th Dec. in the Circus Maximus, where, according to Cicero and Vergil, the Sabine women were carried off. Livy however tells us in 35. 8 that the Circus Maximus was not established until the reign of Tarquinius Priscus.

ll. 23-24. **quantoque . . . concelebrant.** Supply **tanto** with **apparatu** which is the antecedent of **quanto :** ' they celebrated (the games) with as much magnificence as . . .'.

l. 24. **tum sciebant aut poterant,** ' (as) they then knew or could ' = within the existing range of their knowledge or power '.

l. 27. **proximi quique.** Quique is the plural of quisque and the construction is the usual one of superlative + **quisque :** ' all their nearest neighbours '.

l. 32. **eo** =' **in id** ' *or* ' **ad id** '.

l. 35. **forte in quem** = ab eo in quem forte. **raptae (sunt)** agrees in *sense* with its singular subject, which = ' most of the women '.

ll. 36-38. **quasdam . . . deferebant.** This sentence would be better in English if turned into the passive—a device which enables the student also to follow the order of the Latin.

l. 37. **ex plebe,** ' plebeian '.

l. 40. **ferunt,** ' they say '.

l. 42. **clamitatum (est),** impersonal passive, ' they cried '. **ferri,** supply **eam.**

l. 42. **nuptialem.** Cf. Plutarch, *Romulus,* 15 ; ' hence the Romans to this very day, at their weddings, sing Talassius for their nuptial word, as the Greek do Hymenaeus '.

l. 44. **maesti,** adj. for adv., ' in sadness '.

l. 45. **incusantes . . . foedus,** *lit.,* ' expostulating at the treaty of hospitality violated ' = ' expostulating at the violation of the treaty of hospitality '.

violati, hypallage for **violatum.**

l. 46. **per fas ac fidem. per** has the meaning of ' contrary to ', ' in violation of '. The phrase goes very closely with **decepti.**

l. 47. **raptis,** dat. of the possessor. Supply **virginibus.**

l. 49. **patrum,** ' of their fathers', dependent on **superbia,** abl. of cause.

l. 50. **illas** . . . **fore,** ' the daughters, however, would be in marriage (=would be legally married) and in partnership of (=would fully share) all their fortunes, the citizenship and . . .'.

l. 52. **quo,** abl. of comparison. **liberum,** gen. pl. depending on **societate.**

l. 53. **mollirent,** indirect command, ' let them only (**modo**) . . .'.

l. 54. **animos,** ' hearts '.

l. 55. **postmodum** =postea. **gratiam,** ' affection '.

l. 55. **eo melioribus** . . . **viris,** ' they would find their husband kinder for the following reason '. **eo,** abl. of cause.

l. 56. **adnisurus sit** . . . Notice the primary tense, although the strict sequence would require the imperfect subj. So also **expleat** in l. 58. The historians Caesar, Livy, and Tacitus are fond of using primary tenses in the subordinate clauses in a passage of Oratio Obliqua, sometimes using them side by side with the historic tenses demanded by strict sequence.

l. 57. **suam vicem,** adv. acc., ' for his part '.

l. 58. **accedebant : accedo** is often used as the passive of **addo.** Sometimes, as here, it is equivalent to : ' in addition there were . . .'.

l. 59. **purgantium,** *conative* use of pres. partic., ' seeking to excuse '.

l. 59. **cupiditate atque amore,** another hendiadys, ' upon the score of passionate love '.

l. 60. **quae maxime** . . . **sunt,** ' pleas which . . .'.

ad muliebre ingenium, ' over a woman's heart '. Here **ad** = **apud,** as often in Livy.

CHAPTER 10

Line 1. **raptis, a** dat. of the person interested which becomes gen. in English.

l. 4. **indignationes.** Livy uses abstract nouns in the plural almost as the equivalent of more concrete expressions : ' angry feelings '. (Cf. also **irae,** Chap. 7, l. 6.)

l. 5. **Tatium.** Tatius was the ruler of Cures, the most important town of the Sabines.

l. 6. **eo** = ad eum.

l. 9. **lente,** virtually equivalent to **lentius,** ' too slowly '.

l. 10. **inter se communiter.** For this pleonastic expression, cf. the note on Chap. 3, l. 20.

l. 12. **pro ardore iraque.** Hendiadys, ' for the burning anger '.

l. 13. **per se . . . Caeninum. ipsum** emphasises **se** and **nomen Caeninum** is the subject of **facit. Nomen** here means ' people '.

l. 16. **fundit fugatque.** Livy is fond of using alliteration with words of allied meaning.

ll. 20-21. **cum factis . . . ostentator haud minor,** *lit.,* ' not only a hero splendid in his deeds, but also no less a displayer of them ', i.e. ' he was just as eager to display his achievements as he was a splendid hero in their performance '.

l. 21. **suspensa.** Make this perf. part. pass. a main verb, ' he hung the spoils of the . . . on a frame . . . and carrying (it) himself . . .'.

l. 22. **ad id,** ' for that purpose '.

l. 24. **simul cum dono,** *lit.,* ' at the same time with the gift ' =' at the same time as he made the gift '.

l. 25. **templo,** dat.

l. 25. **Iuppiter Feretri**: the title **Feretrius** is derived either from **ferre** (Livy) or from **ferire** (Propert., iv. 10, 45). Fowler (*Roman Festivals* p. 229) regards Jupiter Feretrius as the pure Italian Jupiter who was later overshadowed by the Etruscan god whose temple was established on the Capitol.

On that hill, at this time uninhabited, there stood in later times the temple of Jupiter Optimus Maximus.

The oak (**quercus,** l. 23) was sacred to Jupiter.

l. 26. **Romulus rex regia.** Note the alliteration and the effective juxtaposition of **rex** and **regia.**

l. 28. **sedem opimis spoliis,** ' (as) a resting-place for the **spolia opima** '.

l. 29. **me auctorem sequentes,** ' following my example '.

l. 32. **dis visum.** Supply **est.** ' It seemed (good) to ', (i.e. ' it pleased,) the gods '.

l. 33. **posteros,** ' men in after ages '.

l. 34. **multitudine compotum,** ' by a large number of persons qualified to share it '.

l. 35. **bina . . . opima spolia.** Note the use of **bina** (=duo) with words found only in the plural.

l. 35. **inter** =per. **parta,** from **pario.**
The two occasions were in 428 B.C. when A. Cornelius Cossus slew Tolumnius, king of Veii, and in 222 B.C., when Claudius Marcellus slew Viridomarus, the Insubrian king, cf. Vergil, *Aen.,* vi. 855.

CHAPTER 11

Line 2. **per occasionem ac solitudinem.** Hendiadys : ' taking advantage of the opportunity afforded by their absence '.

l. 3. **ad** =adversus. **legio,** ' a levy ', (*the literal meaning of the word*).

l. 4. **oppressit,** ' surprised '.

l. 7. **raptarum** =captivarum.

l. 9. **rem** =rem publicam, as often in Livy.

l. 9. **impetratum.** Supply **est.** The construction is impersonal passive, common in Latin, impossible in English. We prefer the personal use or an active verb. ' Her request was granted ' *or* ' he granted her request '. Cf. **migratum est** below.

l. 10. **profectus.** Supply **est.**

l. 11. **alienis cladibus,** ' owing to the defeats suffered by others ', abl. of cause.

l. 20. **Tarpeius.** To him was traced the old name of the Capitoline Hill, **mons Tarpeius.** The **saxum Tarpeium (rupes Tarpeia),** which

was so called from its having been the scene of the daughter's
treachery, is usually placed in the south-west corner of the
Capitoline.

l. 21. **arci** =the Capitoline Hill. Tacitus, however, in *Ann.*, xii. 24
tells us : **Capitolium non a Romulo, sed a T. Tatio additum urbi
credidere.**

l. 21. **virginem.** We are told by Varro and Plutarch that she was
a Vestal virgin.

l. 21. **auro.** A different reason is given by Propertius (iv. 4), who
says that she was in love with Tatius and demanded his hand in
marriage as her reward.

l. 23. **sacris,** ' for a sacrifice '. As a vestal, she had to draw water
from the spring of the Camenae.

l. 23. **aquam petitum.** It is interesting to note that the supine
with an object is rarely found in other writers. Caesar and Cicero
prefer the gerundive construction ; e.g. here, **aquae petendae causa.**

l. 24. **accepti.** Supply **in arcem.**

l. 24. **obrutam . . . necavere.** Notice once more : Latin perfect
part. pass. and finite verb are equivalent to two English finite verbs ;
' they overwhelmed and killed '.

l 24. **seu ut . . . seu . . . causa.** Notice how Livy varies his
manner of expressing purpose.

l. 25. **ne quid . . . esset,** *lit.*, ' that not anything anywhere might
be dependable for a traitor ', i.e. ' that no traitor might anywhere
find security '.

l. 27. **quod,** ' because '.

l. 28. **magna specie,** abl. of quality *or* description : ' of great
beauty '.

l. 29. The subj. **habuerint** shows that this causal clause is dependent on **eam pepigisse.**

l. 30. **eo,** ' therefore '.

l. 30. **scuta . . . congesta** (esse). This would be better in the
active in English : ' they heaped upon her (**illi**) '.

l. 31. **sunt qui . . . dicant.** Livy now gives a third account which
represents Tarpeia as a heroine.

l. 31. **ex pacto tradendi,** ' by her stipulation for their handing
over. '

l. 33. **fraude visam agere,** *lit.,* ' (and that) having been seen **to** be acting treacherously ' =' and that when it was seen that she was . . .'.

l. 33. **sua mercede,** ' with her own fee ', **i.e.** ' with the fee she herself had demanded '.

CHAPTER 12

Line 1. **tamen,** ' be that as it may '. We may be uncertain how the citadel was captured, but not about the fact that it was taken.

l. 2. **quod . . . campi,** ' all the level ground '. **campi,** partit. gen.

l. 5. **ira . . . stimulante animos,** abl. absol. The phrase, which is in the act. in Latin, ' anger . . . rousing their courage ', would be better in the passive in English.

l. 6. **in adversum.** Supply **collem,** ' up the hill '.

l. 6. **principes** =**primi,** ' champions '.

l. 7. **ab,** ' on the side of '.

l. 9. **iniquo loco,** abl. absol. Translate ' in spite of . . .'.

l. 11. **veterem portam Palati :** the **porta Mugionia,** which is the northern gate on the Palatine Hill.

l. 12. **fugientium,** ' of the fugitives ' ; participle for noun.

l. 13. **tuis . . . iussus avibus.** The emphasis which falls on **tuis** by its position can be obtained in English only by a circumlocution such as this : ' thine were the birds at whose bidding I . . .'.

l. 16. **media valle,** ' the valley that lies between us '.

l. 17. **arce :** imperative of **arceo.**

l. 18. **Romanis,** dat. of disadvantage, ' from the Romans '.

l. 18. **fugam foedam.** For the alliteration, see Chap. 10, l. 16.

l. 19. **Statori Iovi.** A temple to ' Jupiter the Stayer ' which stood on the Nova Via, near the Porta Mugionia, and had been vowed and dedicated by M. Atilius Regulus in 294 B.C., was later associated with Romulus.

Another temple to he same god was erected by C. Caecilius Metellus Macedonicus in 146 B.C. near the Circus Maximus.

l. 19. **monumentum.** Other writers would prefer the predicative dative. **sit,** final (purpose) subjunctive ; render **quod sit,** ' to be '.

l. 22. hinc, *lit.*, ' from this place ' = ' here '.

l. 25. ab. See l. 7 above. princeps, ' first '.

l. 26. effusos, ' in disorder ' ; *lit.*, ' having been scattered '.

l. 27. toto . . . est. Order for translation : per (tantum) spatium quantum est toto foro. For the partial omission of the antecedent see the note on Chap. 9, ll. 23-24.

toto foro ; in is regularly omitted with nouns qualified by totus, medius, etc. The forum is the Forum Romanum.

l. 30. longe aliud esse . . . cum viris, *lit.*, ' that it is by far one thing to . . . , another thing to . . .' ; i.e. ' that there is a big difference between . . .'.

l. 31. haec gloriantem, ' as he was uttering these boasts '.

l. 33. pelli. Supply eum, ' for him to be put to flight '.

l. 34. alia acies. alia = cetera, ' the rest of the army '.

l. 36. strepitu sequentium. The abl. of cause goes closely with equo trepidante. For sequentium, ' of the pursuers ' = ' of the pursuit ', see the note above, l. 12.

l. 37. averterat. The pluperfect sometimes indicate instantaneous action and is then translated as a perfect.

l. 38. periculo, ' owing to the danger ' ; abl. of cause.

ll. 38-39. et ille . . . evadit, *lit.*, ' and he (Mettius), his men beckoning to (him) and calling to him, courage having been added (to him) owing to the support of many, made his escape '. It will be necessary to recast the abl. absol. phrases to bring this sentence into good English. You might begin : ' Mettius, beckoned to and called by his men, gained courage from the support of so many and . . .'.

CHAPTER 13

Line 3. victo . . . pavore. Make this abl. absol. a causal clause.

l. 3. ausae. Supply sunt.

l. 4. ex transverso, ' from the flank ', to be taken closely with impetu facto. The latter can be made into an active infinitive with ' and ' supplied before dirimere.

l. 5. dirimere . . . iras. This phrase illustrates Livy's fondness for repetition, asyndeton, and the plural of the abstract noun used in a concrete sense, iras being equivalent to iratos.

l. 6. soceri generique, nom. pl., ' that, (being) fathers and sons-in-law, they should not . . .'.

l. 7. partus = liberos.

l. 8. nepotum progeniem = nepotes : similarly liberum progeniem = liberos ; i.e. the dependent genitives mean ' consisting of '.

l. 9. piget. Supply nos (acc.).

l. 12. melius peribimus. The emphasis falls on melius and can be obtained in English by a periphrasis : ' it will be better for us to perish than to live . . .'.

l. 12. cum . . . tum, ' both . . . and ' ; ' not only . . . but also '.

l. 17. conferunt, ' they transferred '.

l. 19. a Curibus. The ancients derived Quirites from the name of the town Cures, but it is highly probable that it was derived from curia, ' ward '. In this case, Quirites would mean ' wardsmen '.

l. 19. appellati. The subject, ' the citizens', is to be derived from geminata urbe.

l. 20. ubi = eum locum ubi. monumentum . . . is in apposition to eum locum, ' (as) a memorial . . . , they called that place where . . . the Curtian Lake '.

l. 21. Curtium lacum. Various explanations of the name are given by the ancients themselves. In addition to the one given here by Livy, we have another account from him (7, 6. 3), where the self-sacrifice of M. Curtius in 362 B.C. is the origin of the name. Varro (L. L., v. 148) gives the last explanation, concerning a C. Curtius, the consul of 454 B.C.

l. 23. ex, temporal, ' after '. repente: the use of an adverb as the attribute of a noun is a marked characteristic of Livy's style. Translate as an adj. and compare Chap. 6, l. 8.

l. 24. ante omnes. Livy prefers this phrase to praecipue, maxime, or in primis.

l. 25. curias, ' wards '. These units were the oldest divisions of the Roman people, created probably for political and military purposes, and consisted of families (familiae) who were neighbours. The members of the curia had certain religious rites in common.

l. 26. nomina earum. Seven names have been preserved, but Plutarch (*Rom.* 20) and Varro reject Livy's explanation of their origin. Plutarch says of this derivation from the names of Sabine women : ' that seems to be false, because many had their names from various places '.

l. 28. mulierum depends on numerus. hoc, abl. of comparison with numero to be supplied from l. 30.

l. 28. aetate. Supply utrum before the indirect question.

l. 29. lectae sint. The subject of this verb (=electae sint)[1] is the unexpressed antecedent of quae . . . darent, ' whether (those) who should give . . . were chosen . . .'.

l. 30. tres centuriae. There were three centuries of knights with ten knights to each of the thirty curiae.

l. 32. Lucerum . . . incerta est. Cicero and Varro derive Luceres from Lucumo, others from Luceres, a king of Ardea, and Plutarch from lucus, the grove where the asylum had stood.

In any case, however, the derivation of all three names is doubtful, and it has been considered that they may represent three different elements in the population, Roman, Sabine, and Etruscan. See, however, C.A.H., VII. pp. 409-410. for the view that the three names are Etruscan, and date from the period of Etruscan influence in Rome.

CHAPTER 14

Line 2. Laurentium. The chief town of the Laurentians was Lavinium, for which see Chap. 1, l. 44.

l. 3. agerent, ' took action '.

l. 4. igitur. The classical use of this conjunction denies it the first place in the sentence. Livy follows the practice of Sallust in placing it first.

l. 5. sollemne sacrificium. Note that sollemnis has here its literal meaning, ' annual '. This festival was probably devoted to the

---

[1] For the use of the simple verb in preference to the compound, see 3. l. 26.

Penates, ' gods of the store ', those gods whom Aeneas, so legend tells us, had brought with him from Troy. Cf. Vergil, *Aeneid* II, 293, (the ghost of Hector speaks to Aeneas) :

Sacra suosque tibi commendat Troia penates :
His cape fatorum comites, his moenia quaere.

l. 7. seu . . . regni, *lit.*, ' whether on account of the mistrustful sharing of royal power ', i.e. ' either from the mistrust that arises from the sharing . . .'.

l. 11. renovatum est. The treaty was renewed annually after the celebration of the Feriae Latinae ; cf. 8, 11, 15.

l. 16. priusquam . . . apparebat, *lit.*, ' before there could be as much strength as it was clear there would be ', i.e. ' before they could be as strong as they obviously would be '.

l. 16. essent. The use of the subj. here is due to the idea of *anticipation* or *prevention*.

l. 17. occupant facere. Livy is imitating the Greek verb φθάνω, ' were the first to . . .'.

l. 18. agri quod . . . est, ' all the land between . . .'. This sentence forms the subject of vastatur. In English, however, it would be better to turn vastatur into the active, ' they ravaged all the land . . .'. agri, partitive gen, *lit.*, ' what of land there is '.

l. 19. Fidenas. Fidenae was an Etruscan town about 5 miles from Rome.

l. 19. ad laevam, ' to the left '. Livy refers to the country on both sides of the Anio north-east of Rome. dextra, abl.

l. 21. tumultus repens . . . illatus, ' the sudden inrush of a crowd '.

l. 22. pro nuntio erat, ' was instead of news ' = ' brought the news first '.

l. 24. mille passuum. Livy uses the partitive gen. after mille (rare in other authors) about as often as the usual mille passus. mille is an acc. of extent, ' a mile away '.

l. 26. locis . . . obscuris. Note the omission of in, quite common with locis, especially when qualified with an adjective.

The text is difficult here and could be improved by the omission

of densa. However, as it stands, the phrase means, ' in dark places about the very thick brush wood growth ', i.e. ' in well-concealed positions where the brush wood had most thickly grown '.

l. 28. **id quod quaerebat,** *lit.,* ' that which he sought ', i.e. to draw out the enemy. Thus we might render this clause closely with **hostem excivit,** ' he achieved his purpose, namely drew out the enemy by riding up to . . .'.

l. 30. **ipsis . . . portis,** dat. dependent on **adequitando.**

l. 31. **fugae,** gen. dependent on **causam minus mirabilem,** ' an excuse less (=not) astonishing ', =' a suitable excuse '.

l. 31. **eadem,** ' the same ', merely equals ' too ', ' also '.

l. 32. **velut . . . equitatu,** ' as the cavalry wavered as if between the plan of fight and flight ' =' as if they were uncertain whether to fight or flee '.

l. 34. **plenis.** In the general eagerness to ' stream out ' the gates of Fidenae became ' suddenly jammed '.

l. 35. **instandi sequendique.** The gerunds depend on **studio,** abl. of cause, and we should render them by English infinitives : ' by their eagerness to . . .'.

l. 38. **addunt pavorem.** Keep the Latin order and turn into the passive : ' additional alarm was caused by . . .'.

l. 38. **mota e castris signa** =' the movement from the camp of the standards '. For the use of the Latin participle where English prefers a noun, cf. note on **inter Lavinium et Albam Longam coloniam deductam,** Ch. 3, l. 16.

l. 40. **prius paene, quam.** **priusquam** is often thus divided (tmesis) : ' almost before '.

l. 40. **quique** =et (ei) qui.

l. 41. **circumagerent,** ' *could* wheel '. The subjunctive is that regularly found with this conjunction (and with **antequam**) when there is present a suggestion of an action anticipated or prevented.

l. 42. **multoque effusius.** effusius, comparative adv., and **multo,** abl. of measure of difference. Cf. **paulo ante** immediately following.

l. 42. **quippe vera fuga.** It is simplest to take **fuga** as nom. to **fuit** understood : ' for (their) flight was genuine '.

l. 43. **qui simulantes.** **Qui** is for **ei qui**, and **simulantes** is acc., object of **secuti erant**, and means ' the pretended fugitives '. **Romanus,** sing. for plural.

l. 45. For the subjunctive **obicerentur,** cf. note on **circumagerent,** above.

l. 46. **velut agmine uno,** ' as though in one body ', i.e. there was no interval at all between the fugitives and their pursuers.

<h3 style="text-align:center">CHAPTER 15</h3>

Line 1. **inritati,** i.e. **inritati sunt,** participle for verb, as often. Three reasons are given for this provocation of the anger of the Veientines, the two first expressed by the causal ablatives **contagione** and **consanguinitate,** the third by the causal clause introduced by **quod.**

l. 4. **essent.** Subjunctive due to virtual oratio obliqua. A clause from the thoughts of the men of Veii is reported.

l. 6. **more,** abl. of manner, ' after the fashion '.

l. 7. **hostium** refers to the Romans, the point of view being that of the Veientines.

l. 9. **Romanus,** sing. for pl. again.

l. 9. **contra,** adv. The Roman attitude was the reverse of that with which the Veientines had made war.

l. 11. **Quem.** Note (i) how Latin writers begin even new sentences with relative words referring to antecedents in the previous sentence ; and (ii) that **quem** refers to **Romanus** (=**Romani**), and, should accordingly be translated ' that they ', being subject to **ponere** and **accessurum esse** in the acc. and infin. construction.

l. 13. **de tectis moenibusque.** **De** =' for ' here.

l. 15. **tantum,** adv., ' solely '.

l. 16. **urbe.** The abl. of separation depends on **abstinuit,** ' refrained from (attacking) their city '.

l. 17. **agros,** etc. The omission of the conjunction is an example of asyndeton. English would link the two main clauses by ' but '.

l. 18. **ulciscendi.** Render by English infinitive dependent on

studio, 'from a desire to ...'. Treat **praedae** (=praedandi) simi-larly.

l. 20. **petitum** is the supine used to express purpose : ' to seek '.

l. 21. **parte,** abl. of separation, ' of a part ', depending on **mul-tatis.** The latter is dative and agrees with eis understood.

l. 23. **ferme** belongs with **haec** : ' these things, speaking gener-ally ' (i.e. no doubt there were other incidents not recorded, but these are the chief).

l. 24. **gesta,** i.e. gesta sunt.

l. 24. **originis,** and **divinitatis,** objective genitives with **fidei,** the latter being dative dependent on **absonum** : ' inconsistent with faith in ...'.

l. 25. **non animus, etc.** Render the three negatives by ' neither ', ' nor ', ' nor '. The sentence is hardly logical, for the nominatives **animus** and **consilium** are in apposition to **nihil,** which stands for ' no *deed* '.

l. 27. **firmandae** agrees with **eius** understood (=urbis).

l. 28. **profecto,** adv.

l. 28. **valuit.** The subject is urbs understood. Study the order of words here. The emphasis falls on **illo,** and can only be retained there by some such device as this : ' for it was undoubtedly owing to the strength given (to it) by *him,* that (the city) ...'.

l. 31. **alios** =ceteros.

CHAPTER 16

Line 1. **ad exercitum recensendum** =ut exercitum recenseret.

l. 2. **campo.** The Campus Martius.

l. 4. **fragore tonitribusque,** hendiadys, ' crash of thunder '.

l. 5. **contioni,** dat. of disadvantage dependent upon a compound verb meaning ' take away '. Cf. **deme terrorem Romanis,** Ch. 12, l. 18.

l. 6. **Romana pubes, etc.** A very Livian sentence which it is worth while to analyse. It opens with the subject of the main verb, which itself comes last in the sentence, five lines away. Next follow in order, (i) an ablative absolute, (ii) and (iii) adverbial clauses of time, introduced by two different words for ' when ', (iv) adverbial clause of concession, (v) adjectival clause, (vi) indirect statement, (vii) adverbial clause of comparison (actually a phrase, **icta,** participle, having been put for **icta esset**). The difficulty of translation into English is eased by taking the earlier part of the sentence in this order : **postquam, ex** (=' after ') **tam turbido die** (=' period '), **serena et tranquilla lux rediit (et) Romana pubes, pavore tandem sedato, vidit regiam sedem vacuam. . . .**

l. 9. **credebat.** The subject is **ea** understood (=**pubes**).

l. 10. **sublimem raptum,** i.e. **(eum) sublimem raptum (esse).**

l. 12. **deum,** ' (as) a god '. So also **regem** and **parentem.**

l. 13. **salvere iubent,** ' hailed '.

l. 14. **exposcunt** has two objects, (i) **pacem,** (meaning ' his favour '), (ii) the **uti** clause. In English both would need to depend on verbs of their own. Therefore insert 'begging ' before translating the second.

l. 15. **volens propitius.** Note two things, (a) adjective used for adverb—English would say ' willing*ly* ', (b) asyndeton.

l. 17. **discerptum regem,** i.e. **regem discerptum esse, acc.** and infin. dependent upon **arguerent.**

l. 17. **taciti.** See note (a) on **volens propitius** immediately above.

l. 17. **arguerent.** The generic subjunctive, used in place of the indicative in relative clauses which have indefinite antecedents. Cf. **sunt qui putent,** ' there are (some) who think '.

l. 18. **perobscura,** adj. for adv. again.

l. 19. **illam alteram,** sc. **famam.**

l. 20. **addita,** i.e. a .lita esse.

l. 21. **sollicita civitate . . . et infensa,** abl. abs.

l. 22. **regis,** objective genitive, ' for the king ', with **desiderio.**

l. 22. **gravis auctor.** See note on **casibus variis,** Ch. 1, l. 5 : (being), as is recorded, a weighty authority in (any) matter, however great '.

NOTES   131

l. 27. **contra intueri,** ' to look him in the face '. Romans prayed with their heads muffled.

l. 29. **caelestes ita velle.** Ita is almost redundant. Render, ' that it is the will of the gods that . . .'.

l. 30. **colant, sciant, tradant,** jussive subjunctives, ' let them . . .'.

l. 33. **Mirum quantum,** etc. In full and in English order, **mirum (est) quantum fidei fuerit illi viro nuntianti haec. fuerit** is perf. subj. (indirect question).

l. 35. **facta fide,** abl. abs., ' once belief had been established '.

CHAPTER 17

Line 1. **certamen et cupido,** hendiadys, ' a greedy struggle '; **regni,** objective genitive.

l. 2. **ad singulos.** This is a conjecture for the MS. reading **a singulis,** which is untranslateable.

l. 3. **pervenerat.** The understood subject is **certamen** : ' it had not extended '.

l. 4. **factionibus inter ordines certabatur. certabatur** is the impersonal passive, and the meaning of **ordo** is defined by the following sentence : ' it was a struggle of faction between the racial strains '.

l. 4. **Oriundi** =**ei qui orti erant,** ' those sprung '.

l. 5. **ab sua parte non erat regnatum,** ' there had been no king of their stock ', _lit._, ' it had not been reigned upon their side ', **regnatum erat** being the impersonal passive.

l. 6. **in societate aequa,** ' in spite of the association's being on equal terms '. For this concessive use of a phrase introduced by **in,** cf. **in variis voluntatibus** below, where, however, the force of the phrase is made clearer by the subsequent **tamen.**

l. 7. **corporis,** ' breed '.

l. 9. **In variis voluntatibus. In** =' despite '.

l. 9. **regnari,** the infinitive of the impersonal passive : ' that there should be a king '.

l. 10. **experta.** The perfect participle, though from a deponent verb, is used with passive meaning.

l. 12. circa, though an adverb, has the force, placed where it is, of an attributive adjective, ' neighbouring '. Cf. the use of **repente,** Ch. 13, l. 23.

l. 12. **civitatium.** The form is several times found. The genitive depends on **animis.**

l. 13. **Et esse.** Et = ' both '.

l. 14. caput is accus., subject to **esse :** ' it was their will that there should be some head '.

l. 14. in animum inducebat. The object of the verb is **concedere,** and the phrase =' was disposed ', *lit.,* ' was accepting into his mind '.

l. 16. **singulis in singulas decurias creatis,** ' individuals being appointed, one for—i.e. to represent—each decury '.

l. 17. **qui praeessent,** final clause.

l. 20. **in orbem,** ' in rotation '.

l. 21. **Id ab re,** etc. The order is **id** (=**intervallum regni) ab re appellatum (est) interregnum, nomen quod tenet nunc quoque.**

l. 22. **Fremere,** ' historic ' infinitive, equivalent in meaning to an inceptive imperfect indicative, ' began to murmur '.

l. 22. **multiplicatam, factos.** Esse is to be supplied with both.

l. 24. **videbantur passuri.** English prefers an impersonal construction, ' it seemed that they would not longer endure (anything) . . .'.

l. 24. **et creatum,** ' and (one) created '.

l. 25. **ea moveri,** ' that these (ideas) were stirring '. Notice that it is the *passive* voice of **moveo** which corresponds to the English intransitive use of ' move '.

l. 26. **offerendum,** i.e. **(id) offerendum (esse),** dependent on **rati,** ' thinking that that, which they were going to lose, ought to be spontaneously offered '.

l. 27. **plus iuris,** ' more of their privilege '.

l. 29. **sic . . . si,** ' only . . . if '. **sic** has limitative force. **id =** ' their choice '.

l. 31. **vi adempta.** In English we should group these words (abl. abs.) with **idem ius,** ' the same right, (though) robbed of its force '.

l. 31. **rogandis.** The presiding officer 'asked' the people, assembled in the **comitia**, their will with regard to the bill, or the candidate, proposed.

l. 32. **ineat.** See note on **circumagerent**, Ch. 14, l. 41.

l. 34. **Tum.** Here Livy returns to the narrative : 'on this occasion '.

l. 34. The relative **quod** refers to the clause that follows. We must say ' May your choosing be . . .'. For the relative to precede its antecedent is very common in Latin, and it is also possible for a wish, done by the ' optative ' subjunctive, to form a subordinate clause.

l. 34. **bonum faustum felixque.** These adjectives are normal in the present formula, by which a blessing is asked upon an undertaking.

l. 36. **dignum,** ' a person worthy '.

l. 36. **qui . . . numeretur,** ' to be accounted a successor to Romulus '. A consecutive **qui** clause is usual after **dignus.**

l. 37. **crearitis,** i.e. creaveritis, fut. perf.

l. 38. **victi beneficio,** ' outdone in generosity ', *lit.*, ' beaten in (the matter of) a good deed '.

l. 39. **id** refers forward and is explained by the **ut** clause : ' this, (namely) that . . .'.

l. 40. **qui = quis. regnaret,** subjunctive in indirect deliberative question, ' should reign '.

CHAPTER 18

Line 2. **consultissimus** has dependent upon it the genitive phrase with which the sentence ends : ' most learned in . . .'.

l. 3. **ut,** ' so far as '.

l. 3. **in illa aetate.** The addition of the preposition is Livian.

l. 4. **iuris.** Even in the still primitive community we already find that preoccupation with law which was distinctive of the Roman race.

l. 4. **Auctorem,** ' (as) the author '. Observe that Latin employs simple apposition in such cases as this, where English requires ' as '.

l. 5. **quia non exstat alius,** ' because no other person is available ', i.e. ' no other name has come down to us '.

l. 6. **quem Servio Tullio, etc.** Translate in the order **quem constat habuisse coetus iuvenum aemulantium studia in ultima ora Italiae, circa Metapontum Heracleamque et Crotona, amplius centum annos post, Servio Tullio regnante Romae,** and observe that **quem** is the subject of **habuisse** in the acc. and infin. construction. Note also the illogical accusative **annos,** replacing the grammatically correct ablative **annis** (abl. of measure of difference). The phrase begins as **annis centum post,** ' later by a hundred years ', **post** being the adverb. For reasons of euphony it became usual to place the monosyllable **post** earlier in the phrase, whereupon it began to be felt as a preposition and to be followed by the appropriate case. **ultima,** i.e. southernmost. The foot of Italy (' Magna Graecia ') was colonised by Greeks, and the cities named were three of their chief settlements. **Crotona** is the acc. case, according to the Greek form, of a nominative **Croton.** Pythagoras, a celebrated philosopher and mathematician, settled in Italy about 530 B.C.

l. 11. **quae fama in Sabinos,** supply **pervenire potuit.**

l. 11. **linguae commercio,** ' common tongue ', *lit.,* ' intercourse of speech '.

l. 13. **Quove praesidio, etc.** This is the last of four arguments against the attribution to Pythagoras of Numa's learning.

l. 13. **sermone moribusque,** abls. of respect.

l. 14. **Suopte igitur ingenio.** Begin with **opinor igitur magis,** and follow with acc. and infin. **animum** (eius = Numae) **temperatum fuisse . . . , instructumque fuisse . . .**
suopte ingenio, ' by his own disposition ' ; **virtutibus,** ' *with* good qualities '.

l. 16. **non tam,** ' not so much '.

l. 17. **quo genere,** abl. of comparison.

l. 19. **inclinari opes videbantur.** English prefers the impersonal construction : ' it was obvious that the power ', etc.

l. 20. **rege ind. sumpto.** The abl. abs. has the force of a conditional clause.

l. **21. neque se quisquam**, etc. **Quisquam** is in apposition to each of the individuals included under **omnes**. Take it immediately after **ausi**, and the latter after **tamen neque** : ' yet, not daring, any one (of them) . . .'.

l. **24. deferendum sc. esse**, gerundive of obligation, 'should be offered '.

l. **25. augurato**, ' (only) after taking the auspices '. Livy is fond of using the perfect participle thus alone as a one-word ablative absolute. **urbe condenda**, ' at the founding of the city '.

l. **26. cui** is the dative of the possessor. Render ' who thereafter as a mark of respec , held that priestly office from the state in perpetuity '.

l. **31. appellarunt**, i.e. **appellaverunt**.

l. **32. Inde ubi prospectu**, etc. We are told in the preceding sentence that Numa faced south. The augur, presumably unveiling his head after the initial prayer, appears to have divided the heavens into areas (**regiones**) by tracing an imaginary line from the eastern horizon, passing through himself to the western horizon ; thereupon he called all that lay to the S. of his line *right* and all to the N. of it *left*. Finally he chose a landmark (**signum**) facing him (**contra**) at the extreme limit of sight. This does not leave us with a clear picture of what the augur did, unless we assume that he actually picked on *four signa*, to S.E., S.W., N.W. and N.E. respectively, thereby creating a square templum over which the gods are prayed to answer by an omen the question as to Numa's fitness for kingship.

l. **34. dextras** and **laevas** are predicates, and **dixit** =' called '.

l. **40. uti adclarassis. Uti** perhaps =**utinam**, which often accompanies the optative (' wish ') subjunctive. Or **adclarassis** (which is an archaic form, equivalent to **adclaraveris**, perf. subj.), may be taken as jussive, with **uti** added, as it often was in the early Latin which Livy is presumably reproducing. The second of these explanations gives the better sense, and the use of a jussive perfect subjunctive is easier to justify than an optative one ; by neither interpretation has **uti** any meaning that can be represented in translation.

l. 42. **vellet,** probably generic subjunctive.

CHAPTER 19

Line 2. **eam** is not wanted and must be ignored. Livy has in‧serted it as if instead of **urbem novam conditam** he had written **quae urbs condita erat.**

l. 2. **iure legibusque ac moribus.** These ablatives may be rendered ' upon justice ', etc.

l. 3. **Quibus.** See note on **quem,** Ch. 15, l. 11.

l. 4. **posse.** Supply some such subject to the infinitive as **populum.**

l. 4. **efferari animos,** acc. and infin. because Livy is still reporting the thoughts of Numa.

l. 5. **mitigandum** sc. **esse.** It, and the following four words, depend on **ratus.**

l. 6. **Ianum,** i.e. ' the *temple* of Janus '. This temple to a native two-headed god of war was only thrice closed (indicating peace) in the first 700 years or so of Roman history, and only once between Numa and Augustus. In the latter's principate it was closed three times.

l. 7. **apertus ut,** etc., i.e. **ut, apertus, significaret civitatem esse in armis, clausus, . . .**

l. 8. **circa,** adv. doing the work of an adjective. Cf. note on **repente,** Ch. 13, l. 23, and the similar use of **circa** again below.

l. 10. **post Punicum,** etc. For the use of the participle **perfectum** (which should be rendered ' the end of '), see note on **inter Lavinium conditum,** etc., Ch. 3, l. 16. The date meant is 234 B.C.

l. 12. **ut videremus** (to be rendered by English present infinitive) is the object of **dederunt,** and **quod** the object of **videremus.**

l. 12. **bellum Actiacum,** i.e. the war between Octavian and Mark Antony, the decisive battle of which was the fleet action off Actium, 31 B.C. The actual closure took place in 29, after the return of Octavian to Italy.

l. 13. **parta,** from **pario.** The sentence reveals approximately the date at which Livy wrote this portion of his history, for not until 27 B.C. did Octavian receive the title Augustus, while in 25 B.C. the temple of Janus was again closed, a fact which, had Livy written after it, must have been mentioned by him.

l. 14. Clauso eo, etc. The cum clause appears to modify clauso.

l. 16. ne luxuriarent, etc. The order is ne animi, quos . . . continuerat, luxuriarent otio.

l. 18. rem . . . efficacissimam. Take this *after* ratus metum deorum iniciendum esse, for rem appears to refer to metus or to the phrase metum inicere.

l. 18. ad multitudinem limits efficacissimam, which agrees with rem : 'a course particularly effective with a populace . . .'.

l. 20. Qui refers to metus deorum.

l. 22. sibi esse, 'that he had', sibi being the dative of the possessor.

l. 22. dea Egeria, an Italian nymph.

l. 22. eius se monitu, etc. To keep the emphasis which Latin places on the word eius by putting it first, begin : 'it was by her counsel that he . . .'.

l. 23. quae . . . essent qualifies sacra.

l. 24. sacerdotes suos, 'priests of their own'.

l. 26. quem, referring to annum, is the object of dispensavit.

l. 26. tricenos singulis. The notion 'each' conveyed by the distributives is needed only once in English.

l. 27. desunt sex dies. There is no numeral in the MSS. But there are indications that either VI or XI may have fallen out.

l. 28. intercalariis mensibus, etc., 'he so ordered it by inserting intercalary months, that, in the twentieth year, when the full courses of all the years were completed, the days should agree with that position of the sun from which they had started out'. meta is the word for the 'turning-point' at the end of the spina or longitudinal wall constituting the long axis of a Roman circus.

l. 30. orsi essent. A verb which, according to the sense required, should be in the indicative mood, is often *attracted* into the subjunctive if the clause in which it occurs is dependent upon one whose verb is in that mood.

l. 31. **idem** is grammatically the subject of **fecit**, but is used idiomatically to mean ' he also '. This use of **idem** is common. Compare **oratio splendida et grandis et eadem in primis faceta** (Cicero), and observe that in this adverbial use the word nevertheless continues to behave as a pronoun/adjective, agreeing in case, number and gender with the noun or pronoun to which it refers.

l. 32. **nihil agi**, *lit.*, ' that nothing should be done ', ' that no appeal should be made to the people '.

l. 33. **futurum erat**, ' it was going to be ', or ' it would be '.

CHAPTER 20

Line 1. **sacerdotibus creandis**, dative of purpose. Cf. **condendae urbi**, Ch. 1, l. 34.

l. 3. **Dialem flaminem**, the chief, as consecrated to the service of Jupiter, of fifteen **flamines**, or priests of particular divinities.

l. 3. **Sed quia** etc. Construe in the order **sed quia putabat in bellicosa civitate fore** (' there would be ') **plures reges similes Romuli quam Numae**, etc.

l. 6. **regiae vicis**, ' of the royal office ', i.e. ' that fell to the share of the king '.

l. 6. **adsiduum sacerdotem.** See note on **auctorem**, Ch. 18, l. 4.

l. 7. **curuli.** The word is connected with **currus**, ' chariot ', and probably indicates that an earlier privilege of principal Roman magistrates, before the time of the chair inlaid with ivory, had been that of riding in these vehicles.

l. 9. **Vestae.** Vesta was a goddess of flocks and herds, and of the household. In her temple burned a fire which was tended by the Vestal virgins and never allowed to go out. The virgins, chosen when young girls, served the goddess for thirty years, after which they might marry if they wished.

l. 12. **de publico.** The latter form is from the noun **publicum**.

l. 12. **virginitate**, etc. Supply **eas** as the object of **fecit.** With it **venerabiles** and **sanctas** agree.

l. 14. **Salios.** The word is connected with **salio**, ' leap ', and the priests were so named from their practice of honouring the god with ritual dances.

l. 14. **Gradivo.** The origin of the title is disputed. It may be connected with **gradior**, ' march '.

l. 16. **ancilia.** According to legend a shield (the **ancile**) fell from heaven as a token from the gods of goodwill towards Rome. To prevent the theft of so sacred a talisman, eleven copies, indistinguishable from the original, were made, and these **ancilia** were in the care of the Salii.

l. 18. **iussit.** The direct object is **eos** understood.

l. 18. **Pontificem,** ' *as* pontifex '. The head of the Roman state religion was called **pontifex maximus.**

l. 19. **ex patribus,** ' (one) of the senators '.

l. 21. **quibus hostiis,** etc. **quibus** is interrogative adjective and introduces a series of indirect deliberative questions, ' with what victims . . . were to be made . . .'.

l. 24. **ut esset quo consultum plebes veniret,** *lit.,* ' that there might be whither the commons might come to consult ', i.e. ' that there might be a person to whom the commons might come for advice '. **consultum** is the supine expressing purpose. Cf. **lusum it Maecenas, dormitum ego Vergiliusque,** where the supines, associated as usual with a verb of motion, mean ' to play ' and ' to sleep '.

l. 25. **quid,** ' aught ' ; say ' any article '. **divini iuris** depends upon it.

l. 26. **nec caelestes modo,** etc. **Nec** = **et non,** and the order for translation is **ut idem pontifex edoceret non modo caelestes caerimonias sed iusta funebria quoque placandosque manes, quaeque prodigia, missa fulminibus quove alio visu, susciperentur atque curarentur.**

placandos manes, ' the appeasing of the dead ', *lit.,* ' ghosts to be appeased '. **quae,** interrogative adjective, ' what ', introduces an indirect question, the last of the four objects of **edoceret.**

quo, indefinite adjective, ' any '. **susciperentur atque curarentur,** indirect deliberative, ' were to be . . .'.

l. 32. **quae suscipienda essent,** ' (as to), what (portents) should be recognized as such '.

CHAPTER 21

Line 1. **Ad . . . procurandaque.** Take this phrase *after* the abl. absolute **multitudine . . . conversa.**

l. 2. The **et** before **animi** (*lit.*, ' both ') may be rendered ' not only ', the succeeding **et,** ' but also '.

l. 3. **deorum adsidua insidens cura. deorum** is objective genitive dependent on **cura** : ' concern with the gods '. **adsidua** belongs in sense with **insidens,** in grammar with **cura** : ' continuing always with them '.

l. 4. **ea pietate. ea** = ' such '. Cf., in the English of the prayer book, ' give us *that* due sense of all thy mercies that our hearts may be unfeignedly thankful '.

l. 6. If **proximo** is right, it goes with **metu,** abl. of attendant circumstances, ' the fear . . . (being) very near '. A suggested emendation, **pro nimio,** ' instead of the excessive fear ' gives a sense more in accord with the rest of the sentence.

l. 7. **Et cum,** etc. The order is **cum homines ipsi formarent se in mores regis velut (in mores) unici exempli.** Render the first **in mores,** ' upon the character ', the second ' upon that '.

l. 10. **eam verecundiam.** For **eam,** see note on **ea pietate** above.

l. 12. **deorum** depends on **cultum.**

l. 12. **violari** has **civitatem** as its subject, and the acc. and infin. is the object of **ducerent** : ' thought (it) impious that a community . . . should be violated '.

l. 13. **quem medium,** ' the centre of which '.

l. 14. **Quo.** Relatives commencing new sentences should be translated by the corresponding demonstratives (e.g. **quo** = **eo,** ' thither ', ' there '), and such demonstratives must occupy their natural places, and not have the artificial prominence of relatives.

l. 15. **Camenis.** These were Italian divinities which, having the same functions as the Greek Muses, were gradually identified with them. The grove dedicated to them by Numa lay outside the Porta Capena, S.E. of the city.

l. 17. **essent** is subjunctive of virtual oratio obliqua, i.e. the mood indicates that the reason given is that offered by Numa : ' because there, he said, took place (**essent**) their meetings '.

l. 18. **id sacrarium,** i.e. that of Faith.

l. 19. Take **usque** before **ad.**

l. 21. **in dexteris.** The right hands of men, clasped in token of of solemn covenant, are temples of Faith.

l. 22. **loca, Argeos.** The name of these chapels, 27 in number, is obscure, as are also the details of the worship annually performed at them. The name **Argei** was also given to certain puppets of rushes, dropped annually into the Tiber from the Pons Sublicius by Vestal Virgins. This ceremony looks as if it might well have been an innocuous substitution for earlier human sacrifices.

l. 23. **maximum** is the subject of **fuit, tutela** its complement. On the latter word depend the genitives **pacis** and **regni.**

l. 25. Observe how Livy uses the adverb **deinceps** as an adjective ; ' successive '. Cf. **repente,** Ch. 13, l. 23.

l. 26. **alius alia via,** ' one by one means (the other by another) '. Notice this idiomatic use of **alius.**

l. 28. **cum, tum,** ' not only ', ' but also ', practically equivalent to **et . . . et.**

CHAPTER 22

Line 1. **res** =res publica, as often.

l. 2. **Hostili,** ' of the Hostilius ', i.e. Hostius Hostilius.

l. 3. **pugna.** See Ch. 12.

l. 6. For **cum** and **tum,** see note on Ch. 21, l. 28.

l. 8. **otio** is abl. of cause, and the order is **ratus civitatem senescere otio.**

l. 10. **praedas,** cattle, of course, as **agerent** makes clear.

l. 13. **missi.** See note on **petiti,** Ch. 2, l. 1, and cf. **acta** below.

l. 14. **priusquam mandata.** **egissent** is readily understood from **agerent.**

l. 15. **Albanum** refers to Cluilius, or else is sg. for pl.

l. 19. **neganti Albano,** dative of disadvantage in association with the compound verb **indico,** but for convenience render by a clause, ' when the Alban refused '.

l. 19. **in tricesimum diem,** ' to commence in 30 days '.

l. 21. **quid petentes venerint.** The indirect question depends on **dicendi,** and the weight of it lies on the participle, not the finite verb : ' what they had come to ask '. Note the sequence. **venerint** and **venissent** are alike possible after historic present.

l. 23. **quod minus placeat,** ' to displease '. **minus** here practically **=non.** The subjunctive, required in any case because the clause is subordinate to an indirect statement, represents a subjunctive (generic) original. For the generic subj., see note on **arguerent,** Ch. 16, l. 17.

l. 24. **repetitum.** The supine expressing purpose. **Res** is its direct object. Cf. **consultum.** Ch. 20, l. 24 and note.

l. 25. **reddantur.** The subject is **res** (understood) and **res reddere =**' make restitution '.

l. 25. **iussos, i.e. se iussos esse.**

l. 27. **testes** is complement of **deos facere,** ' makes the gods witnesses ', or, as we say, ' calls the gods to witness '.

l. 28. **aspernatus dimiserit,** put for **aspernatus sit et dimiserit,** in the Latin manner. When two actions are predicated of the same subject, it is normal to express the first in the form of a participle. Cf. **litteras scriptas obsignavit,** ' he wrote and sealed a letter '. The subjunctives are due to the fact that the clause is an indirect question, dependent on **facere testes.**

l. 28. **in eum,** sc. **populum.**

Chapter 23

Line 3. **Troianam utramque prolem,** ' both (being of) Trojan stock '. **utramque** is attracted to the gender and number of **prolem** ; it should logically be **utrosque,** in apposition with **parentes natosque.**

l. 4. cum =' since '.

l. 7. nec acie certatum est, ' there was no pitched battle '. nec = et non, the et meaning ' both ', which may be omitted. certatum est is the impersonal passive—cf. note on saevitum esse, Ch. 1, l. 2.

l. 11. plus here = amplius, ' more *than* '.

l. 16. ferox, as is shown by the fact that it is modified by morte, abl. of cause = ferox factus, ' made confident ', ' emboldened '.

l. 17. magnumque, etc. The order is dictitansque magnum numen deorum expetiturum poenas ob impium bellum in omne nomen Albanorum, orsum ab ipso capite. Note these points : nomen, ' name ' sometimes means ' those who bear the name ', e.g. nomen Romanum, ' the Roman race ' ; orsum agrees with numen, and, with the following ab, means ' beginning with ' ; capite, i.e. principe, rege.

l. 20. infesto exercitu. The formation with which a commander moves in a campaign is often put in the abl. case without preposition.

l. 21. ducit, sc. exercitum.

l. 21. quam proxime by itself would have meant ' as near as he could ', and potest therefore adds nothing to the sense.

l. 22. legatum praemissum iubet = legatum praemittit et iubet. For this use of the participle, cf. note on aspernatus dimiserit, Ch. 22, l. 28.

l. 23. dimicent. Cf. note on canerent, Ch. 1, l. 27.

l. 24. congressus sit and pertineant are similar subjunctives to dimicent, though the last was no doubt subjunctive (generic) in the original words. congressus sit represents congressus eris of direct speech.

l. 24. scire se allaturum. Another se is wanted, subject of scire.

l. 24. ea quae, ' such proposals as '.

l. 25. nihilo minus, ' no less ', nihilo being abl. of the measure of difference, *lit.*, ' less by nothing '.

l. 26. aspernatus, supply est and verba eius.

l. 27. si, ' in case '. vana adferantur, ' empty things should be put forward ', i.e. ' the suggestions made should prove of no value '.

l. 30. **Iniurias**, etc. The order is **et**—*lit*. ' both ' ; it may be dropped—**ego videor audisse regem nostrum Cluilium** (**dicere** *or* **dicentem** must be supplied here) **iniurias et res quae repetitae sint ex foedere non redditas esse causam huiusce belli.** **res . . . redditas,** ' failure to make the restitution demanded in accordance with the treaty '.

l. 33. **te ferre.** After **nec dubito** the more usual thing would have been **quin tu feras.** (The note refers to the **te** (acc.) immediately after **nec.**)

l. 34. **dictu.** The ' supine in -u ', really an ablative (of respect), modifies **speciosa** : ' things fine in the saying ', i.e. ' fine-sounding words '.

l. 36. **recte an perperam**, i.e. in full **utrum recte an perperam stimulet.**

l. 37. **fuerit ista,** etc., ' let that be for him to determine, who . . .', *lit.*, ' that consideration shall be his '. In such expressions, the verb, which approaches the jussive subjunctive in meaning, is actually future perfect. Cf. **de eventu proelii di viderint.**

l. 38. **gerendo** bello, dative of work contemplated.

l. 39. **illud . . . velim.** Note : (1) **illud**, internal acc. (retained) with the perf. part. pass. **monitum.** (2) **velim**, potential subj. ' Of this I would like you (to be) warned '.

l. 39. **quanta . . . sit,** indirect question depending upon **scis.** Turn by abstract noun, ' the extent of the E. power which surrounds . . .'.

l. 40. **quo propior . . . hoc magis,** ' the nearer . . . the more '. Note the abls. of the measure of difference in both these clauses.

l. 42. **esto,** 2nd pers. sing. imperative of **sum.**

l. 42. **iam cum,** ' at the moment when '.

l. 43. **spectaculo.** Supply ' for the Etruscans '.

l. 46. **in dubiam . . . aleam.** The two genitives **imperii, servitii,** define **aleam,** ' to uncertain hazard ' =' to hazardous uncertainty— sovereignty or slavery '.

l. 47. **utri utris imperent,** indirect deliberative question, dependent on **decerni possit.** The latter is impersonal but would run better if translated personally in the English, ' (that) we may be able to decide '. utris is equivalent to alteris.

l. 50. cum . . . tum, ' both . . . and '. ferocior, ' more warlike '.

l. 51. quaerentibus, dat. of the agent' by (them) seeking on both sides (a solution).'

CHAPTER 24

l. 3. nec ferme . . . alia, ' and scarcely any other ancient tradition '.

l. 4. nobilior, ' better known '.

l. 4. in, ' in spite of (or notwithstanding) an affair so renowned '; i.e. ' the renown of the affair '.

l. 6. auctores utroque trahunt, *lit.*, ' the authorities draw (us) in both directions ' = ' make claims for both sides '. utroque is an adverb, cf. quo, ' where to ', eo, ' thither ', ' there '.

l. 7. qui . . . vocent. Note the consecutive (' generic ') subj., for qui = ' of such a kind that they '.

l. 8. cum . . . agunt, ' propose to '.

l. 9. ibi . . . fuerit, oratio obliqua, giving the proposal of the kings. Note ibi . . . unde, *adverbs*, where English would prefer prepositional phrases, ibi ' with those ', unde ' on whose side '.

l. 11. priusquam dimicarent. In classical Latin, the subjunctive is used in temporal clauses to add an additional idea of ' purpose ' or ' anticipation '. Livy, however, uses the subj. without this implied idea, i.e. in the same sense as the indic. Cf. Ch. 26, l. 1, digrederentur.

l. 12. his legibus, ' on these terms '.

l. 12. ut . . . imperitaret. Order for translation : ut is (populus) cuiusque cives vicissent . . . , imperitaret alteri populo . . .

cuiusque = cuiuscumque. vicissent. The pluperfect subj. represents an original future perf.

cum bona pace, ' in peace and quiet '.

l. 14. foedera alia aliis legibus. For the full expression, we must supply alia aliis again, so that we get, ' some treaties are made on some terms, others on others ', i.e. ' different treaties are made on different terms '.

l. 15. **eodem modo.** Livy naturally assumes that the methods of treaty-making known in historical times were used from the very beginning of Roman history.

l. 15. **tum,** ' on that occasion ' : **ita,** ' as follows '.

l. 16. **ullius,** ' of any (other) '.

l. 17. **fetialis.** The **fetiales,** [1] organised as a college, represented the state in declaring war, and in the making of peace, or treaties. In their duties they were led by a **pater patratus** [2] who acted as their spokesman or plenipotentiary, and ratified the treaty.

For their ritual in declaring war, cf. Ch. 32.

l. 19. **sagmina,** ' tufts of sacred herbage '. These, taken from the citadel and borne by a fetial, gave inviolability to the bearer.

l. 20. **pura tollito.** Supply **sagmina** with **pura** and translate : ' thou shalt take them fresh '. **Pura** might also mean ' untainted ' i.e. ' not cut by a knife '.

l. 22. **facisne me tu regium,** *lit.,* ' dost thou make me royal ' = ' dost thou give to me royal protection '.

nuntium, ' (as) spokesman ', in apposition with **me.**

l. 23. **populi . . . Quiritium.** The phrase ' the Roman people of the Quirites ' is again evidence of the composite character of the population. See the note on Ch. 13, l. 32.

l. 23. **vasa comitesque,** object of **facis** with **regios** supplied. The ' implements ' (**vasa**) were the sacred herbs, the knife, and the sceptre, ' the companions ', the other fetials.

l. 24. **quod . . fiat,** ' may it (**quod,** *lit.* ' which ') be done without harm to myself or to the Roman people '.

l. 26. **Fusium,** from an old form of **Furius.**

l. 27. **verbena** = **sagmina.**

l. 29. **quae . . . est referre,** ' which, recited in a long form, it is not worth while to repeat '. Note **effata,** perf. part. of a deponent verb in passive sense. **operae,** the full phrase is **operae pretium est.**

---

[1] Connected with **fari** and meaning ' speaker ', ' spokesman .

[2] **patratus** = ' that has been made father '.

l. 32. **populus Albanus** : nom. used for voc.

l. 33. **ut,** 'as'. **prima postrema,** *lit.*, ' first last ', i.e. ' from first to last '.

l. 35. **illis legibus,** ' from those terms '.

l. 36. **prior non deficiet,** ' will not be the first to depart '.

l. 36. **defexit** = **defecerit** (fut. perf.).

l. 36. **publico consilio,** ' by public consent '.

l. 37. **ille Diespiter,** ' great Jupiter '. **Diespiter** is another form for **Iuppiter** which is found in old formulas.

l. 39. **quanto . . . pollesque,** ' as thou hast greater strength and power ', *lit.*, ' by so much more as thou art more able and more strong '.

CHAPTER 25

Line 2. **sui,** ' their fellow-soldiers '.

l. 2. **deos . . . manus,** acc. and infin. dependent on ' saying ', which can easily be supplied from the verb **adhortarentur.**

l. 3. **quidquid civium domi (sit),** ' whatever of citizens at home (there) is ', i.e. ' all their fellow citizens at home '.

l. 5. **manus,** acc. pl., obj. of **intueri** ; *lit.*, ' hands ', i.e. ' their prowess '.

l. 5. **pleni . . . vocibus,** *lit.*, ' filled with the shouts of (men) encouraging (them) ' = ' inspired by the shouts of encouragement '.

l. 8. **periculi . . . expertes,** ' free (rather) from immediate danger than from anxiety ', i.e. ' though free from immediate danger (to themselves), yet full of anxiety (as to the result).'

l. 9. **quippe . . . positum,** ' for the empire was at stake, dependent upon . . .'.
The main emphasis falls on **positum** : thus we might render, ' for the supremacy which was at stake depended upon . . .'.
Note these meanings of **ago** and **pono** in the passive.

l. 10. **itaque ergo,** a good example of Livy's fondness for pleonasm.

l. 11. **in,** ' to watch ' ; *lit.*, ' for '.

l. 14. nec . . . fecissent. Obversatur has four subjects, periculum, imperium, servitium, fortuna ; *lit.*, ' their own danger was not present to their minds, (but) the national empire or slavery . . .'.

l. 16. futuraque . . . fecissent, *lit.*, ' and the subsequent fate of their country, destined to be what they themselves made (it) '. fecissent, subj. in virtual oratio obliqua and representing an original future perfect indic.

l. 19. torpebat vox spiritusque, *lit.*, ' voice and breath became sluggish ', i.e. ' they could hardly speak or breathe '.

l. 20. cum iam . . . essent, *lit.*, ' when now not only the motions of their bodies and the movement of weapons and shields, too swift for the eye to follow, but also wounds and blood were for a spectacle ', i.e. ' when all could see not only . . .'. vulnera et sanguis, hendiadys for ' bloody wounds '.

l. 23. vulneratis . . . Albanis, ' while the three A.. . .'.

l. 26. Romanas . . . unius, *lit.*, ' now all hope (but) not yet all anxiety had abandoned the Roman levies, in mortal fear at the plight of their single (champion) '. The Latin order can be retained if we begin, ' now the Roman levies had lost all their hope . . .'. Note legio, ' levy '. There were no ' legions ' at this time.

l. 28. ut . . . sic,   *lit.*,   ' as . . . so ', =' although   no   match . . . yet . . .'.

l. 31. ita . . . sineret, *lit.*, ' having thought that they (eos to be supplied) would pursue in such as way (ita) as the body afflicted with a wound allowed each one '. Note : (i) the necessity to supply eos with secuturos. (ii) sineret, subj. in dependent clause in O.O. ut =' as '. Translate : ' thinking that each one would pursue him with such speed as his wounded body allowed '.

l. 33. cum . . . videt. The indicative mood is used in ' inverse ' cum clauses.

l. 38. qualis . . . solet, *lit.*, ' (such) as is wont (to be the shout) of those-who-cry-encouragement after-being-without-hope ', i.e. ' such as partisans raise at an unhoped-for turn of fortune '.

l. 40. itaque. Strict classical usage demands that itaque should begin a sentence.

l. 40. **alter . . . alterum.** There are two Curiatii left ; therefore **alter** is the third of the brothers, **alterum**, the second. The account of the death of the first is given in l. 37.

l. 41. **nec procul,** an archaic expression for **non** *or* **haud procul.**

l. 41. **et,** ' as well ' as the first.

l. 43. **alterum . . . dabat.** intactum corpus and geminata victoria are nominative. **ferocem** agrees with alterum, obj. The sentence would run better in the passive in English : ' the one was emboldened for the third combat by . . .'.

l. 46. **victus,** ' broken (in spirit) '. **ante se,** ' before his eyes '.

l. 47. **obicitur.** The passive is used in a middle sense here and may be rendered by ' opposed ' or ' met '.

l. 47. **proelium,** ' a (real) battle '.

l. 49. **causae,** dat. **ut . . . imperet,** explanatory of **causae.**

l. 50. **male . . . arma,** ' as his foe could hardly hold up his shield '. **sustinenti** actually qualifies ei understood.

l. 51. **iugulo,** local abl. without a preposition.

l. 53. **maiore . . . quo . . . fuerat,** ' with joy all the greater as the fight (**res**) had been near fear ', i.e. ' had terrified them '. Note the omission of a comparative in the **quo** clause.

l. 54. **nequaquam paribus animis,** ' with by no means similar feelings ' = ' with very different feelings '—an example of litotes.

l. 55. **alteri,** ' the one army ' ; **alteri,** ' the other '.

l. 56. **dicionis alienae facti,** ' brought under a foreign sway '. The predicative gen. of possession is common in Livy.

l. 56. **quo . . . loco,** ' where '.

l. 58. **distantia locis,** ' separated '. **et** =etiam.

CHAPTER 26

Line 1. **digrederentur.** See note on dimicarent, Chap. 24, **11.**

l. 3. **iuventutem,** ' fighting men '. Livy is fond of using collective nouns.

l. 4. **opera,** abl. sing. of **opera.**

l. 5. princeps, ' in advance ' *or* ' at the head '.

l. 6. prae se gerens, ' displaying '.

l. 7. uni, dat. obvia ... fuit, ' met '. It is preceded by its dependent dat., **cui,** l. 6 above.

l. 7. ante portam Capenam. The Porta Capena was below the Caelian Hill, and south east of the Palatine Hill, and gave entrance into Rome from the Via Latina.

l. 11. feroci iuveni, dat. of the person interested, which occurs frequently in Livy and is generally translated by the English possessive.

l. 10. movet animum, ' aroused the anger '.

l. 12. tanto, ' great '.

l. 15. vivi, supply **fratris.**

l. 16. Romana. Order for translation : **sic pereat Romana quaecumque lugebit hostem.**

l. 18. raptus ... regem, ' he was haled before the king for trial '.

l. 19. ne ... esset, *lit.,* ' that he might not be the author of a sentence so stern and displeasing to the people and of the punishment following on the sentence ', i.e. ' that he might not have the responsibility of (passing) so stern and unpopular a sentence and of (inflicting) the ...'.

l. 21. duumviros ... facio, ' I appoint duumvirs '.

Perduellio, ' treason ', and **parricidium,** ' murder of kindred ', were the first crimes to be prosecuted by the Roman state, and, as we learn here, trials for treason were entrusted to a commission of two, the duumvirs.

It has also been suggested that the king handed over the control of this case to the duumvirs in order that an appeal to the people might be open to the accused, for against the king's sentence there was no appeal.

Horatius was guilty of treason, in that by killing his sister he had usurped a right, viz. that of punishment, which belonged to the state.

It may be noticed that Horatius was guilty also of parricidium. If, however, he were tried on this charge and found guilty, there could be no appeal against the sentence, which, as in the case of treason, was always death.

l. 23. **carminis,** ' formula '. The gen. is one of description.

l. 24. **iudicent,** jussive subj.

l. 24. **provocarit.** Supply ' to the people '. The subject (understood) is **quis,** ' a man '.

l. 25. **certato,** 3rd sg. imperative, ' he shall contest (the case) '.

l. 25. **vincent.** The subject is **duumviri** understood.

l. 25. **obnubito.** The subject (again understood) of this and the next two imperatives is **lictor,** the attendant upon the magistrates who was charged with carrying out the sentence. By derivation, the word lictor means ' he who binds '.

An American scholar, Oldfather, believes that the punishment consisted not of hanging nor of crucifixion, but of being fastened to a tree and scourged to death. (*See* Loeb *edition*, p. 92.)

l. 26. **pomerium,** ' bounds (of the city) '. The **pomerium** was originally the line which marked the bounds of a city ; later the name included the strip between the wall and the houses inside it. See the note on Chap. 44, l 16..

l. 28. **ne . . . quidem.** The **ne** must be ignored in translation ; i.e. ' who did not think they could acquit even an innocent person '.

l. 31. **accesserat.** The pluperfect shows that the lictor had moved closer before the order to bind the prisoner's hands was actually given him.

l. 33. **provocatione . . . est,** *lit.,* ' at the appeal it was discussed before the people ; i.e. ' the appeal was discussed ".

l. 35. **P. Horatio . . . proclamante,** abl. absol., ' P. Horatius the father asserting ' =' by the assertion of . . .'.

l. 36. **patrio . . . fuisse,** ' he would have punished his son by the right he had as a father '. Note : (i) **animadvertere in**+acc., ' to punish ' ; (ii) fut. part.+**fuisse** is the infin. which replaces in O. O. imperf. or pluperf. subj. act. of O. R..

The head of each Roman family, **paterfamilias,** possessed an authority over all members of his household and thus had the right not only to punish but also to inflict death upon his children (**ius** vitae necisque). In the exercise of the latter right, he was restrained by custom and a family council consisting of relatives and friends.

l. 37. ne ... orbum facerent, ' not to bereave '.

l. 39. inter haec, ' meanwhile '.

l. 41. Pila Horatia is either neut. pl., (so Livy) ' javelins ', or fem. sing., ' a column ' (so Dionysius, III. 22).

l. 41. huncine. The emphatic form hice is often found with the interrogative enclitic -ne to make hicine. Note here that num hunc would have been more normal in a question expecting a negative answer. To keep the order and therefore the emphasis of the Latin, we might begin, ' is this the man whom just now . . . , (and) can you (endure to) see him . . . '.

l. 42. ovantemque . . . incedentem, ' and advancing triumphant in his victory '.

l. 43. sub furca vinctum, ' bound beneath the fork '. The latter was a V-shaped piece of wood to which the criminal's arms were bound as a preliminary to his being scourged.

l. 45. tam deforme spectaculum. This may be regarded as the antecedent of quod and loosely in apposition with the previous sentence—' so foul a scene that (quod) Alban eyes would scarce be able to endure it '.

l. 48. arbore, local abl. without preposition.

l. 49. modo, ' provided that (it be) '.

l. 52. sua decora, ' the honours he has won '. Sua is emphatic and refers not to the subject of the main verb but to eum.

l. 52. a tanta . . . supplicii, lit., ' from so great a foulness of punishment ' =' from so shameful a punishment '.

l. 53. vindicent. Note the mood—subj., here potential.

l. 53. non tulit, ' could not hold out against '.

l. 54. nec . . . animum, ' or the courage of Horatius himself unwavering in every danger '. Note the doubling of the negatives which here do not cancel out.

l. 55. admiratione . . . iure, abls. of cause, ' from admiration . . . than because of the justice. . . '.

l. 57. **imperatum.** Supply **est** and note how Latin says, ' the father was ordered '.

l. 58. **pecunia publica,** either ' by money paid to the state ', or ' at the public cost '. If the latter is the correct rendering, the meaning is that the people in this way were made to share the guilt of Horatius.

l. 59. **sacrificiis.** These expiatory sacrifices were offered annually to Janus Curiatius and to Juno Sororia to appease the departed spirits of the Curiatii and of Horatia.

Some scholars suggest that the whole story of Horatius might have sprung from this worship of the two deities by the clan of the Horatii.

l. 60. **transmisso . . . tigillo,** ' placing a little beam across the street '. The beam was let into the houses on each side of the street, which led from the Carinae to the Vicus Cuprius.

l. 62. **publice semper refectum,** ' always repaired at the state's expense '.

l. 63. **quo loco,** ' in the place where '.

CHAPTER 27

Line 1. **nec,** ' but . . . not ', a common meaning in Livy.

l. 1. **invidia,** ' resentment '. nom., subj. of **corrupit,** ' broke down '.

Livy likes to make emotions or motives the subject of verbs and thus to add vividness to his narrative. Cf. **cupido cepit** 6, 3.

l. 2. **commissa fuerit,** subjunctive of virtual oratio obliqua.

l. 4. **pravis.** Supply **consiliis,** ' to win back the support of the people by evil ones '. The subj. of **coepit** is ' the dictator '.

l. 5. **ut,** ' just as '. The understood verb is **quaesierat.**

l. 7. **animorum . . . virium,** ' more spirit than strength '.

l. 8. **ad bellum . . . gerendum,** ' to wage war openly and after proclamation '.

l. 9. **suis.** Insert ' but ' or ' while ' before this word.

l. 9. **per speciem societatis,** ' under the disguise of being an ally '.

l. 11. sociis consilii, *lit.*, ' (as) sharers of their plan ', i.e. 'as partners in their design '.

l. 11. pacto ... Albanorum, ' by a promise of desertion (on the part) of the Albans '.

l. 13. Fidenae. This town is east of the R. Tiber and north of the confluence of that river and the Anio.

l. 14. ab Alba. Livy's use of a preposition with names of towns may be regarded as a colloquialism or a mere provincialism.

l. 15. confluentes. Supply fluvios.

l. 20. legionem, ' levy '. Cf. Ch. 25, l. 26.

l. 21. Albano. Supply duci, i.e. Mettius.

l. 23. inde = deinde.

l. 23. satis subisse sese, ' that he had got close enough (to them)'.

l. 23. erigit, ' he led uphill '.

l. 25. consilium erat = constituerat.

l. 25. rem, ' success ', ' victory '.

l. 26. esse, historical infin. The literal translation is : ' at first it was for an astonishment to the Romans who . . .', i.e. ' at first the R. who . . . were astonished '. miraculo is predicative dative. proximi, ' nearest ', i.e. to the Albans.

l. 29. in re trepida, ' in the critical situation '.

l. 29. duodecim Salios. It is not clear from the context whether the twelve Salii are to be given as a priesthood to ' Pallor ' and ' Pavor ' or whether they are the Salii known as Collini, Agonales, or Agonenses, i.e. the twelve Salii who belonged to a god of Sabine origin, Quirinus, worshipped on the Quirinal and possessing functions similar to those of Mars.

l. 33. suo iussu, emphatic as its position in the sentence shows ; ' it was by his command that . . .'.

l. 35. id factum, ' this move '.

l. 35. magnae parti . . . , ' from a large part of the R. army '. The dat. depends on the compound vb. intersaepsit.

l. 37. qui . . . rati, ' (those) who had seen (it), believing what had been heard from the king (to be the case) '.

l. 40. **ut quibus essent,** ' inasmuch as Romans had been attached to them (as) colonists '. For **quippe,** or **ut, qui,** cf. Ch. 1, l. 19.

l. 41. **subito ex collibus** ... **Albanorum,** *lit.,* ' by a sudden charge of the A. down from the hills ' = ' by the A. suddenly charging down from the hills '.

l. 44. **Veientem,** sing. for plural. **redit ... in,** ' turned again upon '.

l. 44. **alieno pavore,** ' by the panic of their neighbours '.

l. 46. **flumen obiectum ab tergo.** Note once again the Latin noun and perf. part. pass. = English abstract noun with genitive. Thus the phrase, ' the river set in the way in their rear ' = ' the barrier of the river in their rear '.

l. 46. **arcebat,** ' prevented (them) '.

l. 46. **quo ... inclinavit,** ' when flight had made-(them)-fall-back there ' (i.e. to the river). Notice that **postquam** prefers perfect, the corresponding English ' when ' pluperfect.

l. 48. **caeci,** adj. for adv., ' blindly '.

l. 49. **inter ... consilium,** ' as they deliberated whether to flee or to fight '.

CHAPTER 28

Line 2. **devictos hostes,** ' on his utter defeat of the foe '. For the translation, see the note above on **flumen obiectum.**

l. 3. **contra,** adv.

l. 4. **quod bene vertat,** *lit.,* ' may which turn out well ' = ' with a prayer for success '.

l. 6. **ut adsolet.** Supply **fieri** with **adsolet,** *lit.,* ' as it is accustomed to be done '. The clause modifies **vocari ... iubet.**

l. 8. **ab extremo,** ' from the outermost (part of the camp) '.

l. 10. **proximi,** ' nearest (to the king) '.

l. 12. **legio,** ' troops ', not ' legion '.

l. 12. **centurionibus,** ' captains ', *not* ' centurions ' (in the later technical meaning.)

l. 14. **si ... virtuti,** ' if ever previously at other times in any war there was (a reason) why you should give thanks, first to ..., next to ...'.

ageretis, consecutive subj. **ipsorum,** emphasises the gen. **vestrae,** ' your *own* '.

l. 17. **dimicatum est,** impersonal pass. English would prefer a verb used personally in the active voice, ' you ...'.

l. 18. **quae ... est.** Take this relative clause after the antecedents **proditione, perfidia.**

l. 19. **ne ... teneat,** *lit.,* ' lest a false belief possess you ', : ' lest you be under a false impression .'

l. 21. **nec ... fuit,** ' and that was not my command but a stratagem and pretended command ', *lit.,* ' pretence of command '.

l. 22. **ut nec ... iniceretur. nec =et non,** et meaning ' both '.

vobis ignorantibus, *lit.,* ' to you (dat. of the person interested) not knowing ', i.e. ' because you did not know '. **deseri vos,** acc. and infin. dependent on **ignorantibus.**

hostibus ... ratis, dat. dependent on **iniceretur,** *lit.,* ' that terror ... might be struck into the enemy thinking ...', i.e. ' that the enemy might be inspired with ... because they believed ...'.

l. 26. **ut et vos ... fecissetis,** ' as you too would have done '.

l. 26. **quo,** ' anywhither ', in modern English, ' anywhere '. **inde,** *lit.,* ' thence ' =' from the battle-field '.

Note **quo :** the use of the indefinite adv. corresponds to that of **quis, quid,** ' anyone ', etc., after **si, nisi, num,** and **ne.**

l. 27. **Mettius ille,** ' Mettius yonder '.

l. 28. **idem,** ' also '.

l. 29. **audeat ... alius,** ' another would dare '. Note that the protasis **nisi ... dedero** is in the indic. where we might expect the present subj.

l. 30. **in hunc,** ' in (punishing) this man '; *lit.,* ' against this man '.

l. 33. **quod ... sit.** See Chap. 16, l. 17.

l. 35. **in animo est,** ' it is my purpose '.

l. 35. **civitatem,** ' citizenship '.

l. 37. **ut,** ' as '. **ex uno quondam.** See Chap. 6, l. 8. **res,** ' state '.

l. 39. **ad haec,** *lit.,* ' at these things ' ; i.e. ' on hearing these words '.

l. 39. **in variis voluntatibus,** ' notwithstanding their different wishes '.

l. 40. **communi . . . cogente,** abl. absol., ' a common fear compelling (them) '. Translate by a passive, ' compelled by a . . .'.

l. 42. **servare,** ' (how) to keep ', depends on **discere.**

l. 42. **vivo . . . esset,** *lit.,* ' that instruction would have been applied by me to you living '. The emphasis falls on **vivo tibi** ; hence translate : ' I should have let you live for me to give you instruction in this '.

l. 44. **at,** ' nevertheless '.

l. 47. **ut . . . gessisti,** ' as a short while ago you had a mind undecided between the cause (**rem**) of Fidenae and of Rome '.

l. 49. **in currus . . . Mettium,** *lit.,* ' he fastened the stretched out Mettius on the chariots '. Cf. **nuntium captum interfecit** = ' he captured and killed the messenger ' : so here, ' he stretched out Mettius and fastened him on . . .'.

l. 50. **in diversum iter,** ' in opposite directions '. The Latin sg. seems strange.

l. 51. **concitati.** Supply **sunt.**

l. 51. **lacerum . . . corpus,** ' torn (halves of his) body '.

l. 53. **ab . . . spectaculi,** ' from so horrible a sight '.

l. 53. **primum . . . fuit.** Begin with **illud fuit.**

l. 54. **exempli parum . . . humanarum,** ' of a type too little mindful of human laws ', i.e. ' of a kind that ignores the laws of humanty '.

l. 55. **in aliis,** ' in other cases '.

l. 56. **gloriari licet,** ' it is possible to boast ' = ' we may boast ': with **nulli . . . poenas,** acc. and infin., dependent on it.

l. 56. **placuisse,** *lit.,* ' have pleased ', with dat. **nulli (gentium)** dependent on it. Render the whole sentence, ' in other cases we may boast that no (other) nation has chosen milder punishments '.

CHAPTER 29

Line 5. **qualis . . . solet.** Supply **fieri** with **solet** and translate : ' (such) as usually occurs on the capture of cities '. **urbium** is dependent on **tumultus et pavor** (understood).

l. 7. **clamor . . . armatorum,** ' the shouts of the enemy and the running (of armed men) through the city '.

l. 8. **omnia . . . miscet,** ' confuse everything ', **i.e.** ' create universal confusion '.

l. 9. **defixit omnium animos,** ' depressed the spirits of all '.

l. 10. **prae metu,** ' from fear '. **Prae** in this sense is usually found in negative sentences, e.g. ' I could not speak for tears ', **prae lacrimis loqui non poteram.**

Some commentators suggest taking **prae metu** not with **obliti** but with **animo deficiente.**

l. 10. **quid relinquerent, quid . . . ferrent,** ' what to leave behind, what to take . . .'. Note the indirect deliberative subj.

l. 11. **deficiente . . . alios,** *lit.,* ' their power of decision failing and some asking-repeatedly others '. It would help the translation of this long sentence if we made these participles main verbs, ' they lost heart and repeatedly questioned each other ', and inserted ' while ' before **nunc.**

l. 13. **ultimum illud visuri domos suas,** *lit.,* ' about to behold for that last time their homes '. **ultimum illud** is an internal acc.

l. 14. **instabat,** ' became insistent '.

l. 15. **ultimis,** ' most distant '.

l. 16. **distantibus,** ' separate ' *or* ' different '.

l. 17. **velut nube inducta,** ' as if a cloud had been drawn over (the scene) '.

l. 18. **quibus . . . elatis.** Order for translation : **elatis (iis) quae quisque poterat.** Note that the relative pronoun is attracted into the case of the unexpressed antecedent **iis.** This is a Greek idiom.

l. 18. **larem ac penates.** The lares are either originally ghosts of the dead, or, according to another view, deities of the farm-land. In any case, each house had its **lar** or deity that protected the household.

The **penates** are the guardian deities of the store-cupboard and were worshipped together with **Vesta** and the **Lares**. Hence **lar ac penates** came to be used in very much the same sense as ' hearth and home ' in English.

l. 20. **migrantium,** *lit.,* ' of (men) emigrating ' =' of emigrants'.

l. 22. **integrabat lacrimas,** *lit.,* ' renewed their tears ', i.e. ' brought tears afresh (to the eyes) '.

ll. 17-25. **raptim . . . deos.** Begin a fresh sentence with **raptim** and split the remainder up into at least three English sentences. It is, therefore, suggested that the first sentence might end with **exirent** (**cum** in l. 18 being ignored), the second might end with **lacrimas** and the third begin at **voces etiam.**

l. 22. **voces,** ' cries '.

l. 26. **Romanus,** collective again for ' the Romans '. Cf. 15, 2 ; 25, 12.

l. 27. **una hora,** nom.

l. 27. **quadringentorum,** i.e. 300 years before Rome's foundation (said to be 753 B.C.) together with 100 years, the time passed since that date.

l. 28. **quibus,** abl. (for the more usual acc.) of duration of time.

l. 28. **steterat,** ' had stood (secure) ', a meaning common in Vergil.

l. 29. **dedit,** ' gave (over) '.

l. 29. **templis,** dat. dependent on **temperatum est,** impers. pass. English prefers to say, ' the temples were spared '. **deum,** gen. pl.

CHAPTER 30

Line 2. **Caelius mons.** The Caelian Hill is the hill south-east of Rome at the foot of which to the west is the Porta Capena.

l. 2. **quo.** Why **quo** and not **ut**? **habitaretur,** impersonal passive.

l. 3. **sedem,** ' (as) the site '. Note that **eam** which refers to **mons** (*masc*). is attracted in gender to the predicate noun.

l. 4. **principes . . . legit.** In Chap. 28, 7, Tullus had announced his intention of enrolling the leading men of Alba into the senate.

In Chap. 8, l. 29, Romulus appointed a hundred senators ; Tullus now adds nobles from Alba,[1] a third hundred is to be added later by Tarquinius Priscus (Chap. 35, l. 27) ; and 300 remained the usual number until the time of Sulla (80 B.C.).

l. 7. **templumque,** etc. **templum** is in apposition to **curiam,** direct object, ' (as) a holy place '. This **Curia Hostilia** was burned down in 52 B.C., when a riotous mob built in it a pyre for the murdered tribune Clodius.

l. 13. **Hac fiducia virium** =his **viribus fretus,** ' relying on this might '. Livy's phrase will not go literally into English, because, by a sort of hypallage (cf. note on **maiora rerum initia,** Ch. 1, l. 14) he has made the adjective qualify **fiducia** instead of **virium,** and because such an objective genitive as **virium** has no close parallel in our language. **Fiducia** is an abl. of cause.

l. 17. **mercatu frequenti,** abl. abs., ' when . . .'. Great fairs were held on the goddess's feast day in the groves sacred to Feronia.

l. 18. **comprehensos,** sc. **esse.** Cf. **retentos** below.

l. 18. **Sabini,** sc. **querebantur.**

l. 18. **prius,** i.e. before the arrests complained of by the Romans.

l. 18. **lucum.** The asylum established by Romulus.

l. 19. **causae,** ' (as) the causes '.

l. 20. **haud parum,** *lit.,* ' not too little ' =' very well '. It modifies **memores** and is an example of litotes, deliberate understatement for literary effect.

l. 20. **memores** has dependent upon it two indirect statements, **partem locatam** (esse) and **Romanam rem auctam** (esse). The **et** following **memores** =' both '.

l. 23. **circumspicere.** Cf. note on **fremere,** Ch. 17, l. 22. The following **et** =' also '.

l. 24. **Inde** =Veiis (abl.).

l. 24. **ob residuas,** etc. The order after **inde** is animis maxime sollicitatis ad defectionem ob iras residuas bellorum. Previous wars against Veii were recorded in Chs. 15 and 27.

---

[1] Presumably 100, as Livy obtains a total of 300.

l. 27. **plebe.** i.e. the commons of Veii.

l. 27. **publico auxilio**, ' official help ', contrasted with the help offered, from the two motives mentioned above, by private individuals.

l. 29. **de ceteris.** It was more surprising that the Veientines, being of a different race, should be loyal to the treaty.

l. 29. **pacta** belongs in grammar with **fides** (= ' sanctity ' here), in sense with **indutiarum.** Cf. note on **ad maiora rerum initia,** Ch. 1, l. 14. **verti**, ' to depend '. It is the *passive* voice of **verto** which corresponds to the English *intransitive* active.

l. 31. **in eo,** ' on this '. What ' this ' is is explained by the indirect deliberative question **utri . . . inferrent,** ' which side should attack first '.

l. 32. **occupat,** cf. Chap. 14, l. 17.

l. 34. **et . . . quidem,** ' partly, indeed '. This is answered by **ceterum plurimum,** ' but chiefly '.

l. 36. **invectis.** The passive voice of **veho** and its compounds often corresponds to an English intransitive active. Thus **invehor** here = ' ride against '.

l. 37. **nec pugna,** etc., *lit.*, ' nor thereafter could the battle become static for them nor flight be spread out ', i.e. ' and after that they could not bring the foe to a standstill, or scatter in flight '.

CHAPTER 31

Line 4. **lapidibus pluvisse.** Elsewhere Livy has **lapides,** acc., which corresponds to English usage.

l. 4. **Quod** is nom., subject to **posset.** Translate by ' this ', and read again the note on **quem,** Ch. 15, l. 11.

l. 5. **missis,** abl. abs., agreeing with **quibusdam,** ' certain persons ', understood. But turn into a principal clause.

l. 5. **haud aliter quam,** by litotes for **perinde ac.** ' just as '.

l. 7. **Visi,** i.e. **visi sunt.**

l. 8. **summi cacuminis.** We should say ' *on* the summit of the mountain '.

l. 8. **ut . . . facerent.** The clause is an indirect petition dependent on the verbal idea readily supplied from **vocem,** ' crying that the S. should . . .'.

l. 9. **velut** belongs with the abl. abs. **dis relictis,** which should be translated by a clause.

l. 11. **et aut Romana,** etc. These clauses are not logically co-ordinate with the relative clause which precedes, and are best done with an English participle, ' having either adopted . . .'.

l. 11. **ut fit,** ' as does happen ', ' as is usual '.

l. 12. **Romanis.** The dative of the agent, so called : ' by the Romans '.

l. 13. **ab,** ' in consequence of '.

l. 17. **nuntiaretur.** The subjunctive with **quandoque** is Livian and became increasingly common in later writers to express indefinite frequency.

l. 18. **multo,** abl. of measure of difference, *lit.,* ' by much ', modifying **post,** an adverb here, meaning ' later '.

l. 18. **pestilentia** is abl. of cause, and **laboratum est,** impersonal passive : ' the state fell into distress through pestilence '.

l. 19. **Unde,** relative for demonstrative **inde,** as so commonly. It modifies **oreretur.**

l. 19. **militandi.** The genitive, being the only case in which one noun may depend upon another, expresses many relations between nouns for which the conventional rendering ' of ' is quite inappropriate. Say here ' reluctance to take the field '.

l. 21. **credente.** Render the participle by a relative clause, ' who believed ', and take **etiam** (=' actually ') with it.

l. 21. **iuvenum.** According to Roman ideas one remained a **iuvenis** till the age of 40 or so. One was even called **adulescens** when well into the thirties, and Sallust uses the diminutive **adulescentulus** for Julius Caesar at 33.

l. 22. **implicitus est.** In the English metaphor a disease ' *attacks* ', in Latin it ' entangles '.

l. 23. **illi.** A dative is often found where we should expect a genitive or possessive adjective. **illi** =' his '.

l. 24. **qui,** i.e. is qui, ' he who '.

l. 24. **ratus esset.** The subjunctive is regularly used in relative clauses which have adverbial force. Here the clause does the work of an adverbial clause of concession (' although ').

l. 25. **dĕdĕre.** Observe the quantities.

l. 26. **superstitionibus,** dative with **obnoxius.**

l. 29. **unam opem,** etc., ' thought that the one remedy left . . . (was) if . . .'. The *if*-clause is unnatural in English : say ' lay in obtaining . . .'.

l. 31. **volventem.** The word is appropriate to the scrolls on which the **commentarii** would have been written. The actual meaning here is ' *un*rolling '.

l. 32. **ibi,** i.e. in the **commentarii.**

l. 33. **facta** =facta esse.

l. 33. **operatum,** ' devoting himself to '. The deponent verb **operor** is almost synonymous with **operam dare,** and like that phrase is joined with the dative. Note the perfect participle of a deponent verb used, as it frequently is, with present meaning.

l. 34. **sed non rite,** etc. The construction is still acc. and infin. dependent on **tradunt** above, and the three clauses each have different subjects : **id sacrum non rite initum . . . esse, nullam speciem . . . oblatam** (esse), **eum** (=regem) **ictum** (esse . . . et) **conflagrasse.**

CHAPTER 32

Line 1. **iam inde ab initio,** ' from the very first '.

l. 3. **quo** =eo =interrege.

l. 5. **filia,** abl. of origin with **ortus,** ' born of his daughter '.

l. 6. **et** before **avitae** ='both ', and introduces the first of two reasons why the new king thought and acted as he did. For **avitae gloriae memor,** then, say (to balance the **quia** clause), ' because he remembered his grandfather's fame '.

l. 7. **cetera,** acc. of respect with **egregium,** ' outstanding as regards other matters '.

l. 7. **ab una parte,** ' *in* one respect ', we say.

l. 8. **aut neglectis religionibus,** etc.   The ablative absolutes sug-gest alternative reasons for the preceding statement.

l. 9. **antiquissimum,** acc. sg. neuter, agreeing with **facere,** which is the subject, in the acc. and infin. construction, of **esse** understood : 'thinking that it was by far the most important thing to per-form. . . .'

l. 11. **in album,** with **elata,** ' on to a white tablet '.

l. 12. **elata proponere** = **efferre et proponere.**   Cf. note on **asper-natus dimiserit,** Ch. 22, l. 28.

l. 13. **facta.**   Cf. note on **petiti,** Ch. 2, l. 1.

l. 14. **abiturum.**   **abire in,** *lit.,* ' go off into ' may be rendered ' imitate '.

l. 17. **Romanis,** dative.

l. 18. **desidem,** ' (being) disinclined for action '.

l. 20. **medium,** *lit.,* ' central ', i.e. partook of both natures '—the pious and the warlike.

l. 22. **cum in novo,** etc.   More readily seen if the order is changed, **in populo cum novo tum feroci,** the **cum, tum,** meaning ' both ', ' and '.

l. 23. **etiam.**   After this word **credebat** is to be taken a second time, with the following words in this order : **se haud facile habit-urum . . . id otium quod contigisset illi.**   For the order Livy uses (relative before antecedent and attracting a portion of the latter into its own clause), cf. **in qua parte hostes densissimos videtis, eam aggredimini.**

l. 24. **temptari patientiam,** etc.   A continuation of the reported thoughts of Ancus Marcius.

l. 25. **et temptatam,** ' and once proved '.

l. 26. **Tullo regi,** ' to a King Tullus '.

l. 27. **instituisset.**   The subjunctive is one of virtual oratio obliqua.   The clause gives the reason present in the mind or speech of Ancus for doing what he did.

l. 29. **ab antiqua gente Aequicolis.**   Cf. **urbs Roma,** ' city of Rome '.   The A. were near neighbours of the Romans.

l. 29. **ius,** ' the legal formula '.

l. 30. **fetiales.** Livy has already mentioned these officials (Ch. 24) and recorded a formula used by them in the making of treaties.

l. 32. **unde =a quibus.**

l. 34. **fas,** ' the right ', is subject of the jussive subjunctive **audiat.**

l. 36. **legatus** is a participle = ' commissioned ', and the adverbs belong with it.

l. 36. **fides sit** = credatur.

l. 39. **dedier** = dedi, pres. infin. pass. of dedo. It is an obsolete form. Notice the use of the acc. and infin. instead of **ut** + subjunctive, the normal construction with verbs of asking and ordering.

l. 40. **siris** = siveris, perf. subj. This tense, with negative **ne** (here included in **nunquam**) is a regular formula for prohibitions, and therefore alternative to **noli** + infinitive.

l. 41. **quicumque ei,** etc., i.e. ' to the first man who comes in his way ', *lit.,* ' (to that) man who shall have met him first '. But, of the antecedent **ei viro, ei** has been omitted and **viro** transferred to the relative clause and attracted into the case of the relative pronoun.

l. 42. **paucis verbis,** etc., ' with the alteration of a few words in the formula and in the drawing up of the oath '.

l. 44. **quos exposcit.** Supply **ei** as antecedent.

l. 49. **ius persolvere,** ' pay what-is-justly-due '.

l. 52. **ad consulendum.** The verb is here used absolutely : ' for consultation ', ' in order to take counsel '.

l. 53. **consulebat.** Notice the change of tense. The imperfect is that of habitual action : ' the King would, *or* was wont to, consult '.

l. 53. **Quarum rerum litium causarum.** Whatever construction the genitive in this formula was originally intended to have, it is hard to trace any in the sentence as it stands. And yet the sense is plain enough : ' As regards the things, the suits, the causes, touching which the pater patratus of the Roman People of the Quirites made demands upon the pater patratus of the Prisci Latini . . .'.

l. 57. **dari oportuit,** ' ought to have been given '. Notice the asyndeton here, **dari fieri solvi,** and in **rerum litium causarum** above.

l. 58. **quem primum sententiam.** **quem** and **sententiam** are both objects of **rogabat,** ' whom he was wont to ask for his opinion first '. For other verbs that take double accusative of the direct object cf. **doceo, celo.**

l. 60. **quaerendas** (esse) agrees with **eas** understood (=**res lites causas).**

l. 63. **Fieri solitum** (est) **ut fetialis,** ' it was usual for the fetial to . . .'.

l. 64. **hastam,** etc., ' a lance, iron-tipped, or hardened by fire, (and) stained with blood '.

l. 66. **Quod . . . fecerunt deliquerunt.** It is simplest to take **quod** as a conjunction, ' whereas ', and the verbs as intransitive, ' have acted and offended '. The following **quod** is similar, ' (and) where- as '.

l. 74. **dixisset.** The subjunctive was used by Livy in imitation of the Greek optative of indefinite frequency. This can be suggested by rendering **ubi** by ' whenever '.

CHAPTER 33

Line 6. **Et cum circa,** etc. **cum** is causal, ' since ', or ' as '. For the relative positions of the four hills mentioned, see the map, p. 48. **Circa** probably means here ' on both sides of '.

l. 9. **Aventinum.** The neuter noun is an alternative to **Mons Aventinus.**

ll. 9, 10. **datum, additi.** Supply **est** and **sunt.**

l. 10. **eodem,** adverb, *lit.,* ' to the same place ', but obviously meaning here ' to the same multitude '.

l. 10. The very local nature of this stage of Roman history can be deduced from the situation of Tellena and Ficana, which lay not more than fifteen miles or so S.W. of Rome.

l. 12. **vacuum** agrees with **id** (understood) =**Politorium,** ' (when left) empty '—by the removal to Rome of its inhabitants as described above.

l. 13. **diruendae urbis eius,** ' of that city's being destroyed '.

l. 15. **Medulliam compulso,** ' having been centred upon M.' Apparently the meaning is that the whole military effort of the warring peoples was directed to the attack and defence of the one town. Medullia lay in the acute angle between the Tiber and the Anio.

l. 16. **Marte incerto, varia victoria,** ' the fighting being indecisive (and) victory inclining now to one side, now to the other '.

l. 16. **nam et urbs,** etc. The et =' both '.

l. 20. **acie,** ' in a regular engagement '.

l. 24. **ad Murciae,** sc. **aram.** Venus, under the name of Murcia, had an altar at the foot of the Aventine, at which sacrifice was offered to her as the patroness of the slothful. **datae,** i.e. **datae sunt.**

l. 25. **inopia,** abl. of cause, ' from lack '.

l. 25. **quando.** Distinguish this indefinite adverb =' at any time ', from the interrogative ' when '.

l. 26. **ea.** Observe that this pronoun has been made to agree with the complement **arx** rather than with the noun **Ianiculum** to which it refers. The Janiculum was a ridge lying on the Tuscan bank of the river.

l. 26. **Id non muro,** etc. Begin with **placuit,** which has its common meaning of ' it was decided '. The subject of **placuit** is the acc. and infin. **id coniungi,** ' that it should be joined '. **id** = **Ianiculum.**

l. 27. **itineris,** ' of passage to and fro '.

l. 27. **ponte sublicio.** A bridge entirely of wooden construction.

l. 28. **in Tiberi.** In Latin a bridge is built not ' over ' or ' across ' but ' on ' a river.

l. 30. **a planioribus aditu locis,** ' at the places more level (and consequently easier) to approach '. For this use of **a,** cf. **a tergo,** ' in the rear '.

l. 31. **rebus,** say ' population ' or ' numbers '.

l. 32. **discrimine recte an perperam facti confuso,** ' the distinction between right and wrong actions having become blurred '. The expression is a condensed form for something like **discrimine, utrum quid recte an perperam factum esset, confuso.**

l. 36. **Veientibus,** dative of disadvantage with **adempta,** ' from the Veientines '. The Maesian Forest lay north of the Tiber and not far from the coast.

l. 39. **egregie rebus bello gestis,** *lit.*, ' operations having been excellently conducted in the war '. Say ' in view of the striking success of the military operations '. The phrase gives the reason for what follows.

CHAPTER 34

Line 1. **Lucumo.** This, which the Romans regarded as a proper name, was actually a title among the Etruscans, denoting priestly or princely rank.

l. 2. **cupidine ac spe,** abls. of cause, modifying **commigravit** : ' *from* the desire . . .'.

l. 3. **cuius adipiscendi,** ' of obtaining which ', depends on **facultas. Tarquiniis** is locative.

l. 4. **ibi quoque,** and not merely at Rome.

l. 6. **qui ob seditiones,** etc. It is worth while to notice the very Latin way in which the four statements about Lucumo are made— how the use of the participle **ducta,** of the quasi-participle **profugus,** and of the **cum** clause keep the ideas they express in proper sub-ordination to the chief notion intended to be conveyed—the birth of the sons. Our own language does not take kindly to this hier-archical pattern, and we might say ' who was exiled . . . , settled . . . , married . . . , and begot . . .'

l. 9. **heres.** Deal with this as if you had **et . . . heres fuit.** But it is, of course, a parallel case to **casibus variis,** Ch. **1, l. 5,** on which see the note.

l. 11. **manet superstes,** a mere variation for **superest. filio =** Arruns ; **pater =** Demaratus.

l. 11. **qui,** i.e. Demaratus. In spite of the order of words, **qui** is the subject of the **cum** clause ; ' as he (**qui**), unaware . . .'.

l. 14. **Egerio,** made to agree, in the common Latin manner, with

puero rather than logically with **nomen. Egerius,** connected with **egeo,** ' need ', suggests ' pauper '.

l. 15. **Lucumoni contra,** etc. A very Latin sentence, beginning literally as follows : ' for Lucumo, on the other hand, the inheritor of all the property, whereas **(cum)** his riches were creating pride, Tanaquil married **(ducta in matrimonium)** increased (it) ' . . . Notice particularly how **Tanaquil ducta** represents what we express in English by ' his marriage with Tanaquil ', and cf. note on **inter Lavinium conditum,** etc., Ch. 3, l. 16.

ll. 17-19. **et quae,** etc., *lit.,* ' and such a woman as not easily to permit those things into which she had married (to be) lower than those things in which she had been born ', i.e. ' one who would ill endure that her fortune as a wife should be inferior to that into which she had been born '. Note the generic subjunctive **sineret** and the use of the adverb **quo,** ' whither ', for **in quae. iis** is abl. of comparison.

l. 19. **innupsisset.** The mood of the verb is perhaps due to attraction, but it may possibly be a Hellenism, with the subjunctive expressing *indefiniteness* ; ' whatever fortune she should marry into '.

l. 20. **ortum,** giving the reason for **spernentibus,** ' (as) being sprung '.

l. 23. **ab Tarquiniis.** It is characteristic of Livy to insert the preposition. Cf. **a Curibus** below.

l. 23. **ad id,** ' for her purpose '.

l. 24. **visa :** The colon, as often, indicates the point of transition to reported speech. The next two sentences give Tanaquil's thoughts.

l. 25. **ex virtute,** ' the result of merit '.

l. 25. **futurum,** sc. esse.

l. 28. **nobilem una imagine Numae,** *lit.,* ' noble by reason of one portrait, Numa's ', i.e. ' having only one distinguished ancestor, Numa '. It was the custom for noble Roman families to display in the atria of their houses the masks or the busts of those ancestors who had distinguished themselves by attaining high office.

l. 29. **cupido** is attracted into the case of **ei,** which must be supplied with **persuadet**. But proceed as if the text read **ut qui cupidus esset.**

l. 29. **et cui Tarquinii**, etc., ' and (one) for whom T. was only his mother's home '. Observe that the verb **esset** agrees not with its plural subject, **Tarquinii**, but with the singular complement. For the mood of the verb, cf. note on **ut qui**, Ch. 1, l. 19.

l. 30. Sublatis, from **tollo.**

l. 31. **ventum erat**, impers. pass., = **venerant.**

l. 32. **ibi ei carpento**, etc. The dative **ei** belongs with **aufert** : ' from him, sitting . . . an eagle . . . removes the cap .' For **carpento**, see the note on Chap. 48, l. 20.

l. 35. **ministerio**, dat. of purpose with **missa.**

l. 36. **laeta**, adj. for adv., very frequent in Latin.

l. 37. **perita mulier**, ' (being) a woman instructed '.

l. 37. **Etrusci**, sc. **sunt.**

l. 38. **excelsa et alta**, acc. pl. neuter ; **complexa**, nom. sg. fem.

l. 39. **eam alitem**, etc. See the note on **visa** : above. In this sentence **is** = **talis** as in **ea pietate**, Ch. 21, l. 4· ' Such a bird it was, coming from such a quarter óf the sky and bringing-a-message from such a god '. These are the reasons why Tanaquil bids her husband ' hope for a high and lofty destiny '.

l. 40. **summum culmen**. The adjective is pleonastic. Say ' the very crown of a man's head '.

l. 42. **decus**, i.e. th. **pilleus.**

l. 42. **ut . . . redderet**,   only) to replace it upon the same head with divine approval '.

l. 46. **et ipse fortunam**, etc. The order is **et ipse adiuvabat fortunam benigno adloquio, comitate invitandi, conciliandoque sibi beneficiis (eos) quos poterat. comitate invitandi**, ' by the courtesy of his offers of hospitality '.

l. 51. **in familiaris amicitiae iura adduxerat**, ' he had developed . . . into the privileges of close friendship '.

l. 53. per omnia expertus, 'after being tested in all'. The participle of the deponent verb experior is used here in a passive meaning, as in Ch. 17, l. 10.

CHAPTER 35

Line 2. belli pacisque et artibus et gloria, ' both in the arts of war, and peace, and in the renown he won from them '.

l. 3. par, ' (being) equal '.

l. 4. eo magis, ' the more on that account '.

l. 4. instare, historic infinitive.

l. 6. venatum. See note on consultum, Ch. 20, l. 24.

l. 6. Isque primus dicitur, ' and he is said to have been the first b th to . . .'. Cf. with this quippe qui non primus peregrinus regnum adfectet below, ' since he was not the first foreigner to seek the kingship '. (Notice in this latter sentence examples of both historic and primary subjunctives, the latter being put, in the Greek manner, for greater vividness of effect, just as the historic present indicative is used for the same purpose.)

l. 10. quod, ' (a thing) which '.

l. 13. ignarum urbis, non petentem. This has concessive force, ' (though) knowing nothing of the city and not seeking (such elevation) '.

l. 14. ultro. ' Actually ', perhaps the best single word to keep in mind as an equivalent, will do reasonably well here. The adverb is used to distinguish statements that introduce what is unexpected, e.g. mihi petere dubitanti ultro dedisti, ' though I hesitated to ask, you gave *of your own accord* '.

l. 14. ex quo, usually ' since ', here ' as soon as '.

l. 16. aetatis eius, i.e. the period from his coming of age to the moment of which he is speaking.

i. 16. qua, ' during which '.

l. 18. haud paenitendo magistro, ' a teacher not to be repented of ' = ' no mean teacher '—litotes.

l. 22. certasse. The subject is se, understood.

l. 22. **ingenti,** ' extraordinary '.

l. 23. **Ergo virum,** etc. The grammatical order is **ergo ambitio, quam in petendo habuerat, secuta est virum, egregium cetera, etiam regnantem.** But it is best to retain the Latin order as far as may be, which involves making ' man ' the subject and putting the verb in the passive. **habuerat,** ' had employed ' ; **cetera,** accus. of respect with **egregium,** ' otherwise noble '. **ergo,** because it was **ambitio** which had gained him the throne.

l. 26. **regni sui firmandi,** ' of fortifying his own position as king '.

l. 27. **centum,** sc. **viros.**

l. 27. **in patres legit,** ' selected for admission to the senate '.

l. 27. **minorum gentium** depends on **patres** (nom.) understood, with which **factio** is in apposition.

l. 28. **haud dubia,** litotes for ' completely reliable '.

l. 30. **primum,** adjective.

l. 30. **ibi,** i.e. in their territory.

l. 31. **quam quanta belli fama fuerat,** ' than reports about the war had led people to expect ', (*lit.*, ' than (so great) as had been the reputation of the war ').

l. 36. **spectacula,** ' seats *or* stands (for viewing the games) '.

l. 37. **furcis,** etc. Construe as follows : **furcis sustinentibus** (abl. abs.) **spectacula duodenos pedes alta ab terra.** Translate : ' from seats raised on props twelve feet high from the ground '.

l. 38. **fuit,** ' consisted of '.

l. 39. **Sollemnes** is complement of **mansere, annui** attributive to **ludi.**

l. 40. **appellati,** ' being called '.

l. 41. **et,** ' also '.

l. 41. **aedificanda,** ' for building *on* '.

CHAPTER 36

Line 2. **intervenit.** The indicative is regular in ' inverse **cum** clauses ', i.e. when the clause grammatically subordinate is in sense principal.

l. 3. **priusquam.** Observe the division of this conjunction.

l. 5. **trepidatum est,** ' there was great alarm ', impersonal passive, as is **pugnatum est** following.

l. 9. **equitem,** sg. for pl.

l. 10. **quas centurias.** Reverse these in translating.

l. 12. **inaugurato,** ' (only) after taking auspices '. For this one-word abl. abs., cf. **tranquillo, ut aiunt, quilibet gubernator est,** ' when-it-is-calm, anyone is a helmsman as they say '.

l. 13. **negare,** historic infin. Translate by ' asserted '. See the next note.

l. 14. **neque mutari neque novum constitui posse,** ' that there could be no change, nor could a new thing be instituted '. **mutari posse** is impersonal passive. Observe that the negatives **negare** and **neque** do not cancel one another, and that in English only one negative must appear.

l. 16. **regi,** though dat., answers to an English possessive gen.

l. 17. **fierine** := num **fieri.**

l. 19. **futuram,** i.e. **eam** (=rem) **futuram esse,** ' that it would happen '.

l. 19. **hoc,** acc.

l. 23. **quo in loco,** i.e. **in eo loco in quo,** ' at the spot where '.

l. 25. **sitam fuisse** (=esse), pf. infin. pass. of **sino.**

l. 28. **accessit,** ' accrued '.

l. 28. **belli domique,** locatives both, **belli** being put for the more usual **militiae.**

l. 29. **auspicato.** Cf. note on **inaugurato** earlier in this chapter.

l. 29. **concilia** begins a second consecutive clause, and might have been preceded by **et ut.**

l. 29. **exercitus vocati,** ' the calling out of armies '. For the use of the participle, see the note on **inter Lavinium conditum,** etc., Ch. 3, l. 16.

l. 30. **summa rerum,** a Livian variation for **res summae,** ' the most vital affairs '. In the phrase **summa** is neut. pl.

l. 32. **numero alterum tantum adiecit,** *lit.,* ' to the number he added another so great ', i.e. ' he doubled their number '.

l. 33. **mille et octingenti.** Livy's arithmetic seems at fault. If the number 600, comprising the 300 equites of Romulus (Ch. 13) and the 300 added by Tullus (Ch. 30) be doubled, we can make no more than 1200 of the result.

l. 34. **Posteriores** is the *complement* of **appellati sunt** ; the subject of it is (ei) **qui additi sunt.** For posteriores, say ' newer knights '.

l. 34. **sub iisdem nominibus.** For the names, see Ch. 13.

l. 35. **quas,** i.e. **eas.** See note on **quem,** Ch. 15, l. 11.

CHAPTER 37

Line 2. **confligitur,** impers. pass.

l. 2. **viribus,** abl. of respect, ' in strength '.

l. 4. **missis,** abl. abs., ' (men) being sent '.

ll. 4-5. **qui . . . conicerent,** final clause.

l. 5. **ardentem conicerent** = incenderent et conicerent, ' to set on fire and throw '.

l. 6. **pleraque** is parenthetic and limitative: ' and driven, most of it, against . . .'.

l. 7. **cum** appears very late in the sentence. It means ' since ' and should be the first word translated.

l. 8. **in pugna,** ' during the fighting '.

l. 8. **effusis,** dative of disadvantage, ' to (them) routed ' = ' in their rout '.

l. 9. **cum,** ' although '.

l. 11. **arma,** ' shields '. As they were made of wood or wicker-work, they would float.

l. 11. **cognita,** ' (being) recognised '.

l. 12. **insignem,** ' known '.

l. 14. **utrimque . . .** Begin with **ferunt,** ' they say '. **positos,** in agreement with **eos** (understood), subj. of **incurrisse.**

l. 15. **peditum suorum,** ' (consisting) of their own infantry '.

l. 17. instantes, acc. in agreement with **Sabinas legiones** and having dependent on it **cedentibus**, ' (who were) pressing hard upon (the Romans) as they were giving ground '.

l. 18. **averterent,** ' put ', *lit.*, ' diverted '.

l. 19. **tenuere,** ' reached (them) '.

l. 20. **Tarquinius . . . inducere.** In this sentence make **ratus** a main verb, and insert ' therefore ' before the two abl. absols. which should be translated in the active voice as main verbs, ' he sent . . . he burnt ' and add ' and ' before **pergit. instandum.** Supply **esse** with this gerundive of obligation.

l. 22. **spoliis,** i.e. weapons, armour and clothing of the enemy.

l. 24. **quamquam . . . erat,** ' although the thing had been done badly ' = ' although they (i.e. the S.) had been unsuccessful '.

l. 25. **gesturos.** Supply **se**.

l. 26. **quia . . . spatium,** ' because the situation did not allow time of deliberating (= for deliberation) '.

l. 27. **tumultuario milite,** ' with soldiers hastily levied '.

l. 28. **perditis . . . rebus,** ' their cause being already practically lost '.

CHAPTER 38

Line 1. **Collatia.** This Sabine town was situated about 13 miles due east of Rome.

l. 1. **citra,** ' on this side of '—from the standpoint of Rome, i.e. ' west of '.

l. 1. **agri,** partitive gen dependent on **quidquid,** ' all the land ',

l. 2. **ademptum.** Supply **est.** The verb has two subjects but agrees only with the nearer one.

l. 2. **fratris . . . regis,** ' he was the son of the king's brother '.

l. 4. **accipio,** ' I understand ', or ' I am told '.

l. 5. **rex.** The king, not the fetials, received the surrender.

l. 5. **oratores,** ' spokesmen '.

l. 6. **vos,** acc.

l. 8. **in sua potestate,** ' in its own power ' = ' its own master '.

l. 12. **at,** ' then '.

l. 14. **ubi . . . ventum est,** *lit.*, ' where they came nowhere to the struggle of the whole affair '. **ubi** = in **quo**, the latter being the coordinate relative. Thus we may render, ' in this (campaign) they came at no point to a decisive struggle '.

l. 16. **arma,** ' his strength ', obj. of **circumferendo.**

l. 16. **nomen,** ' people ' *or* ' race ', a meaning in which Livy often employs the word.

l. 19. **de,** ' from '. **aut qui,** ' or (from those) who '.

l. 20. **capta.** Supply **sunt.** All these towns were placed north of the Anio and situated not more than 10-15 miles north-east of Rome.

l. 21. **maiore . . . bella,** *lit.*, ' after this the tasks of peace were begun with enthusiasm greater than the degree of effort (**mole**) with which he had waged his campaigns '. The full expression is **tanta mole quanta . . .** English would prefer the active here, ' the king began the tasks of peace . . .'.

l. 23. **fuisset.** The subjunctive is due to attraction.

l. 27. **quia . . . aquas,** ' because (the citizens) could **not** easily carry off the (flood-)waters from the level (ground) '.

l. 28. **cloacis . . . ductis,** abl. abs., ' by constructing drains with a downward slope into the Tiber '.

l. 29. **aream ad aedem,** ' site for a temple '.

l. 30. **iam . . . loci,** *lit.*, ' his mind now having a preconception of the grandeur of the place destined-one-day-to-be ' = ' inasmuch as he had a preconception of the grandeur the place would one day have '.

Chapter 39

Line 1. **prodigium . . . mirabile,** ' a portent wonderful in its appearance and in its sequel '. Note the abls. of respect, **visu, eventu.**

l. 2. **puero dormienti,** dat. of the person interested, to be translated as a gen. with **caput.** Begin the sentence with **ferunt,** ' they say '.

l. 2. **Servio Tullio.** For the attraction of this to the case of the relative pronoun, see the note on **Troiano,** Chap. 1, l. 12

l. 3. **caput arsisse.** For a similar portent, see Vergil, *Aen.* II, 681 sqq.:

namque . . .
ecce levis summo de vertice visus Iuli
fundere lumen apex tactuque innoxia mollis
lambere flamma comas et circum tempora pasci.

l. 4. **ad miraculum,** *lit.,* ' at the marvel of so great a thing ' =' at so great a marvel '.

l. 5. **excitos reges,** acc. and infin., dependent upon **ferunt. reges,** ' the king and queen '.

l. 6. **retentum.** Supply **eum** and **esse.**

l. 7. **sedato eam tumultu,** ' after calming the uproar, (she) . . .'.

l. 8. **experrectus esset.** This pluperf. subj. represents a fut. perf. of direct speech.

l. 10. **viden** =**vides ne.**

l. 11. **scire licet . . .,** ' you may be certain that . . .'.

l. 12. **rebus nostris dubiis,** ' to our dubious fortunes '. Tarquin had no son and had sent away the sons of Ancus, his predecessor.

l. 13. **regiae adflictae,** dat., ' to the royal house distressed ' =' to the royal house in time of distress '.

l. 13. **materiam ingentis decoris,** ' the means of great distinction ' =' one who will bring great distinction (to us) '.

l. 15. **liberum loco,** ' as a free child ' ; *lit.,* ' in the place of the free (ones) '. **liberum** is gen. pl. The phrase means, ' as a son '. **Liberi,** ' the free ones ', as opposed to the slaves ; hence ' children of the house ', and ' children ' generally.

l. 15. **coeptum** (esse) **haberi,** ' began to be treated '. Note that when the verb **coepi** has dependent upon it a passive infinitive, it is used in the passive itself.

Finally, notice that Livy has returned to oratio obliqua, but **quibus . . . excitantur** has its verb in the indicative because it is an addition by Livy.

l. 16. **quibus . . . excitantur,** ' by which dispositions are roused to the cultivation of great fortune ' =' whereby men are inspired to court great fortune '.

l. 17. **quod . . . esset,** 'since it was pleasing to heaven'. **cordi,** predicative dat., and **esset,** subj. in causal relative clause.

l. 20. **ulla arte,** ' in any activity ', abl. of respect.

l. 21. **hic . . . credere prohibet,** *lit.*, ' this so great honour on what- ever grounds conferred upon him (**illi**) prevents (our) believing ' = ' the conferring upon him of this great honour, no matter upon what grounds, . . .'.

l. 22. **serva,** abl. of origin. **parvum,** ' (as) a child '.

l. 24. **qui . . . domo.** Order for literal translation : **qui ferunt capto Corniculo uxorem S. T. . . . gravidam viro occiso, qui . . . fuerat cum cognita esset . . .**

The sentence in this order is awkward in English because **viro occiso** refers also to **Servi Tulli.** Thus we might render after **capto Corniculo,** ' S. T. who had been . . . , being slain, his wife who was pregnant was recognised . . . and . . .'.

l. 27. **prohibitam servitio,** ' rescued from slavery '.

l. 29. **inde,** ' in consequence '.

l. 29. **tanto . . . auctam,** *lit.*, ' by so great kindness both intimacy between the women was increased '. The women are Tanaquil and Ocrisia. We might make ' so great (an act of) kindness ' the subj., and continue ' increased the intimacy between . . .'.

l. 31. **in domo a parvo,** ' in the royal family from childhood '.

l. 33. **venerit,** perfect subj. The historians often retain the tenses of oratio recta in subordinate clauses in oratio obliqua.

l. 33. **ut . . . crederetur.** The strict historic sequence is used here (although Livy has, as explained in the previous note, retained the tense of O.R. in the case of **venerit**), because **crederetur** depends directly on the historic **fecisse.** This is Livy's usual practice. For a full discussion of this problem, see the appendix in Dr. R. S. Con- way's edition of Livy, Book II.

l. 33. **ut . . . fecisse,** *lit.*, ' caused that he was believed born of a slave-woman '. **serva,** abl. of origin.

CHAPTER 40

Line 1. **duodequadragesimo . . . coeperat,** i.e. from 616 to 578 B.C.

l. 1. **ex quo,** ' since '.

l. 4. **etsi . . . habuerant,** ' although previously they had always considered it a great wrong '.

l. 6. **regnare.** Supply et before this acc. and infin. : ' and that there should be reigning at Rome . . .'.

l. 6. **non modo** =non modo non, as often.

l. 7. **sed ne Italicae quidem stirpis.** In Chap. 34, 2, Livy has told us that the father of Tarquinius had settled in Italy after being banished from Corinth by political unrest.

l. 7. **tum . . . crescere.** Note carefully that Livy has changed the shape of his sentence. He began with a nom., **Anci filii duo** and we should now naturally expect to have the main verb to which that nom. belongs. Instead, however, a new nom., occurs, **indignitas.** Such a change of grammatical construction is known as anacoluthon. In this passage, it is not very harsh because ' the two sons of A. ' remain the virtual if not the grammatical subject throughout the sentence. Consequently, we can suggest translating this ' although the two sons of A. (l. 4) . . . ., then they felt their indignation the more fiercely increased in that (si) . . .'.

l. 8. **si** almost equals **quod,** especially after a verb of emotion.

l. 9. **inde** =a **Tarquinio.**

l. 9. **ad servitia.** Note the abstract for the concrete, ad servitia being equivalent to **ad servos,** ' into the (hands of) slaves '. Livy does not accept the story of the servile origin of Servius.

l. 10. **post . . . quam Romulus . . . regnum,** ' a hundred years after R. . . . held the sovereign power '.
Note : (i) **postquam** divided (tmesis), (ii) post with **centesimum annum** is similar grammatically to the use of **ante** in dates ; **ante quintum diem Kalendas Martias.**

l. 12. **tenuerit, fuerit, possideat.** Tenses of O.R. are again retained.

l. 13. **Cum . . .tum,** ' not only . . . but also '. **Romani nominis,** gen., where English would prefer dat. Similarly **domus suae.**

l. 14. **Anci . . . salva,** abl. absol., ' the male stock of king Ancus (being) safe ', i.e. ' while the sons of . . . were alive '.

l. 20. **rex futurus erat,** ' the king was likely to be '.

ll. 17-20. **sed et . . . privatus.** Livy begins this sentence with **et** ' both ', and then after the second **et** gives us not a second sentence coordinate with the first but a causal clause. The sense is clear, however ; they had two incentives to an attack on Tarquin rather than on Servius, their indignation at the insult and the knowledge that the king, if he survived, would avenge the crime more severely than a subject could.

ll. 20-22. **tum . . . videbatur,** *lit.,* ' then, Servius slain, (the king) seemed likely-to-make (as) his heir of the throne the same (man), whomsoever else he chose (as) his son-in-law ' ; i.e. ' then, if Servius were slain, it seemed that the king would make his heir to the throne whomsoever . . .'.

delegisset. The pluperfect subj. represents a future perf. of oratio recta ; **faciet . . . delegerit.**

l. 26. **specie rixae,** ' with the appearance of a quarrel ' =' feigning a quarrel '.

l. 30. **vociferari . . . obstrepere,** historic infinitives.

l. 30. **certatim . . . obstrepere,** ' in rivalry the one shouted the other down ' =' strove to shout each other down '.

l. 32. **rem orditur,** ' began (to state) his case '.

l. 33. **totus,** adj. for adv., ' wholly '.

l. 34. **elatam . . . deiecit,** a good example of the Latin participle replacing finite verb as explained in the note on **aspernatus dimiserit,** Chap. 22, 28, ' he raised aloft his hatchet and brought it down '.

CHAPTER 41

Line 1. **qui** =**ei qui.**

l. 2. **fugientes,** ' as they fled '.

l. 3. **mirantium.** The participle is plural although it qualifies the sg. collective **populi.**

l. 3. **clamor . . . concursus.** Supply the verb **erat.**

l. 3. **quid rei esset,** ' what was the matter '. Note **rei,** partitive gen. dependent upon **quid.**

l. 5. **quae . . . sunt,** *lit.,* ' what things are wanted for healing a wound '. **opus,** ' necessary ', is often used with *a dat. of the person who needs* and *abl. of the thing needed* : e.g. **opus est mihi equo,** ' I need a horse '. In this passage, however, the *thing needed* is the subj. and **opus,** used as an indeclinable adjective, is the complement or predicate.

curando vulneri, dat. of work contemplated.

l. 6. **simul . . . simul,** ' both . . . and '.

l. 7. **si . . . molitur.** The protasis **si destituat spes,** ' in case her hope should fail (her),' has for apodosis not **molitur,** but an unexpressed clause which can be supplied from **praesidia,** ' measures-of-protection (which she could use), if her hopes should fail '.

The present subj. (**destituat**) is used to retain the actual condition present to the mind of Tanaquil at the time she acted. This is comparable with Livy's fondness for retaining the tense of oratio recta in oratio obliqua.

l. 10. **inimicis ludibrio.** Note the predicative dat. accompanied as it commonly is, by a second dat.

l. 11. **non eorum,** ' not of those ' = ' not theirs ', referring to the sons of Ancus.

l. 13. **deos duces,** ' the gods (as your) guides ' = ' the guidance of the gods '.

l. 14. **divino . . . igni,** *lit.,* ' by divine fire formerly poured round ' = ' by encircling it of old with divine fire '.

l. 15. **excitet.** Notice the mood.

l. 16. **et nos peregrini,** ' We too (though) foreigners '.

l. 17. **re subita,** ' in this sudden crisis '. The construction is abl. absol.

l. 20. **per . . . versas,** ' through a window looking out (*lit.,* turned) upon New Street '. The latter ran around the north slope of the Palatine and began at the Porta Mugionia.

l. 21. **ad Iovis Statoris.** Supply **templum,** ' by the temple of Jove the Stayer.'

Compare the English use of ' St. Paul's ' for ' St. P's. Cathedral'. For this temple, associated by tradition with Romulus, but actually not built until 294 B.C., see the note on Chap. 12, l. 19.

l. 22. **bono animo,** abl. of quality or description, ' of good cheer '. Note the short staccato sentences which Livy puts into the mouth of Tanaquil to illustrate her determined character.

l. 24. **iam ... redisse,** ' had already recovered consciousness '.

l. 25. **omnia ... esse,** ' all (the symptoms) were favourable '.

l. 27. **iubere.** The subject is **regem** understood. **dicto audientem esse,** ' to obey '.

l. 30. **sede regia,** local abl. without the preposition **in,** a use imitated from poetry.

l. 30. **alia ... de aliis,** ' some (cases), (but) about others '.

l. 32. **per ... vicis,** ' on the pretext of performing another's office '. Note that **fungor** (like **utor** and **fruor**) was a transitive verb in old Latin and that in the personal use of the gerundive here, where one would normally expect the gerund and the ablative case, it continues to show its former transitive nature.

l. 35. **primus regnavit,** ' was the first to reign '.

l. 36. **iniussu ... patrum,** ' without the authorisation of the people, (but) with the consent of the fathers '. The latter phrase implies passive acquiescence, not formal confirmation (=**auctoritas**). Note once again the Latin fondness for asyndeton.

l. 37. **ut,** ' when '.

l. 37. **iam tum,** ' before this ', i.e. at the time of the murder.

l. 39. **exsulatum,** acc. of the supine used to express purpose.

CHAPTER 42

Line 2. **munire,** historic infin.

l. 2. **ne ... esset.** Order for translation : **ne animus liberum (gen. pl.) Tarquini esset talis adversus se qualis (animus) liberum Anci fuerat adversus Tarquinium.**

l. 4. **filias,** i.e., the two Tullias. The elder is generally regarded as the wife of Lucius, the younger, as the wife of Arruns.

l. 5. **nec rupit,** ' he could not break '.

l. 6. **quin . . . faceret,** *lit.,* ' so that jealousy of his power even . . . did not make all things disloyal and hostile '.

quin is regularly used to introduce an adverbial clause of result and in such cases = **ut non.**

l. 9. **ad . . . status,** *lit.,* ' for the tranquillity of the present state ' = ' for the tranquil maintenance of the present state of things '.

l. 10 **indutiae.** A hundred years' truce was granted the Veientes in the reign of Romulus (15, l. 21), i·e. about 140 years before the events Livy is now describing. Chap. 33, l. 36, however, seems to suggest that there might have been a war during this long interval, for there it is stated that in the reign of Ancus the Veientes had the Maesian forest taken from them.

l. 13. **haud dubius . . . rediit,** ' he returned to Rome, no doubtful king, whether . . .', i.e. ' his claim to the throne no longer doubted . . .'.

l. 16. **divini iuris,** ' of religious law '.

l. 19. **ita . . . ferrent. famā ferrent,** ' should celebrate '.

quibus . . . interlucet, ' by which some difference appears between the degrees of rank and fortune '.

fuisset : the subjunctive is due to attraction.

l. 21. **ex quo . . . fierent.** The relative introduces a purpose clause, ' in order that in consequence the duties . . . might be performed '. **Ex quo = ut ex eo.**

l. 21. **viritim,** ' man by man ' = ' indiscriminately ' ; i.e. treating each man as the equal of his fellow without regard to the question of property.

l. 22. **classes. classis** literally means ' calling ' and then, ' those called out ' and thus is used sometimes in the meaning of **exercitus.**

l. 23. **hunc,** ' the following '.

Chapter 43

The following table will make Livy's account of the census more intelligible :

Class	Centuries	Property Qualification	Equipment of Infantry
First	80	100,000 asses	galea, clipeus, ocreae, lorica, hasta et gladius
(Fabri)	2	. . . . . .	No arms
Second	20	75,000	As First, but with scutum and without lorica
Third	20	50,000	As above, without ocreae
Fourth	20	25,000	Only hasta et verutum
Fifth	30	11,000	fundae lapidesque
Musicians	2	. . . . . .	
Exempt	1	Under 1,000	
New Equites	12⎱	⎰ Extra	from the leading men of
Old ,,	6⎰	⎱Classem	the state (ex primoribus)

On the dating of this reconstruction of the Roman army which has traditionally been imputed to Servius Tullius, see Cary, *A History of Rome*, pp. 80 sqq., and his authorities there quoted. Cary puts it in the middle of the 5th century B.C. See also *Cambridge Ancient History*, II, 432 sqq., 482 sqq.

Line 1. **centum milium aeris.** Supply **censum** on which this gen. depends. **aeris** = assium. The rating refers to capital, not income.

l. 3. **seniorum,** i.e. 46-60 years of age; **iuniorum,** 17-45 years of age. The latter would form the striking force of the army.

l. 3. **prima classis** is the complement to **appellati (sunt).**

l. 5. **arma his imperata galea . . . ,** ' the arms (which were) demanded from them (were) the helmet . . .'.

l. 9. **fabrum,** gen. pl.

l. 9. **quae . . . stipendia facerent,** ' to serve . . .' ; purpose clause.

l. 10. **machinas.** It is extremely doubtful whether, at the time of which Livy is writing, the art of war had developed so far as to call for war-engines.

l. 11. **intra centum . . . censum,** ' within a rating of 100,000 as far as (that) of 75,000 '.

l. 14. **scutum pro clipeo,** ' oblong shield instead of the round one '. While the **clipeus** was a round shield, the **scutum** was oblong, and of convex form for the better protection of the sides as well as the front of the body. It was made of wood and covered with leather. It afforded sufficient protection for the bearer to be without a breastplate.

l. 15. **tertiae . . . voluit,** *lit.,* ' he wished the rating of the third class to be a 50,000 (rating) '.

l. 16. **totidem . . . factae,** ' these centuries too were made the same number (as in the 2nd class) and with the same distinction of ages '.

l. 17. **aetatium,** a Livian form for the regular aetatum.

l. 17. **nec . . . mutatum (est),** ' and no change was made . . .'.

l. 18. **tantum,** *adv.,* ' only '.

l. 21. **verutum,** a dart, 3′ or 4′ long. The **hasta** of the first class was a lance which could be either thrown or used for thrusting. It was much longer than the **pilum** of the legionary soldier of the 1st century B.C. and later.

l. 21. **quinta classis aucta,** ' the fifth class was increased ' = ' was made larger ' ; i.e. than the previous four classes.

l. 23. **his accensi . . . distributi,** ' enrolled in addition to them (were) the horn-blowers and trumpeters, divided into two centuries '.

l. 24. **undecim milibus,** ' at 11,000 ' ; abl. of price.

l. 25. **hoc minor census,** ' the rating less than (=below) this '.

l. 26. **habuit,** ' included '.

l. 26. **inde =ex ea,** ' from it ', i.e. ' the rest of the population '.

l. 27. **immunis militia,** ' exempt from military service '. **militia,** abl. of separation.

l. 29. **scripsit=conscripsit,** and illustrates once again Livy's fondness for using a simple verb instead of its compound.

These 12 centuries of cavalry were enrolled from citizens of the **highest rating.**

l. 30. sub iisdem ... nominibus, 'under the same names with which they had been inaugurated '.

For the three centuries of knights which Romulus had instituted, see Chap. 13, l. 30.

Servius arranged the cavalry into 18 centuries, 12 drawn from citizens of the top rating, and 6 reserved for the patricians. Names for the latter were obtained by doubling the old names of the original three of Romulus.

When the comitia centuriata was used as a political body, these six centuriae (known also as sex suffragia) voted first of the 18 centuries of knights, just as the latter voted before the centuries of the first class.

l. 32. quibus. The antecedent is bina milia aeris. The order for translation will then be : viduae attributae quae penderent in annos singulos bina milia aeris quibus equos alerent.

Note : penderent, alerent, purpose subj. viduae, unmarried women. attributae (sunt), 'were told off ', i.e. for this maintenance of the horses.

This yearly allowance was later known as the aes hordearium, ' money for barley-fodder '.

l. 35. a pauperibus, ' from the poor '. This phrase means poor patricians, for at this time only the patricians had any political rights and privileges and amongst these one of the most important was the right to fight in the levies of the day. The organisation attributed to Servius distributed this right more equitably amongst all sections of the community except the poorest, and from now on a man's position in the exercitus depended not on his birth, but upon his wealth and his ability to provide himself with offensive and defensive equipment.

The next step was the making of political responsibility as well as military obligations dependent upon wealth.

l. 35. est additus. Supply divitibus.

l. 36. ut ... reges. This sentence will run better in English if the Latin order is followed and the verb servaverant is turned into the passive, ' in accordance with the tradition laid down by R. and observed by . . .'.

l. 37. **suffragium . . . iure,** ' a suffrage of the same power and privilege '.

In the **comitia curiata,** ' assembly by wards ', the majority of citizens in each curia determined the block vote of the curia, and, thus, in theory at any rate, the poor citizen had a vote of the same power and privilege as the wealthy one.

l. 39. **ut neque . . . esset,** ' so that while no one . . . , yet all power . . .', (*lit.*, ' so that both not anyone . . . and . . .').

Under the Servian organisation every citizen had the right to vote as before, but his individual importance as a voter was now dependent on the class to which his wealth entitled him to belong. For example, in the lower classes and the one century of all those outside the lowest rating, an individual vote could be made politically insignificant, in that the 18 centuries of the **equites** together with the 80 centuries of the 1st class gave these, the leading men (**primores**), an absolute majority over all the remaining centuries.

l. 41. **vocabantur,** ' were called (to vote) '. The century voting first was known as the **centuria praerogativa.** (Its vote often determined that of those that followed.)

l. 42. **si variaret,** *imperson.*, ' if ever there were a difference of opinion '. The subj. is used by Livy to express indefinite frequency.

l. 43. **secundae classis.** Supply **centuriae vocabantur.**

l. 43. **nec mirari . . . non convenire,** ' nor ought (we) to be surprised that the present organisation which now exists after the tribes were made up to thirty-five, their number doubled in-respect-of the centuries of juniors and seniors, does not agree with the total instituted by Servius '.

This is another difficult passage about which scholars are not fully agreed. The centuriate assembly was reorganised, probably about 241 B.C., in such a way as to equalise the votes within the five classes and to correlate the voting groups (the centuries) within the classes with the local tribes. Thus we may suppose that each of the five classes was divided by tribes into thirty-five groups and that each of these was divided into two sub-divisions of juniors and seniors. Thus we get, 18 of knights $+ 5 \times (35 \times 2) + 5$ (artisans + proletarii) $= 373$.

l. 45. **qui nunc est.** Notice the indicative mood, the use of which shows that the relative clause is an addition by Livy.

l. 46. **duplicato earum numero,** abl. absol. Translate : ' and their number was doubled '.

l. 49. **collibus qui habitabantur,** ' according to the hills which were inhabited '.

l. 50. **tribus.** They were called Sucusana, Esquilina, Palatina, Collina. The last three are derived from the names of hills, the first from the district Sucusana. Hence some MSS. include **regionibus** before **collibus** and insert **que.**

l. 50. **a tributo.** The **tributum** was a tax which during the republican period until 167 B.C. was levied from time to time to pay the cost of wars. As it was regarded as a compulsory loan rather than as a tax, it might be repaid after a successful campaign.

Livy's derivation of tribes from **tributum** is quite wrong, in fact the very reverse of the truth, for **tributum** is probably derived from **tribus.**

l. 51. **nam . . . ratio est,** *lit.,* ' for the method of contributing it equitably according to the rating was entered upon also by the same man ', i.e. by Servius. This sentence would run better in English in the active : ' Servius also planned the method of . . .'.

l. 53. **quicquam pertinuere,** ' had anything to do ', *lit.,* ' concerned in anyway '. **quicquam,** adverbial acc.

CHAPTER 44

Line 1. **metu . . . mortisque,** ' by the fear of a law passed concerning unregistered persons with the threats of imprisonment and death ', i.e. ' by the fear of a law which threatened with . . . those who did not register '.

l. 4. **in campo Martio.** This field obtained its name from the altar of Mars erected there. Being outside the pomerium it was used for army musters and parades and therefore for the meeting of the comitia centuriata. Today, it is the most densely populated part of Rome.

l. 5. **instructum exercitum . . . lustravit.** Note the Latin use of the participle; ' having marshalled all his army there he purified it '.

l. 5. **suovetaurilibus.** The three victims were no doubt carried or led in solemn ceremonial procession round the army and then offered as a sacrifice of atonement and purification to Mars, with a prayer that the god might keep away all manner of evil from the land and its inhabitants.

l. 6. **conditum . . . appellatum. conditum lustrum =**' the close of the purification ', and is the complement after **appellatum** (est). Note once again the translation of the Latin participle.

l. 7. **quia . . . est,** *lit.*, ' because in taking the census the end was made ' =' because it brought the taking of the census to an end '.

l. 9. **Fabius Pictor.** This Roman senator and historian lived in the second half of the 3rd century B.C. and wrote, in Greek, a history of Rome from the earliest times to his own day.

l. 10. **ad,** ' in view of ', ' to meet '.

l. 11. **urbs . . . visa est,** ' the city also seemed necessary to be enlarged ' =' it seemed that the city should be enlarged '. Note the personal use of **videor** and the nom. of the gerundive to express ' ought ', ' must '.

l. 12. **Viminalem . . . Esquiliis,** ' he increased the Viminal by (the inclusion of) the Esquiline '. The latter (the name means ' out-district ') included the eastern plateau formed by the Oppian and Cispian hills.

l. 14. **aggere, fossis, muro.** The city wall of republican Rome, an elaborate work, was traditionally ascribed to Servius Tullus, but scholars are in disagreement about its actual date. Perhaps we might accept the view that while the familiar city wall was mainly the work of 378 B.C., after the capture of Rome by the Gauls, a date at which we are told by Livy in Books VI and VII extensive repairs were carried out, there had stood on the same line an earlier wall which may have been constructed in the reign of Servius Tullius.

Those who accept only the later dating confine the original work of Servius to the **agger**—that part which crossed the plateau be-tween the Quirinal and Oppian hills.

l. 16. **verbi . . . intuentes,** ' those who look only at the etymology of the word '.

l. 16. **postmoerium,** ' (the part) behind the wall '. This, regarded from the point of view of the enemy, means the space between the wall and urban property.

l. 17. **circamoerium,** ' (the part) on both sides of the wall ', i.e. the ground adjacent to the outer as well as to the inner face of the wall.

Livy's explanation is definitely wrong, for the original meaning of **pomerium** referred only to the space between the wall and the houses inside the wall.

l. 19. **qua,** relative adv., ' where '.

l. 19. **certis circa terminis,** ' with fixed boundaries on either side (of it) '.

l. 20. **ut neque . . . continuarentur,** ' so that the buildings on the inner side might not be carried up to the city walls '.

l. 22. **puri aliquid . . . soli,** ' some ground might be kept free from human use '.

l. 23. **hoc spatium,** obj. of **appellarunt,** with **pomerium** as a complement to the obj. To keep the order of the Latin, turn the sentence into the passive, ' this space was called by the R. the pomerium . . .'.

l. 24. **non magis . . . id,** *lit.,* ' not more because . . . , but because ' =' as much because the wall was behind it as because . . .'.

l. 25. **esset.** Subjunctive due to virtual oratio obliqua.

l. 27. **tantum . . . proferebantur.** Translate this main clause before the correlative clause **quantum . . . erant.**

The earliest known boundary (that of Servius) included the Capitoline, Quirinal, Viminal, Oppian, Caelian, and Palatine hills and remained unaltered until it was extended by Sulla and Caesar in the first century B.C., i.e. it remained the boundary of the city for 500 years.

CHAPTER 45

Line 1. **magnitudine** =**incremento,** ' enlargement ', instrumental abl.

l. 2. **omnibus,** neut. pl., ' all his arrangements '.

l. 3. consilio, ' by statesmanship ' ; opposed to armis, ' by force of arms '.

l. 4. iam tum. The worship of Diana (the Artemis of the Greeks) reached Rome from Ephesus by way of Massilia, which was founded by Greek colonists (Phocaean) about 600 B.C. The temple of Artemis at Ephesus was one of the seven wonders of the world.

l. 6. factum fama ferebat. Note the alliteration. fama ferebat, ' tradition related '.

l. 6. Asiae, i.e. of Asia Minor. The coast of Asia Minor was dotted with Greek towns which had been established, like those in Eastern Sicily, and in South and West Italy, during a vigorous period of Greek expansion throughout the 8th and 7th centuries B.C.

l. 7. laudare, historic infin. deos consociatos, ' gods united ' = ' unity of worship '.

l. 9. hospitia . . . iunxerat, ' he had assiduously contracted (ties of) hospitality and friendship ', i.e. ' he had worked hard to contract . . .'.

l. 10. perpulit, ' he got his way'.

l. 11. fanum Dianae. Most scholars accept this transfer of the cult of Diana to the Aventine hill by Servius as historical. Dionysius of Halicarnassus (end of 1st century B.C.) has two passages in his historical work in which he states that in his time the temple contained a fifth-century document and a stele on which was preserved a treaty made with the Latins in the time of Servius.

l. 12. ea . . . , ' this was an admission that . . .'. Note ea attracted into the gender of the complement. de quo, ' concerning which question '.

l. 14. id, ' this controversy '. omissum, supply esse.

l. 15. ob rem . . . armis, ' on account of the thing so often unsuccessfully tried by force of arms ' =' on account of their frequent and unsuccessful use of armed force '.

l. 16. uni, dat. se dare, ' to offer itself '.

l. 17. bos . . . specie. Note : (i) the personal use of dicitur, (ii) nata ; supply esse, (iii) miranda . . . specie, abl. of quality or description. Render : ' it is said that a heifer of wonderful size and beauty was born . . .'.

l. 21. **ut erat,** ' as indeed it was '.

l. 21. **prodigii loco.** See the note on Chap. 39, 15.

l. 21. **cecinere . . . imperium.** Order for translation : **vates cecinere imperium fore ibi** (=in ea civitate) **cuius civis . . . immolasset,** pluperf. subj. representing an original future perfect in the direct speech.

l. 25. **bovem . . . deducit.** Note the Latin use of the participle. Translate : ' drove the heifer to Rome and brought her to the shrine '.

l. 27. **celebrata fama,** *lit.,* ' celebrated in report ', i.e. ' much talked of '.

l. 28. **memor responsi,** ' mindful of the prophecy '.

l. 30. **quin,** ' why not '.

l. 30. **perfunderis.** The Latin passive is equivalent to the English intransitive verb, ' bathe '.

l. 30. **vivo . . . flumine,** ' in a running stream '. Local abl. without a preposition. Cf. **infima valle** l. 31.

l. 31. **praefluit** =praeterfluit.

l. 32. **qui . . . cuperet.** Qui is here causal, ' inasmuch as he . . .'.

CHAPTER 46

Line 1. **usu,** ' by prescriptive right '. **usus,** a legal term, implies ownership which has been acquired by use or employment of a thing for a certain length of time.

l. 2. **iactari voces,** ' that remarks were thrown out '.

l. 4. **conciliata . . . diviso.** Make the first abl. absol. a main verb in the active and render the second by a gerund, ' he won over . . . by dividing . . .'. Finally insert ' and ' before **ausus est.**

l. 6. **vellent iuberentne.** The position of the enclitic **-ne** shows that these two verbs are to be regarded as forming one expression.

l. 7. **quanto . . . ante.** Grammatically the verb to be supplied in this comparative clause is **est declaratus.** If, however, we translate **quanto** by ' as ' we may supply ' enjoyed ' as the verb.

l. 8. **Tarquinio,** dat. of the person interested. Render by English possessive.

l. 9. **impensius,** with **criminandi.**

l. 9. **quia . . . agi,** *lit.,* ' because he had realised that it was being done about land of the people, the wish of the fathers (being) opposed ' = ' because he had realised that the action being taken in giving land to the people was opposed to the wishes of the fathers '.

l. 11. **crescendi,** ' of growing ', i.e. ' of increasing his power '.

l. 12. **et ipse.** Two phrases follow giving reasons for Tarquin's persistence : ' both (being) himself a young man . . . and with his wife Tullia . . . goading '. The construction is obscured by the deficiency of Latin in the matter of a word for ' being ' and by the fact that the first of the two balanced phrases is nom. in agreement with the subject, the second abl. absol.

l. 14. **tulit,** ' produced '.

l. 15. **regum,** ' for kings '. Note the obj. gen., dependent on **taedio.**

l. 15. **ultimum . . . foret.** ultimum is predicative and should be translated last. **foret** = esset. **partum** from **pario.**

l. 16. **hic,** demonstrative adjective.

l. 18. **parum liquet,** ' it is not clear ', has dependent upon it **(utrum) Prisci . . . fuerit.** -ne = ' or '.

l. 18. **pluribus auctoribus,** abl. absol., *lit.,* ' (there being) more authorities ' = ' on the evidence of the majority (of historians) '.

l. 19. **ediderim,** perfect subj. (potential), ' I should declare '.

l. 19. **filium,** i.e. **eum filium esse.**

l. 22. **longe** = valde, ' very '.

l. 22. **ne . . . iungerentur** is a noun clause subject to **inciderat.**

l. 23. **fortuna,** abl., ' owing to the (good) fortune of the R.P. '.

l. 24. **quo** introduces a purpose clause which contains a comparative **(diuturnius).**

l. 26. **ferox Tullia,** ' the Tullia who had spirit '.

l. 26. **materiae,** ' stuff ', partit. gen. dependent upon **nihil.**

l. 26. **neque ... neque,** ' either ... or '. The negatives do not cancel, but emphasise, the preceding **nihil.**

l. 27. **tota,** ' entirely ', adj. for adv.

l. 28. **mirari ... dicere ... spernere,** historic infin.

l. 28. **virum,** predicative, ' him she called a man '.

l. 30. **virum nacta,** ' having got a man (for a husband) '.

l. 30. **muliebri cessaret audacia,** *lit.*, ' was idle in respect of enterprise of a woman ' =' lacked enterprise as a woman '. The subj. in this causal clause gives the reason which existed in the mind of the spirited Tullia.

l. 33. **Ea ... virum : secretis** with **sermonibus. viri alieni,** ' the other's husband '. **parcere,** historic infin., with **nullis ... contumeliis** dependent on it. **de viro,** etc., ' about her husband to his brother and about her sister to her (=her sister's) husband '.

ll. 35-8. **et se ... esset,** ' she asserted (**contendere,** histor. infin.) that it would have been fairer for her (to remain) unmarried and for him (to be) without a wife than to be tied to an inferior so that they had to remain inactive through the cowardice of others '.

l. 38. **quo.** Note the abl., dependent upon **digna.** We say ' *of* whom she was worthy ' =' whom she deserved '.

l. 41. **Arruns Tarquinius et Tullia minor.** These words are bracketed by the editor of the Oxford Classical Texts as their retention involves either attributing a slip to Livy (i.e. he wrote **Arruns** instead of **Lucius**) or taking the clause **Arruns ... fecissent** as referring to the victim,[1] and entailing an awkward change of subject in the case of **iunguntur.**

l. 42. **prope continuatis funeribus,** ' by deaths which followed hard upon one another ' ; those, that is, of the unambitious Tarquin and Tullia, who are murdered by their consorts.

l. 44. **magis ... approbante,** *lit.*, ' Servius rather not-preventing than approving '; ' not-preventing ' =' permitting '. Therefore we get, ' with the permission rather than the approval of S.'.

[1] A view which is unsuitable to the meaning of the words and disagrees with our other authority, Dionysius.

CHAPTER 47

Line 3. **spectare, pati,** historic infins.

l. 5. **non . . . serviret:** oratio obliqua. Tullia is referring to her life with her first husband ; *lit.,* ' there had not been lacking to her (one) to whom she was said to be married nor (one) with whom she was a slave in silence '.

Render : ' she had not lacked a man . .'.

l. 5. **defuisse . . . ,** ' (but) she had lacked (a man) to think . . .'.

l. 10. **sin minus,** ' but if not '.

l. 10. **eo peius,** ' for the worse ' ; *lit.,* ' by this the worse '. **eo** merely anticipates the **quod** clause.

l. 11. **quin** =qui-ne, ' how-not? ', ' why not? '

l. 11. **accingeris.** The passive is here equivalent to active voice with acc. of the reflexive pronoun, ' you gird yourself '.

l. 12. **non tibi necesse est,** ' it is not necessary for you '. **ab Corintho,** ' (coming) from Corinth '. **ut patri tuo,** ' as (it was) for your father '.

l. 13. **peregrina regna moliri,** *lit.,* ' to work at (=to toil to win ') a foreign throne ' (=' a throne in a foreign land ').

l. 14. **patrii.** Supply **di,** ' and your ancestral gods '.

l. 19. **devolvere,** imperative passive.

l. 19. **ad stirpem,** ' to your family ' =' to the level of your family '.

l. 20. **increpando.** See the note on Chap. 4, l. 28.

l. 21. **si,** ' in that '. See the note on Chap. 40, l. 8.

l. 21. **cum,** ' whereas '.

l. 24. **ipsa,** i.e. Tullia. **regio . . . orta,** *lit.,* ' sprung from royal seed ', means no more than ' the daughter of a king '.

l. 28. **pro eo,** ' in return '.

l. 29. **cum . . .tum,** ' not only . . . but also '.

l. 29. **regis criminibus** =regem criminando, ' by slandering the king '. **crescere,** ' he gained influence '.

l. 31. **agendae rei,** either dat. (work contemplated); or possibly gen. dependent upon **tempus.** In any case, translate by ' for action '.

l. 33. **pro curia,** ' in the front part of the Curia '.

l. 34. **ad regem Tarquinium,** ' before Tarquin (as) king '.

l. 36. **metu ne ... esset,** *lit.*, ' through fear that not to have come might be for a harm (to them) ' = ' through fear that their staying away might do them harm '.

l. 37. **et iam rati,** ' and thinking that it was all over with Servius '. Notice this meaning of the passive of **ago** when used impersonally.

l. 38. **maledicta.** Supplied ' uttered ' as the verb.

l. 38. **ab stirpe ultima orsus,** ' beginning with his most distant ancestor '.

l. 40. **non ... inito,** *lit.*, ' an interregnum not having been entered into ', i.e. ' without the interregnum being observed '.

' Without ' should also be used in translating the three following phrases.

l. 44. **odio ... honestatis,** ' through hatred of the nobility of others '.

l. 44. **ereptum agrum ... divisisse.** Note this use of perf. part. passive again : in English we say, ' had taken land from ... and divided it out ...'.

l. 45. **sordidissimo cuique** is the regular Latin for ' all the lowest (citizens) ' ; or, ' the riff-raff of the nation '.

l. 46. **inclinasse.** Supply **eum** (i.e. **Servius**) as the subject.

ll. 47-9. **ut insignis ... largiretur,** ' in order that the prosperity of the wealthier (citizens) might be a mark[1] for envy and accessible (for him), that from it (**unde** = **ut ex ea (fortuna)**), whenever he wished, he might make lavish grants to the most needy '.

CHAPTER 48

Line 3. **quid hoc ... rei est.** See the note on **quid rei**, Chap. 41, l. 3

l. 5. **cum ille.** Supply **dixisset** as the verb.

l. 6. **se ... tenere,** ' that he was occupying '.

[1] *lit.*, ' obvious ', ' conspicuous '.

l. 7. **potiorem,** ' preferable ', in agreement with **heredem. filium regis** is in apposition with **se.**

l. 7. **illum,** i.e. **Servius,** and subj. of **insultasse.**

l. 8. **per licentiam,** ' presumptuously '.

l. 8. **eludentem** is equivalent to **elusisse (dominos et).**

l. 8. **dominis.** Servius had been a house-slave of the Tarquinii.

l. 11. **qui vicisset.** The antecedent of **qui, eum** (to be supplied) is the subject of **regnaturum** (esse). **Vicisset** represents a fut. perf. of oratio recta.

l. 11. **etiam,** i.e. in addition to his own ambition, and his wife's prompting.

l. 12. **ultima audere,** *lit.,* ' to dare the last things ' = ' to stop at nothing '.

l. 12. **multo ... validior. Multo,** abl. of the measure of difference with **validior ; aetate et viribus,** abls. of respect.

l. 13. **medium,** i.e. ' by the middle ', ' round the waist '.

l. 13. **elatumque ... deiecit.** Cf. **ereptum ... divisisse** of the previous chapter and translate **elatum** by a present part. or a finite verb which is *active* in voice.

l. 14. **in inferiorem partem per gradus,** i.e. ' down the steps '.

l. 20. **carpento.** This carriage was a two-wheeled vehicle, with an arched covering or hood. Note the instrumental abl. It can also be regarded as abl. of place where.

l. 21. **id quod ... constat,** ' what is generally agreed '. The clause is loosely in apposition with the whole sentence. We would prefer to say in English : ' there is general agreement at any rate **(certe)** that she rode in her carriage ... (and) summoned ...'.

l. 21. **invecta** is properly the perf. part. pass. of **inveho.** The passive voice of this verb is frequently used for ' travel ' when artificial aids are mentioned or implied : e.g. for ' ride ', ' drive ', ' sail '. **Feror** is used of unaided motion.

l. 21. **nec reverita,** *lit.,* ' nor having stood in awe of ' = ' without feeling any awe before '.

To appear in this way before an assembly of men was regarded as indecorous for a Roman matron.

l. 23. **prima appellavit.** Note the Latin for—' was the first to call '.

l. 25. **Cyprium vicum.** See the map of Rome.

l. 26. **flectenti,** dat. of the present participle, in agreement with ei understood, and grammatically dependent upon **restitit,** *lit.,* ' (to her) turning to the right ', i.e. ' as she sought to turn to the right '.

l. 27. **restitit . . . inhibuit.** The subject is **is qui iumenta agebat.**

l. 30. **traditur.** Supply **factum esse,** ' to have occurred '.

l. 31. **quo,** *lit.,* ' where ' ; better, ' for there '.

l. 31. **amens . . . viri,** *lit.,* ' maddened, the avenging furies of her sister and her husband driving (her) ', i.e. ' goaded to madness by the . . .'.

The idea of the ' avenging spirits ', or ' furies ' is borrowed by Livy from Greek tragedy where they pursue relentlessly those who have committed unnatural murder. Cf. Vergil, *Aeneid* IV, 471, **Agamemnonius scaenis agitatus Orestes,** ' Orestes, son of Agamemnon, hounded across the stage '.

l. 32. **Tullia . . . fertur,** ' Tullia is said '.

l. 33. **sanguinis ac caedis paternae,** *lit.,* ' of the blood and of the murder of her father ' ; probably a hendiadys for ' of the blood of her murdered father '.

l. 36. **quibus iratis . . . sequerentur,** *lit.,* ' who (being) angry, results similar to the evil beginning of the reign soon followed ' ; i.e. ' so that their anger (at the crime) soon brought results similar to the evil . . .'.

propediem. The similar results did not, however, follow until 25 years later.

quibus iratis = ut eis iratis, introducing an adverbial clause which gives the result of her action.

l. 40. **difficilis aemulatio esset,** ' emulation was difficult ' =' it was difficult to emulate (him) '.

l. 40. **id . . . accessit.** **Accedere** is regularly used as the passive of **addere** : hence we get : ' this too was added . . .'.

l. 43. **quia unius esset,** ' because it was of (=belonged to) one (person) '.

l. 44. **quidam auctores sunt,** ' there are some authors ' = ' some authors state ', has the preceding acc. and infin. dependent upon it.

l. 44. **ni . . . intervenisset.** Note this protasis of a conditional clause, unreal in past time. The true apodosis has to be supplied, ' and he would have done so, had not . . .'.

l. 45. **intestinum,** ' of one of his family '.

l. 45. **consilia agitanti.** The dat. depends upon the verb **intervenisset,** *lit.,* ' (him) thinking over plans ' = ' him as he . . .'.

CHAPTER 49

Line 1. **cui Superbo cognomen.** For the attraction of **Superbo** to the case of **cui,** see the note on Chap. 1, l. 12, **Troiano.**

l. 3. **sepultura prohibuit,** ' stopped from burial ' = ' denied the rites of burial '. The deprivation of a burial in accordance with the rites of one's religion was regarded with horror by the ancients as they believed that the soul of such an unburied corpse wandered about for a hundred years along the banks of the river Styx, which it was unable to cross to gain access to Hades.

l. 5. **conscius . . . posse,** ' aware after this that the example of the throne's being unlawfully sought by himself could be taken (as) a precedent against himself '.

l. 7. **corpus,** ' his person '.

l. 8. **neque . . . ad ius regni quicquam,** ' nor anything in relation to the right of the throne ' = ' no claim at all to the throne '.

l. 9. **ut qui . . . regnaret,** ' inasmuch as he was ruling '.

l. 10. **eo accedebat.** If you read again the note on the preceding chapter (48, l. 40), you will appreciate that ' it was added to this (**eo**) that ' merely equals ' in addition '.

l. 10. **in caritate . . . esset. reponenti** agrees with **Tarquinio** (understood), a dative of the agent with **regnum tutandum esset ;** *lit.,* ' by T. putting naught of hope in the affection of his (fellow)-citizens the power was to be safeguarded by fear ' ; i.e. ' as T. could put . . . , he had to . . .'.

l. 12. **quem** = metum.

l. 12. **cognitiones capitalium rerum,** ' investigation of capital charges ' ; i.e. cases which involved the life, freedom or civic rights of a citizen.

l. 13. **sine consiliis,** *lit.,* ' without consultations ' = ' without advisers '.

l. 14. **causam,** ' pretext '.

l. 15. **non suspectos . . . invisos,** ' not only those he suspected or disliked '.

l. 16. **unde = (eos) ab quibus. posset.** The subj. shows that the relative clause denotes a *class* ; hence it is called a *generic* subj.

l. 19. **per se nihil agi,** *lit.,* ' that nothing was done through them ' = ' that they transacted no state business '.

l. 21. **de omnibus,** ' on all occasions ', **omnibus** being neut. pl.

l. 22. **domesticis consiliis,** ' by household consultation ' = ' on the advice of his own household '.

l. 25. **conciliabat.** Notice the force of the (conative) imperfect here : ' he tried to win over '.

l. 30. **Circa.** During his long journey home after the siege and capture of Troy, the Greek prince Ulysses was detained in the island of Aea by the witch Circe, reputed daughter of the sun. Mamilius was said to have been the son of Mamilia, daughter of Telegonus, son of Ulysses and Circe.

l. 31. **ei Mamilio.** These words resume the sentence after the parenthesis and must be omitted in translation.

l. 31. **nuptum,** a free use of the acc. of the supine, expressing purpose.

CHAPTER 50

Line 2. **cum . . . indicit,** ' when he declared for a certain day that they should meet . . .'. The **ut** clause is the object of **indicit.** Hence we may say ' when he prescribed for a certain day a meeting at the grove of Ferentina '.

The latter was a grove and a spring (Chap. 51, l. 39) in the valley of Marino, north of Alba Longa. As this grove was associated with the Latin league and the form of the word suggests a title rather than the actual name of a goddess, it is possible that this Ferentina is the same deity as the Diana mentioned in Chap. 45.

l. 3. esse . . . , ' there were, (he said), (matters) which . . .'.

l. 6. antequam . . . occideret. The subj. in this temporal clause suggests that Tarquin's time of arrival was deliberately chosen to anticipate the setting of the sun.

l. 7. toto die, abl. of time within which.

l. 7. variis sermonibus, ' in various speeches '.

l. 8. ab Aricia, ' from Aricia ', i.e. ' of Aricia '.

l. 9. haud mirum . . . Indirect speech now begins and continues until l. 25.

l. 10. Superbo. For the agreement with ei, dat. (to be supplied) rather than with cognomen, cf. Egerio, Chap. 34, l. 14. and Superbo, 49, l. 2.

l. 10. iam . . . appellabant. Take iam ita closely with appellabant, and note the contrast which exists in the Latin between clam quidem mussitantes and vulgo tamen ; ' secretly in whispers, yet commonly enough '.

l. 12. an quicquam superbius esse, ' or could anything be more . . '. Note that rhetorical questions in the 1st or 3rd person occurring in direct speech become acc. and infin. in indirect speech.

l. 14. excitis. Supply se (*pl.*) as the word with which excitis agrees.

l. 14. qui indixerit. Note the primary tense, perfect subj. For this and similar primary tenses in the following clauses, see the note on Chap. 1, l. 31.

l. 16. obnoxios, ' (them) while they were in his power '.

l. 16. cui . . . apparere, rhetorical question   hence acc. and infin. in oratio obliqua.

l. 17. in, ' over '.

l. 17. quod, i.e. imperium. So also illud, l. 18.

l. 17. si sui bene crediderint . . . The emphasis falls on bene and can be obtained in English by a periphrasis, ' if his fellow-citizens had done well to entrust this (power) (to him) '.

l. 18. et non, ' and not rather '.

l. 19. credere et . . . debere, ' the Latins also should entrust (it to him)—although not even then (sic) since he was of foreign birth '. alienigenae is dat. in agreement with ei (to be understood).

l. 20. suos, ' his own subjects ', i.e. the Romans.

l. 21. alii super alios, ' one after another '.

l. 22. quid . . . portendi, another rhetorical question, ' what better expectation was held out . . .' spei, partitive gen.

l. 23. se, Turnus, the speaker.

l. 25. haec . . . pertinentia, ' these (words) and others (lit., pertaining to the same, i.e. of the same) import ', acc. pl., obj. of dissereret.

l. 27. cum maxime, ' when especially ' = ' just at the moment when '.

l. 31. id temporis, ' at that time ' = ' so late '. id temporis is an idiomatic variation for eo tempore.

l. 32. cura, abl., ' in his anxiety '. reconciliandi depends upon it.

l. 34. ne id quidem . . . ferunt, ' they say that (he) (eum to be supplied) made not even this (remark) uncommented upon (tacitum) by Turnus '.

l. 35. dixisse. Supply eum, i.e. Turnum.

l. 37. ni pareat . . . esse. This sentence gives us ' the few words ', paucis verbis, ' unless he (i.e. the son) obeyed his father, he would get into trouble '.

CHAPTER 51

Line 1. increpans. The present participle denotes according to strict usage an action contemporaneous with that of the main verb. Here Livy is using it with the sense of a perfect participle *active*, the absence of which, except in the case of deponent verbs, is acutely felt in Latin.

l. 1. Aricinus, ' he of Aricia ', i.e. Turnus.

l. 2. aliquanto . . . ferens, ' resenting this incident (quam rem), considerably more than he appeared to '.

l. 6. pro imperio, ' in virtue of his authority '.

l. 9. **vim,** ' quantity '.

l. 12. **quasi . . . perturbatus,** ' as if alarmed by a strange event '.

l. 13. **velut . . . inlatam,** *lit.,* ' as though caused by a kind of providence of the gods ' = ' somehow by the providence of heaven '.

l. 14. **saluti . . . fuisse,** ' had been for a salvation to himself and to them ' = ' had proved his and their salvation '. Note the predicative dat. with a second dat. associated with it.

l. 14. **dici,** oratio obliqua, *lit.,* ' it was told him, (he said) '. **A Turno** belongs to **parari** and **primoribus** is dat,

l. 16. **Latinorum** is dependent upon **imperium.**
teneat. Note the primary tense.

l. 16. **adgressurum fuisse,** ' he had been going-to-attack '. Note the infinitive form of the **adgressurus erat** of direct speech.

l. 17. **dilatam rem esse,** ' the attempt had been put off ', would be better in the active in English.

l. 18. **quod . . . peteret.** Order for translation, **quod auctor concilii quem peteret . . .**
Note once again **afuerit** (primary sequence) and **peteret** (historic sequence) in the same sentence.

l. 19. **absentis,** obj. gen., ' against (him) in his absence '.

l. 21. **ubi . . . ventum sit,** impersonal passive, ' when they had come '.

l. 22. **instructus,** ' furnished '.

l. 24. **ad eum,** ' to his quarters '.

l. 24. **id vanum . . . sit,** alternative indirect question (with **utrum** to be supplied) ' (whether) this was false or not ', the subject of **sciri posse.**

l. 26. **suspectam fecit . . . Tarquini.** The verb **fecit** though singular has three subjects ; **ingenium, oratio, mora.** The order of the Latin can be retained in the English translation if the sentence is turned into the passive, e.g. ' the accusation (**rem**) was made plausible by . . .'.

l. 27. **quod videbatur . . . potuisse.** Note the personal use of **videbatur,** the regular idiom in Latin. We prefer the impersonal verb : i.e. for ' the massacre seemed to have been able . . . ', we say, ' it seemed that the massacre could have . . .'.

l. 29. **nisi.** The conjunction is used to bring out the conditional force of the abl. absol. which follows.

l. 31. **Turnum . . . excitatum circumsistunt . . . ,** ' guards wakened T. from sleep and surrounded (him) '.

l. 38. **indicta causa,** abl. absol., ' the cause not pleaded ' = ' without a hearing '.

l. 39. **deiectus . . . mergeretur,** *lit.*, ' that (**ut**) . . . having been plunged into the source of the Ferentine Water, a hurdle thrown on above, and stones heaped upon (it), he was drowned '. Translate : ' he was plunged . . . and drowned by having **a** hurdle thrown upon him, upon which stones were then heaped '.

CHAPTER 52

Line 2. **Turnum novantem res.** As **novare res** is the regular Latin for ' to attempt a revolution ', we may render the phrase here by ' the revolutionary attempt of T.'

l. 2. **qui . . . adfecissent.** Note the subjunctive of virtual oratio obliqua, ' who (said he) had visited . . . with a punishment (that was) well-deserved in view of his flagrant treason '.

l. 4. **vetusto iure,** ' in accordance with an ancient right '.

l. 5. **eo foedere . . . imperium,** ' were bound by that treaty by which in the time of Tullus, all the Alban state with its settlers had come into Rome's power '. (For the treaty, see Chap. 24, l. 11.)

l. 8. **utilitatis.** This gen. is dependent upon **causa** and has dependent upon **it omnium** ; ' he thought it (was) more in the interest of all '.

l. 9. **secunda fortuna,** abl. dependent upon **fruantur.**

l. 14. **superior . . . erat,** ' the Roman interest was dominant '.

l. 15. **capita . . . rege videbant,** ' they saw that the chief men **of** the Latin people took the side, and shared the views, of the king '.

l. 17. **si adversatus esset.** The pluperfect subj. represents the future perfect of direct speech.

l. 17. **documentum,** ' a demonstration '. **cuique** is dat., ' to each (man) there was a demonstration . . .'. Translate : ' each man had had a demonstration of the danger (he would incur) if he offered any opposition '.

l. 21. **ad,** ' (in obedience) to '.

l. 22. **secretum,** ' separate '.

l. 23. **manipulos,** ' companies '. Livy does not mean ' the maniple ' which in later times signified a regular unit of the Roman army of the Republic.

l. 24. **ex binis . . . imposuit.** In saying that Tarquin made one company of two, and two of one, Livy means that he made new companies by dividing the old companies into two and then uniting them into a new one with one half from a Latin company and the other half from a Roman company. Tarquin did not actually double the companies as Livy's use of **geminatis** might suggest.

CHAPTER 53

Line 1. **ut . . . ita,** ' although . . . yet '. **belli,** locative, ' in war '.

l. 2. **quin.** Here the conjunction means ' moreover '. In this sense it is commonly followed by **etiam** and by the indicative mood. The subjunctives in the sentence are conditional.

l. 3. **degeneratum.** Livy occasionally uses the neuter of the perfect participle passive as a noun. The construction may have been suggested by the use in Greek of the neuter definite article with the perf. part. or perf. infin. passive.

Thus **degeneratum in aliis,** ' his degeneracy in other respects ' is the subject of **offecisset.**

l. 4. **Volscis,** dat., ' against the V.' **in,** ' which was to last for '.

l. 4. **amplius,** ' more (than) ' has no effect grammatically on **ducentos annos.**

l. 7. **talenta.** These talents were probably equivalent to about £8,800[1] in all. Comparisons of money-values are always difficult

[1] If we reckon the talent = £220 sterling at pre-1914 value of the pound sterling.

owing to the fluctuations in the value of money, i.e. in the amount money can buy.

l. 7. eam . . . templi, *lit.*, ' such a grandeur of a temple of Jupiter ' =' a temple to Jupiter so grand '.

l. 8. quae . . . esset, ' that it was worthy . . .'. Quae here introduces an adverbial clause of result, and is equal to ut ea.

l. 10. captivam pecuniam, ' the money from the spoil '.

l. 12. excepit. The subject is Tarquinius. Many MSS. have eum after deinde, in which case the subject is bellum.

l. 12. quo, ' in which '.

l. 12. lentius spe, ' more tedious than his expectation ', i.e. ' more tedious than he expected '.

l. 14. pulso, dat. in agreement with ei (understood), and dependent on the compound verb adempta esset.

l. 15. minime arte Romana, *lit.*, ' by a not-at-all Roman method '. We are to understand from this expression that the good faith of a Roman was proverbial.

l. 16. fundamentis, operibus are datives dependent on intentum.

l. 16. velut, ' apparently '. posito = deposito =' having been given up '.

l. 21. iam ab alienis. . . . The passage down to l. 36 is in oratio obliqua. It will be noticed again that the original tenses (present and perfect) are found in the subordinate clauses. See again the note on Chap. 1, l. 31, audierit.

l. 21. vertisse superbiam. The latter is the obj. of vertisse (trans.), eum (understood) being the subj.

l. 22. liberorum . . . taedere, ' he was weary of the large number of his children too '.

l. 22. ut . . . relinquat. Order for the beginning of the translation: ut (consecutive) faciat domi quoque solitudinem quam fecerit in curia. . . .

ne . . . relinquat is a purpose clause, ' in order that he might leave no heir . . .'.

l. 24. ne errarent . . . simuletur, ' let them not be mistaken, for them the war which was pretended to have been abandoned was waiting '.

l. 28. quod si, ' but if '.

l. 33. tegere . . . sciant, ' knew (how) to protect '.

l. 33. forsitan . . . inventurum. aliquid is the object, se the subject of inventurum (esse).

l. 34. ardoris aliquid, ' some enthusiasm '. Note the partitive gen.

l. 36. Cum . . . videretur. Note : (i) the personal use of videor (we prefer the impersonal, i.e. ' it seemed that he would leave . . . ') ; (ii) nihil morari, ' not to heed '. Supply eum as the object.

morarentur is subj. in virtual oratio obliqua, i.e. the mood indicates that the clause is a reported version of the thought in the mind of the Gabines.

l. 38. vetant. Supply eum as the object.

l. 38. mirari si. For the use of si after mirari, see the notes on Chap. 40, ll. 7, 8, tum . . . crescere, and si.

l. 41. futurum credere . . . ut . . . transferatur. Take credere (with se understood) first and futurum ut bellum transferatur as a periphrasis for bellum translatum iri, fut. infin. passive.

CHAPTER 54

Line 1. adhiberi. Historic infin., ' he was invited '.

l. 2. veteribus Gabinis, ' long-established residents of Gabii '.

l. 3. auctor esse. Historic infin., ' he was the adviser of ' = ' he advised '. Livy uses many historic infins. and historic presents in this chapter.

l. 5. nosset . . . sciret . . . potuissent. The subjunctives are due to virtual oratio obliqua, i.e. the mood indicates that the reasons given are those of Sextus.

nosset, ' he was acquainted with ' ; sciret, ' he knew ' (i.e. with more exact knowledge).

l. 7. ad rebellandum, i.e. ad bellum renovandum.

l. 9. praedatum, acc. of the supine, used to express purpose.

l. 10. **dictis . . . instructis**, abl. absol., best translated as a causal clause, ' as all his words and deeds were designed to cause deception '.

l. 12. **inscia . . . ageretur**, ' the population not knowing what was happening '. Note that the indirect question **quid ageretur** is dependent on the adj. **inscia** (which has the force of a pres. partic.).

l. 13. **proelia parva**, ' skirmishes '.

l. 15. **summi infimique**, nom. pl.

l. 17. **apud milites . . . esset.** Order for translation : **esse** (historic infin.) **vero tanta caritate apud milites obeundo periculo . . .** **tanta caritate** is abl. of description, and equivalent in meaning to **tam carus.**

l. 20. **conlectum.** Supply **esse.** The subj. is **satis,** and the whole is acc. and infin. dependent upon **videbat.**

l. 22. **sciscitatum,** acc. of the supine used to express purpose.

l. 22. **quando . . . dedissent.** Order for translation : **quando quidem di dedissent ei ut unus posset omnia publice Gabiis.**

ut . . . Gabiis, *lit.,* ' that alone he could everything in the state at Gabii ' = ' had sole power in every department of state at Gabii '. **ei,** irregularly for **sibi.**

l. 25. **voce,** ' by voice ' = ' in words '.

l. 28. **dicitur . . . decussisse.** Note once again Latin's preference for the personal construction.

l. 29. **interrogando exspectandoque,** abls. of cause, modifying **fessus.** But we can say : ' tired of asking (questions) and . . .'.

l. 30. **ut re imperfecta,** ' as though his mission was unaccomplished '.

l. 33. **Sexto ubi . . . patuit,** ' when it was clear to Sextus what . . .'.

l. 35. **alios . . . opportunos,** *lit.,* ' others, exposed-to-attack by their own unpopularity ', i.e. ' by attack to which their personal unpopularity exposed them '.

l. 36. **in quibus . . . futura,** ' in (the case of) whom an accusation was likely to be less plausible ' = ' in whose case it would not look well to make any accusation '.

l. 39. **iuxta atque,** ' as well as '. **divisui fuere,** ' were for a distributing ' =' were available for distribution '. Note the dat. of purpose.

l. 40. **largitiones . . . praedaeque.** Supply a verb, ' came '.

l. 41. **sensus,** nom. pl.

l. 42. **adimi,** historic infin.

CHAPTER 55

Line 1. **receptis** = captis.

l. 2. **cum Tuscis.** We are told in Chap. 42, 2, that Servius undertook a war with the people of Veii and the other Etruscans.

Perhaps the treaty here referred to is the official restoration of peaceful relations between the two peoples.

l. 4. **Iovis templum.** This temple was actually dedicated, in the first year of the republic (509 B.C.), to a group of three deities, Jupiter Optimus Maximus, Minerva, and Juno. The original platform of the temple still exists. This famous temple (with additions) lasted until 83 B.C., when it was burned down.

l. 4. **in monte Tarpeio.** The Tarpeian rock from which murderers and traitors were thrown is located at the south-west corner of the Capitol.

l. 5. **Tarquinios . . . perfecisse.** The acc. and infin. is dependent (upon a verb of saying implied in **instrumenta relinqueret.**) Translate, **T. reges ambos** as a gen., ' of the two Tarquins, both kings '.

For the vow of the elder Tarquin, see Chap. 38, l. 30.

l. 7. **a ceteris religionibus,** ' from all other religious claims '.

l. 7. **tota.** Supply ' and ' before this word, ' and (belong) entirely to Jupiter and his temple '.

l. 8. **quod inaedificaretur.** The subjunct. is due to attraction.

l. 8. **exaugurare.** There seems to be no doubt that the cult of the three deities was an alien (i.e. Etruscan) imposition and it is interesting to note that the site had to be cleared of local shrines and sanctuaries to make way for the newcomers.

l. 9. **quae aliquot,** ' several of which '.

l. 10. **in ipso . . . pugnae,** 'at the critical moment in the battle against R.'

l. 12. **inter,** temporal, 'at'.

l. 13. **movisse . . . deos :** order for translation, **traditur deos movisse numen ad indicandam . . .**

l. 15. **aves,** nom. pl.

l. 15. **in,** 'in the case of'.

l. 16. **acceptum est,** 'was taken, 'i.e.' understood'.

l. 17. **non motam . . . finibus,** *lit.,* 'the seat of T. not having been moved and him alone of the gods not having been called forth from the place consecrated to him'. Translate : 'the fact that the seat of T. had not been moved and that he alone . . .'. The whole phrase is subj. of the following infin., **portendere.**

The god Terminus who, as we learn from this passage, had been on the Capitol before the building of Jupiter's temple and refused to move to make way for him, was probably a kind of concentration of the numina attached to all boundary marks. Accordingly this god, probably originally a stone pillar set up in prehistoric times, was left inside the temple, and, as he had to be under the open sky, an opening was left in the roof above. See Ovid, *Fasti,* ii, 669 ff. and 638 ff.

l. 21. **caput.** From this story came the derivation of the first part of the word **Capitolium** from **caput.** See also Livy, V, 54. 7, **hic Capitolium est, ubi quondam capite humano invento responsum est eo loco caput rerum summamque imperii fore.**

l. 22. **aperientibus fundamenta,** 'to those opening the foundations' = 'to the men digging the foundations'.

l. 24. **rerum,** 'of the world'. See the quotation from Livy, V above.

l. 25. **quique . . . quosque,** 'both (those) who . . . and (those) whom'.

l. 27. **animus,** 'inclination'.

l. 28. **ad culmen,** 'up to the gable', i.e. to completion.

l. 30. **Fabio.** For this historian, see note on Chap. 44, l. 9.

l. 31. **crediderim.** Potential subj. With it is to be taken **eo magis.**

l. 32. **Pisoni.** Lucius Calpurnius Piso Frugi (consul, 133 B.C.) wrote seven books of Annals to cover the history of Rome from the earliest times to his own day.

l. 32. **quadraginta milia pondo argenti.** Supply **librarum** after **milia** and translate ' 40,000 pounds of silver '.

pondo, an old abl., was often used (with **librarum** understood) to denote weight in pounds. The sum given here would amount to about twelve times as much as the 40 silver talents. See also Chap. 53, l. 6.

l. 33. **summam . . . exsuperaturam,** the accusatives are in apposition with **quadraginta milia** ; *lit.*, ' a sum of money not to be hoped for from the spoil of a single city of those days (**tum**) and not likely to exceed the costs of the foundations of none not even of these buildings '.

In the second half of the sentence, Livy is referring to buildings of his own time, begun or completed before the date of this book (27 B.C.).

The two negatives ' none ', ' not ' cancel out. Thus we get ' of any building even in modern times '.

CHAPTER 56

Line 2. **pecunia publica,** money raised by taxes, i.e. ' state funds '.

l. 3. **operis etiam ex plebe,** ' workman from the populace '. Note the use of the abstract **opera,** ' work ', ' service ', for the concrete **operarius,** ' workman '. Cf. **ad servitia** = **ad servos** (40, l. 9).

l. 3. **qui,** coordinating relative with **labor,** = ' this '.

l. 4. **militiae,** dat., not locative. **et ipse,** ' in itself ' to be taken with **haud parvus.**

l. 5. **gravabatur,** from the deponent verb and followed by acc. and infin.

l. 6. **ad alia . . . opera.** Order for translation : **ad alia opera ut minora specie sic aliquanto maioris laboris.**

ut . . . sic, ' while . . ., yet '. Supply ' which were ' with these

212 LIVY, BOOK ONE

phrases, i.e. 'which, while they were . . .'. **minora specie**, ' less in appearance ' =' less pretentious '.

l. 7. **foros . . . faciendos, cloacam . . . agendam.** The accusatives are in apposition with **alia opera.**

l. 8. **cloaca maxima.** This ' main drain ' in Rome was a canalised stream which drained north-east Rome from the Argiletum to the river Tiber via the Forum, under the Vicus Tuscus and Velabrum. The present remains are not earlier than the 3rd century B.C., although there are still some branch drains which belong to the 5th century. Tradition, therefore, may be right in ascribing the original drain to the regal period.

l. 10. **nova haec magnificentia,** 'the new splendour of modern times '. See the note at the end of the last chapter.

vix quicquam adaequare potuit, ' has hardly been able to produce anything equal '.

l. 13. **rebatur.** The subject is Tarquinius. **oneri** is a predicative dat. with **urbi** dependent on **oneri esse.**

l. 15. **praesidia futura,** in apposition with **colonos,** ' to be safeguards to ' =' to safeguard '.

l. 18. **cum,** ' although '.

l. 21. **tantum,** ' only '.

l. 28. **iuvenis . . . induerat,** *lit.,* ' a young man of a temperament far other than (was the temperament) whose assumed appearance he had put on '. Say : ' a young man of a very different temperament from the one he had in appearance assumed and put on '.

l. 30. **primores . . . interfectum.** The sentence is grammatically irregular, for we might have expected **in quibus frater suus esset.** The meaning, however, is perfectly clear. Note that the perf. infin. pass. has been made to agree with its nearest subj. **fratrem** rather than with the more distant one **primores.**

l. 31. **neque . . . quicquam,** ' nothing '. The gerundives **timendum, concupiscendum** are in agreement with it. Though they are passive in Latin, they will be rendered here most conveniently by the pres. infin. act.

l. 33. **contemptuque tutus esse,** ' and to be safe (i.e. to secure his safety) in being ignored '.

l. 34. **esset.** The subj. is due to virtual oratio obliqua ; ' in a case where (as he thought) there was little protection . . .'.

l. 34. **ex industria factus . . . stultitiae,** *lit.*, ' deliberately shaping himself to the imitation of idiocy '. The perf. part. pass. **factus** is used here as the equivalent of the (non-existent) perfect part. act. and reflexive pronoun.

l. 36. **Bruti.** The name means ' stupid ', ' dull ', We have here another example of an aetiological story, i.e. the name **Brutus** is the cause, not the result of the story.

l. 38. **liberator . . . animus,** ' that spirit destined to free the Roman people '.

l. 39. **tempora sua,** ' its proper opportunities '.

l. 39. **Is . . . ingenii sui.** Note : (i) the personal use of **dicitur.** Translate impersonally : ' it is said that . . . (ii) the phrase in apposition with **is, ludibrium . . . comes,** ' more (as) a butt than (as) a companion '.

Take with **aureum baculum** (a) **donum A.,** ' as a gift to A. ' (b) **per ambages . . . sui,** ' as an enigmatical symbol of his own temperament '.

l. 40. **corneo . . . baculo,** ' in a wand of cornel-wood hollowed out for that purpose '.

l. 44. **cupido . . . iuvenum,** *lit.*, ' desire seized the hearts of the young princes '. We should prefer this in the passive.

l. 46. **ex infimo specu,** ' from the depths of the cave '. Actually the Pythian priestess sat on a tripod over a cleft in the rocks from which issued sulphurous vapours. When inspired by the god, she uttered her oracular response in hexameters.

l. 53. **Brutus . . . vocem,** ' B., thinking that the Pythian response looked elsewhither (= had another meaning) '.

l. 53. **velut si . . . recidisset,** ' as if he had . . .' =' pretending to stumble and fall '.

l. 55. **esset.** See the note on l. 34 above.

l. 56. **reditum.** Supply **est** and note the impersonal pass.

Chapter 57

Line 1. **ut in . . . ,** ' for . . .'.

l. 3. **cum . . . tum,** ' not only . . . but also '.

l. 6. **praeter . . . infestos.** **infestos** agrees with **animos** and may be translated as a causal clause, ' for in addition to this general arrogance, they were also hostile to the monarchy because . . .'.

aliam. **alius** may be translated by ' general ' when, as here, it precedes and therefore points to a particular instance.

l. 9. **si,** ' (to see) if '.

l. 10. **obsidione munitionibusque,** ' with siege-works ', hendiadys.

l. 10. **coepti . . . hostes.** Supply **sunt** with **coepti** and note once again that when **coepi** has dependent upon it a pass. infin. **coepi** is put into the pass. as well.

l. 17. **Egeri.** See Chap. 38, l. 2.

l. 17. **incidit . . . mentio,** ' wives were mentioned '.

l. 18. **miris modis =**' wonderfully ', *or* ' enthusiastically '.

l. 18. **inde . . . accenso,** ' then when their rivalry became impassioned '.

l. 21. **quin,** ' why . . . not? '

l. 23. **id . . . sit,** jussive subj., *lit.*, ' let that be the most tested for each (wife) ' =' let that be the decisive test of each (wife) '.

l. 25. **Romam.** The ride would be about 30 miles.

l. 27. **Collatiam.** Collatia was about 13 miles east of Rome.

l. 29. **nocte sera,** ' (though) late at night '.

l. 30. **deditam lanae,** ' wholly-given-up to her wool (-spinning) '.

l. 31. **muliebris . . . fuit,** ' the honour in this contest about their wives fell to Lucretia '.

Chapter 58

Line 2. **ubi,** coordinate relative adv. Translate as if the text read **et ibi.**

l. 5. **postquam . . . videbantur,** ' when it seemed that (everything) about (him) was safe and all were asleep '.

l. 9. **vocem,** ' a sound '.

l. 12. versare . . . animum, 'used every form of pressure on her woman's mind '.

l. 15. iugulatum. Translate the perf. part. pass. as an active verb.

l. 17. quo terrore, ' by this terrifying threat '.

l. 18. profectus, to be taken with esset.

l. 18. ferox . . . muliebri, ' exulting in having violated a woman's honour '.

l. 20. tanto malo, ' at so dire an evil '.

l. 22. facto . . . esse, ' there was need of action and haste ', i.e. ' action and haste were needed '. The abl. sg. neut. of the perf. part. pass., used as a noun, is commonly found with the phrase opus est.

l. 27. obortae (sunt), ' welled up '.

l. 28. satin salve. satin =satis ne. With salve (adv.) understand agis, ' do you do well enough ' =' are you quite well? '

l. 32. dexteras fidemque, hendiadys, ' your right hands as a pledge '.

l. 32. haud . . . fore ; supply rem, *lit.*, ' that (the deed) will not be without punishment for the violator '.. ' the violator will not escape punishment for his deed '.

l. 33. hostis pro hospite, ' enemy instead of guest ', i.e. ' repaying my hospitality with his hostility '.

l. 35. pestiferum, to be taken closely with mihi . . . estis, ' baneful for me, and for him if you are men '.

l. 36. animi, loc. ' in mind ', with aegram, which agrees with eam understood.

l. 37. ab coacta, ' from her who had been forced '.

l. 38. mentem peccare, acc. and infin. with the emphasis on mentem, ' it was the mind that sinned . . .'.

l. 38. inde . . . abesse, ' where there was no intention, there was no sin '.

l. 39. videritis, either fut. perfect, ' you shall determine,' or perfect subj. (jussive) a construction which is rare without a negative.

l. 41. nec ulla ... vivet, ' nor hereafter shall any unchaste woman live through the example of Lucretia '.

l. 43. in vulnus, ' over the wound '.

CHAPTER 59

Line 2. extractum. Translate the perf. part. pass. by an active participle or finite verb.

l. 3. ante regiam iniuriam, to be taken closely with castissimum (which is in agreement with sanguinem), ' most chaste before the royal outrage ', i.e. ' until the prince outraged it '.

l. 9. stupentibus miraculo ... ingenium, ' amazed at the wonder of the thing, whence (had come) this new spirit . . .', i.e. ' in amazement, wondering from where had come . . .'.

l. 11. toti, ' altogether '.

l. 12. iam inde, ' straightway '.

l. 14. elatum. The passive participle (again) will be best replaced by an active finite verb in English. Efferre is the technical word for ' carrying out ' for burial.

l. 15. miraculo ... indignitate, ' by the wonder ... and the indignity ', i.e. ' in wonder ... and resentment at ', a phrase which will have to be translated after homines (obj. of concient).

l. 17. Brutus castigator ... auctorque, ' B. the critic ... and adviser . . .' =' Brutus' criticisms of ... and advice to take up arms . . .'.

l. 19. quod ... deceret, ' as befitted . . .'. The subj. is due to virtual oratio obliqua, and quod is literally ' (that) which '.

l. 20. adversus hostilia ausos, ' against men who had dared hostile things ', i.e. ' to act as enemies '.

l. 21. voluntarius, ' offering his services '.

l. 22. patre, i.e. ' Lucretia's father '.

l. 28. quidquid ... rentur, ' they believed that whatever it was, it was not without purpose '.

l. 28. nec minorem ... animorum, ' no less resentment '.

l. 31. **ad tribunum Celerum.** For the Celeres, see the note on Chap. 15, l. 32.

l. 33. **oratio habita (est).** Translate in the active : ' he delivered a speech '.

l. 34. **nequaquam . . . fuerat,** ' by no means of that sentiment and temper . . .', i.e. ' quite inconsistent with the mind and disposition . . . he had hitherto counterfeited '.

l. 38. **addita (est) superbia . . . ,** *lit.,* ' the pride . . . was added ', i.e. ' he also touched upon the pride . . .'.

l. 40. **Romanos homines . . . ,** indirect speech, ' (he said) that . . .'.

l. 42. **factos (esse),** ' had been made ', i.e. ' had been turned into '.

l. 43. **memorata (est) caedes.** Make active again, ' he mentioned the shameful murder . . .'.

l. 43. **invecta . . . filia.** This phrase is grammatically the subj. of **memorata (est).** In our translation, it will become the object, ' the daughter's riding in her accursed chariot over her father's body '.

l. 44. **invocati . . . di,** *lit.,* ' the gods were called upon . . .'. In the active, ' he called upon the gods who avenge parents '.

ll. 45-7. **his . . . memoratis.** Begin with **memoratis,** in the act., ' having said these and other, methinks more savage, words . . .'.

l. 45. **quae . . . subicit,** ' which the immediate (feeling of) indignation suggests,—and they are by no means easy for historians to relate—'.

l. 54 **inter,** temporal, ' during '.

l. 56. **parentum,** gen. dependent upon **furias,** ' the spirits that avenge the wrongs done to parents '.

CHAPTER 60

Line 1. **re nova,** ' by the strange turn of events '.

l. 6. **Tarquinio,** a good example of the dat. of disadvantage : we may render : ' Tarquin found the gates closed . . .'.

l. 7. **liberatorem.** To keep the order of the Latin and thus retain the contrast, **Tarquinio . . . liberatorem,** turn this sentence into the passive.

l. 14. **regnatum (est),** impersonal pass., ' there were kings '.

l. 14. **ab condita . . . liberatam.** The perf. partics. pass. are to be rendered here by English nouns : ' from the foundation of the city to its liberation '.

l. 16. **consules.** Actually these two magistrates who took over the functions of the kings were called praetors until the time of the decemvirate.

l. 16. **comitiis centuriatis,** ' at the assembly by centuries '. It is very doubtful whether this assembly was in existence at this time. See the notes on Chap. 43, ll. 30, 37, 43.

l. 16. **a praefecto urbis.** The praefectus is presiding over the election in the capacity of interrex. The latter name is actually given by one historian Dionysius (V, 84) to Lucretius, father of Lucretia.

l. 17. **ex commentariis,** ' in accordance with the memoranda of S.T.'

VOCABULARY

(*In the following vocabulary only irregular verbs are given their principal parts in full. Otherwise the figures* (1), (2), (3), (4), *following a verb denote that it is a regular example of that conjugation. No conjugation number is given in the case of* -io *verbs like* capio. *References are to* section *nos.*)

a, ab, *prep. with abl.*, from, by ; on, in consequence of, after.

abdo, -ere, -didi, -ditum (3), conceal, hide away.

abduco, -ere, -duxi, -ductum (3), lead away.

abeo, -ire, -ii, -itum, go away, depart ; withdraw.

abhorreo (2), shrink from.

abigo, -ere, -egi, -actum (3), drive away.

ablego (1), send away.

abnuo, -ere, -ui (3), refuse.

abolesco, -ere, -levi (3), vanish, disappear.

Aborigines, -um, *m. pl.*, the earliest inhabitants of Italy.

abrogo (1), cancel, take away, abrogate.

absens, -ntis, absent.

absolvo, -ere, -vi, -utum (3), acquit.

absonus, -a, -um, out of harmony, incompatible.

abstergeo, -ere, -si, -sum (2), wipe away.

abstineo, -ere, -ui, -entum (2), forego ; refrain from attacking.

abstuli, *see* **aufero.**

absum, -esse, afui, be absent, distant.

abundans, -antis, excessive, superfluous.

abundo (1), overflow.

ac, *see* **atque.**

accedo, -ere, -cessi, -cessum (3), go to, approach, be joined, added to.

accendo, -ere, -di, -sum (3), set on fire, *or* ablaze, inflame.

accenseo, -ere, -ui, -nsum (2), reckon among.

acer, -cris, -cre, sharp, keen ; fierce, violent.

accingo, -ere, -nxi, -nctum (3), prepare for action.

accio (4), summon ; invite (35. 3).

accipio, -ere, -cepi, -ceptum, receive, admit, adopt (32. 14) hear, be told.

acceptus, -a, -um, popular, welcome, acceptable.

accola, -ae, *m.*, neighbour.

accuso (1), accuse.

Achivi, -orum, *m. pl.*, the Greeks.

acies, -ei, *f.*, line of battle, pitched battle, army ; **acie,** in the field.

acriter, *adv.*, keenly, vigorously.

Actiacus, -a, -um, of Actium.

ad, *prep. with acc.,* to, at, for, near ; towards, until, in answer **to** ; corresponding to.

adaequo (1), level.

adclaro (1), manifest.

adcresco, -ere, -crevi, -cretum (3), grow, increase.

addico, -ere, -xi, -ctum (3), (*of omen*) give assent, be favourable.

adduco, -ere, -xi, -ctum (3), bring to, develop (into).

adedo, -ere, -edi, -esum (3), eat up, consume.

adeo, *adv.,* to such a degree, so.

adeo, -ire, -ii, -itum, approach.

adequito (1), ride up to.

adfecto (1), aim at, aspire to ; seek.

adfero, -ferre, attuli, -latum, bring forward ; strike (*terror*) into.

adficio, -ere, -feci, -fectum, affect ; *with* **poena,** punish.

adfinitas, -tatis, *f.,* connection by marriage.

adfirmo (1), affirm, strengthen, establish.

adfligo, -ere, -xi, -ctum (3), afflict, distress, crush.

adgredior, -i, -gressum, attack ; advance.

adhibeo (2), invite, apply ; employ (7. 12).

adhortor (1), encourage.

adicio, -ere, -ieci, -iectum, add, apply ; turn (20. 1).

adimo, -ere, -emi, -emptum (3), take away (*with dat.*).

adipiscor, -i, adeptus (3), obtain.

adiectio, -ionis, *f.,* addition.

adiungo, -ere, -xi, -ctum (3), add.

adiuvo, -are, -iuvi. -iutum (1), assist.

adlicio, -ere, -lexi, -lectum, allure, entice, attract.

adloquium, -i, *n.,* address, speech.

adloquor, -i, -locutus (3), address, speak to.

administro (1), administer, govern.

admiratio, -ionis, *f.,* admiration.

admiror (1), wonder at, admire.

admitto, -ere, -misi, -missum (3) approve.

admodum, *adv.,* greatly, very.

admoneo (2), remind.

admonitus, -us, *m.,* advice, instance, suggestion.

admoveo, -ere, -movi, -motum (2) bring up.

adnitor, -i, -xus (sus) (3), strive.

adnuo, -ere, -ui, -utum (3), nod.

adolesco, -ere, -evi, -ultum (3), grow up.

adoperio, -ire, -ui, -ertum (4), cover up.

adorior (4), attack.

adorno (1), distinguish, honour.

adpeto, -ere, -ii (ivi), -itum (3), aim at ; *intrans.,* approach.

adprobo (1), approve.

adquiro, -ere, -sivi, -situm (3), gain, acquire.

adscisco, -ere, -scivi, -scitum (3), adopt.

adsentio, -ire, -si, -sum (4), agree.

adsiduus, -a, -um, perpetual.

adsoleo (2), *only 3rd pers.,* be wont.

adsto, -are, -stiti (1), stand before.

adsuefacio, -ere, -feci, -factum, accustom.

adsuesco, -ere, -suevi, -suetum (3), become accustomed.

adsum, -esse, -fui, be present, help, assist (*often with dat.*)

adsumo, -ᴇɾᴇ, -mpsi, -mptum (3), enrol ; assume.

adulescens, -ntis, *m.*, young man, youth.

adulter, -eri, *m.*, adulterer.

adulterium, -i, *n.*, adultery.

aduncus, -a, -um, hooked.

advena, -ae, *c.*, foreigner ; *as adj.*, foreign.

advenio, -ire, -veni, -ventum (4), arrive.

adventus, -us, *m.*, arrival, coming.

adversor (1), resist (*often with dat.*).

adversus, -a, -um, facing, opposing ; adversa pugna, defeat.

adversus, *prep. with acc., and adv.*, towards, against, in face of (2. 4).

advoco (1), summon.

aedificatio, -ionis, *f.*, building.

aedificium, -i, *n.*, building.

aedifico (1), build, build on.

aedes, *or* aedis, -is, *f.*, temple ; *in pl.*, house.

aeger, -gra, -grum, sick.

aegre, *adv.*, with difficulty ; with pati, ferre, to feel aggrieved or resentment at, to feel vexed at.

aegritudo, -inis, *f.*, mortification, melancholy.

aemulatio, -ionis, *f.*, act of rivalling.

aemulor (1), aspire to.

Aeneas, -ae, *m.*, Aeneas.

Aeneas Silvius, -ae, -i, *m.*, Aeneas Silvius.

aeneus, -a, -um, of copper *or* bronze.

aequalis, -e, equal ; *as noun*, friend (of same age).

aequaliter, *adv.*, equally.

Aequi, -orum, *m. pl.*, the Aequi (*Italian tribe*).

Aequicoli, -orum, *m. pl.*, the Aequicoli.

aequo (1), equalise ; equal, match.

aequus, -a, -um, level, even ; equal.

aes, aeris, *n.*, copper ; money, asses.

aetas, -tatis, *f.*, age, generation, period, time, youth.

age dum, *interjection*, come.

ager, agri, *m.*, land, territory, field, country.

agger, -eris, *m.*, mound.

agitatio, -ionis, *f.*, play (of weapons).

agito (1), ponder, think over *or* of.

agmen, -inis, *n.*, column, band ; procession (29. 5).

agnosco, -ere, -novi, -nitum (3), recognise.

ago, -ere, egi, actum (3), do, drive, carry along (12. 4) ; spend (*of reign*, 32. 3) ; hold (*of festival*).

agrestis, -e, rustic ; *as noun*, peasant, countryman.

Agrippa, -ae, *m.*, Agrippa (*Alban king*).

aio, *defect. vb.*, say.

ala, -ae, *f.*, wing.

Alba, -ae, *m.*, Alba (*Alban king*).

Alba Longa, *f.*, Alba Longa.

Albanus, -a, -um, Alban, of Alba.

album, -i, *n.*, white tablet.

alea, -ae, *f.*, hazard.

ales, -itis, *c.*, bird.

alias, *adv.*, at other times ; otherwise.

alienigena, -ae, *c.*, foreigner.

alienus, -a, -um, of others, strange (58. 7) ; inappropriate (20. 3) ; *as noun*, stranger, alien.

alio, *adv.*, in another direction.

aliquamdiu, *adv.*, for some time.

aliquando, *adv.*, sometimes.

aliquanto, *adv.*, considerably.

aliquantum, *adv.*, considerably.

aliquantus, -a, -um, considerable ; aliquantum spatii, for some considerable distance (25. 8).

aliqui, -ae, -quod, some, any.

aliquis, -quid, some one *or* thing.

aliquot, *indeclin.*, some, several.

aliquotiens, *adv.*, several times.

aliter, *adv.*, otherwise.

alius, -a, -um, other, different, another ; alii ... alii, some ... others.

alluvies, -ei, *f.*, inundation, overflow.

alo, -ere, alui, altum (3), support, keep, maintain.

Alpes, -ium, *f. pl.*, the Alps.

alte, *adv.*, deeply, deep ; on high.

alter, -a, -um, one of two, other, one's neighbour.

altercatio, -ionis, *f.*, altercation.

altus, -a, -um, high ; deep.

alveus, -i, *m.*, hollow vessel, basket.

ambages, -ium, *f. pl.*, riddle ; tacitae ambages, unspoken enigmas ; haud per ambages, in no enigmatical fashion.

ambigo, -ere (3), argue.

ambitio, -ionis, *f.*, currying of favour.

ambitiose, *adv.*, by canvassing.

ambitiosus, -a, -um, canvassing.

ambo, -ae, -o, both.

amens, -ntis, frantic, infatuated.

Ameriola, -ae, *f.*, Ameriola (*town of Prisci Latini*).

amicitia. -ae, *f.*, friendship.

amicus, -i, *m.*, friend.

amigro (1), emigrate.

amitto, -ere, -misi, -missum (3), lose.

amnis, -is, *m.*, river.

amo (1), love, like.

amor, -oris, *m.*, love.

amplector, -i, -plexus, (3) clasp, embrace.

amplifico (1), enlarge.

amplitudo, -inis, *f.*, grandeur.

amplius, *adv.*, more (than).

amplus, -a, -um, large, grand.

Amulius, -i, *m.*, Amulius (*king of Alba*).

an, or, whether (*in questions*).

anceps, -ipitis, too swift for the eye to follow (25. 5) ; wavering (28. 9).

Anchises, -ae, *m.*, Anchises (*father of Aeneas*).

ancile, -is, *n.*, sacred shield (*of Mars*).

ancilla, -ae, *f.*, handmaid.

Ancus Martius, -i -i, *m.*, Ancus Martius (*4th king of Rome*).

ango, -ere (3), distress, vex.

anguis, -is, *m.*, snake.

animadverto, -ere, -ti, -sum (3), notice ; punish (26. 9).

animus, -i, *m.*, mind, heart, purpose ; spirit ; courage (25. 3) ; anger (26. 2 etc.) ; attention (28. 5) ; pride (34. 4) ; *pl.*, affection ; resentment.

Anio, -ienis, *m.*, Anio (*a tributary of the Tiber*).

annus, -i, *m.*, year.

annuus, -a, -um, annual, lasting for a year.

ante, *prep. with acc., and adv.*, before ; longe ante, far beyond.

antea, *adv.*, before, formerly.

ante-eo, -ire, -ii, -itum, go before, take the lead (59. 6).

Antemnates, -ium, *m. pl.*, men of Antemnae.

Antenor, -oris, *m.*, Antenor (*a Trojan*).

antiquitas, -tatis, *f.*, antiquity, old times.

antiquus, -a, -um, ancient, of first importance.

antistes, -itis, *c.*, priest ; priestess.

anulus, -i, *m.*, ring.

anxius, -a, -um, anxious.

aperio, -ire, -ui, -tum, (4) open, disclose.

aperte, *adv.*, openly.

apertum, -i, *n.*, the open.

apertus, -a, -um, open.

Apiolae, -arum, *f, pl.*, Apiolae.

apparatus, -us, *m.*, magnificence.

appareo (2), appear, be plain.

apparitor, -oris, *m.*, attendant.

appello (1), name, call ; appeal to (40. 5).

appono, -ere, -posui, -positum (3), place *or* set before.

apte, *adv.*, deftly.

aptus, -a, -um, suitable, suited.

apud, *prep. with acc.*, among, at the house of, in presence of, with.

aqua, -ae, *f.*, water, stream.

aquila, -ae, *f.*, eagle.

ara, -ae, *f.*, altar.

arbiter, -tri, *m.*, witness.

arbitror (1), think.

arbor, -oris, *f.*, tree.

Arcadia, -ae, *f.*, Arcadia (*district of S. Greece*).

Arcadicus, -a, -um, Arcadian.

Arcas, -adis, *m.*, an Arcadian.

arceo, -ere, -ui, -ctum (2), repel, save.

arcesso, -ere, -ivi, -itum (3), summon.

arcuatus, -a, -um, covered, tilted.

Ardea, -ae, *f.*, Ardea.

ardeo, -ere, -si, -sum (2), burn.

ardor, -oris, *m.*, ardour, eagerness.

area, -ae, *f.*, open space, site (38. 7, 55. 2).

Argei, -orum, *m. pl.*, see *note on* 21. 5.

argentum, -i, *n.*, silver.

Argiletum, -i, *n.*, Argiletum (*district of Rome*).

arguo, -ere, -ui, -utum (3), allege, charge ; censure (28. 6).

Aricia, -ae, *f.*, Aricia.

Aricinus, -a, -um, of Aricia.

aries, -etis, *m.*, battering-ram.

arma, -orum, *n. pl.*, arms ; shields.

armentum, -i, *n.*, herd.

armilla, -ae, *f.*, bracelet.

armo (1), arm ; armati, *m. pl.*, armed men, in arms.

aro (1), plough.

arripio, -ere, -ui, -eptum, seize.

Arruns, -ntis, *m.*, Arruns (*son of Demaratus and brother of L. Tarquinius Priscus*).

ars, artis, *f.*, art, skill ; *pl.*, qualities, studies.

arx, arcis, *f.*, citadel, stronghold.

Ascanius, -i, *m.*, Ascanius (*son of Aeneas*).

Asia, -ae, *f.*, Asia (Minor).

aspernor (1), disdain, reject.

asylum, -i, *n.*, sanctuary, place of refuge.

at, *conj.*, but, still, then.

atque, and, and moreover.

atqui, and yet, but.

atrox, -ocis, fierce, revolting, horrible (26. 5), frightful (58. 5).

attonitus, -a, -um, bewildered, annoyed.

attribuo, -ere, -ui, -utum (3), assign, deliver.

Attus, -i, *m.,* Attus.

Atys, -yos, *m.,* Atys (*Alban king*).

auctor, -oris, *m.,* instigator, proposer, author, authority ; counsellor (1. 1), doer (58. 9), convener (51. 4) ; **auctor fio,** I authorise (+in +*acc.*).

auctoritas, -tatis, *f.,* influence.

audacia, -ae, *f.,* boldness ; enterprise (46. 6) ; assurance (48. 1.)

audeo, -ere, ausus sum (2), *semi-dep.,* dare, venture.

audio (4), hear.

aufero, -ferre, abstuli, ablatum, take away, remove, steal (58. 8).

aufugio, -ere, -fugi, flee away, run.

augeo, -ere, -xi, -ctum (2), increase ; strengthen, exalt.

augur, -uris, *m.,* augur.

augurato, *adv.,* after auspices taken.

augurium, -i, *n.,* augury.

auguror (1), take auspices.

augustus, -a, -um, reverend, majestic ; venerable (29. 5).

Augustus, -i, *m.,* Augustus.

aureus, -a, -um, golden, of gold.

aurora, -ae, *f.,* dawn.

aurum, -i, *n.,* gold.

auspicato, *adv.,* after auspice-taking.

auspicium, -i, *n.,* auspice, omen.

aut, or, either ; **aut . . . aut,** either . . . or.

autem, but, moreover.

auxilium, -i, *n.,* aid, help.

avaritia, -ae, *f.,* rapacity, greed.

aveho, -ere, -vexi -vectum (3), carry away ; *in pass.,* ride away.

Aventinum, -i, *n.,* the Aventine.

Aventinus, -i, *m.,* Aventinus (*Alban king*).

Aventinus, -a, -um, Aventine.

averto, -ere, -ti, -sum (3), turn away ; appropriate (7. 5).

aversus, -a, -um, turned away ; turned the other way (7 5).

avidus, -a, -um, desirous, greedy.

avis, -is, *f.,* bird.

avitus, -a, -um, of a grandfather.

avoco (1), summon away.

avolo (1), fly away.

avunculus, -i, *m.,* uncle.

avus, -i, *m.,* grandfather.

baculum, -i, *n.,* staff.

bellator, -oris, *m.,* warrior.

bellicosus, -a, -um, warlike.

bellicus, -a, -um, of *or* belonging to war.

bellum, -i, *n.,* war.

bene, *adv.,* well.

beneficium, -i, *n.,* benevolent action, benefaction, kindness, favour.

benigne, *adv.,* kindly.

benignitas, -tatis, *f.,* kindness.

benignus, -a, -um, kind, kindly, good-natured.

bigae, -arum, *f. pl.,* pair of horses.

bini, -ae, -a, two each.

bis, *adv.,* twice.

blande, *adv.,* courteously, graciously.

blanditia, -ae, *f.,* flattery.

blandus, -a, -um, flattering, agreeable.

bonus, -a, -um, good ; *n. pl.*, goods, property.

bos, bovis, *c.*, bull, cow, ox.

bracchium, -i, *n.*, arm.

brevi, *adv.*, soon.

brevis, -e, short.

Brutus, -i, *m.*, L. Junius Brutus.

cacumen, -inis, *n.*, top, peak.

Cacus, -i, *m.*, Cacus.

cado, -ere, cecidi, casum (3), fall.

caecus, -a, -um, blind.

caedes, -is, *f.*, slaughter, murder, loss ; death (59. 8).

caedo, -ere, cecidi, caesum (3), kill, slay.

caelebs, -ibis, unmarried.

caelestis, -e, heavenly, of *or* from heaven ; divine ; *in pl., as noun* = the gods.

Caelius, -a, -um, Caelian.

caelum, -i, *n.*, heaven.

Caeninenses, -ium, *m. pl.*, men of Caenina.

Caeninus, -a, -um, of Caenina.

Caere, *n., indecl.*, Caere (*town in Etruria*).

caerimonia, -ae, *f.*, ceremony ; observance.

Caesar, -aris, *m.*, Caesar (*title of the Roman Emperors*).

Camena, -ae, *f.*, Camena (*Italian muse*).

Cameria, -ae, *f.*, Cameria (*town in Latium*).

campus, -i, *m.*, plain.

cano, -ere, cecini, cantum (3), sing, prophesy, sound.

Capena (porta), -ae, *f.*, the Capene Gate (*in Rome*).

capesso, -ere, -ivi, -itum (3), take to (*of flight*).

Capetus, -i, *m.*, Capetus (*Alban king*).

capillus, -i, *m.*, hair.

capio, -ere, cepi, captum, take, take up, form *or* adopt (*a plan*) ; capture ; choose.

capitalis, -e, involving life, capital.

Capitolinus, -i, *m.*, the Capitoline (hill).

Capitolium, -i, *n.*, the Capitol.

Capra, -ae, *f.*, Capra (*a pool in Campus Martius*).

captivus, -a, -um, captive ; *as noun*, captive.

caput, -itis, *n.*, head ; capital ; leader.

Capys, -yos, *m.*, Capys (*Alban king*).

carcer, -eris, *m.*, prison.

caritas, -tatis, *f.*, affection.

carmen, -inis, *n.*, formula ; prophecy ; hymn.

Carmenta, -ae, *f.*, Carmenta (*Roman goddess of prophecy*).

carpentum, -i, *n.*, carriage.

carus, -a, -um, dear.

castigator, -oris, *m.*, chider.

castitas, -tatis, *f.*, purity, chastity.

castra, -orum, *n. pl.*, camp.

castus, -a, -um, chaste, pure.

casus, -us, *m.*, fall ; chance, destiny.

catena, -ae, *f.*, chain.

cauda, -ae, *f.*, tail.

causa, -ae, *f.*, cause ; *abl.*, causā, for the sake (of).

cavo (1), hollow.

cedo, -ere, cessi, cessum (3), retire, yield.

celeber, -bris, -bre, famous.

celebro (1), celebrate ; attend (22. 5).

Celeres, -um, *m. pl.*, the Celeres (*bodyguard of Romulus*).

celeriter, *adv.*, quickly.

celo (1), conceal.

cena, -ae, *f.*, dinner.

ceno (1), dine.

censeo, -ere, -ui, -nsum (2), rate, take the census ; think, propose.

census, -us, *m.*, census, rating, rateable property.

centesimus, -a, -um, hundredth.

centum, hundred.

centuria, -ae, *f.*, a century.

Centuriata, -orum, *n. pl.* (comitia), assembly by centuries.

centurio, -ionis, *m.*, centurion.

cera, -ae, *f.*, (waxed) tablet.

cerno, -ere, crevi, cretum (3), perceive.

certamen, -inis, *n.*, contest, struggle, conflict.

certatim, *adv.*, with rivalry, enthusiastically.

certe, *adv.*, at any rate.

certo (1), fight, vie, struggle.

certus, -a, -um, certain, fixed ; unmistakable ; unquestioned (23. 9).

cesso (1), be dull, wanting.

ceterum, *conj.*, but.

ceterus, -a, -um, the rest of ; rest, remaining ; the others.

cibus, -i, *m.*, food.

cieo, -ere, civi, citum (2), rouse. pugnam ciere, to lead the fighting.

cingo, -ere, -xi, -ctum (3), surround.

Circa, -ae, *f.*, Circe.

circa, *prep. with acc., and adv.*, around, on both sides ; near by.

circamoerium, ' the part on both sides of the wall.'

Circeii, -orum, *m. pl.*, Circeii (*town in Latium*).

circumago, -ere, -egi, -actum (3), wheel ; *in pass.*, revolve.

circumduco, -ere, -xi, -ctum (3), lead around.

circumdo, -are, -dedi, -datum (1), put *or* station round ; *in pass.*, surround.

circumeo, -ire, -ii, -itum, go round ; canvass (47. 7).

circumfero, -ferre, -tuli, -latum, carry *or* lead round, parade (38. 4).

circumfundo, -ere, -fudi, -fusum (3), shed *or* pour round.

circumsaepio, -ire, -si, -tum (4), fence round.

circumsisto, -ere, -steti *or* stiti (3), surround.

circumspicio, -ere, -spexi, -spectum, look round for.

circumsto, -are, -steti (1), stand round, surround.

circumvenio, -ire, -veni, -ventum (4), surround.

circus, -i, *m.*, circus.

cito (1), hasten ; summon ; equo citato, *and in pl.*, at full gallop.

citra, *prep. with acc., and adv.*, on this side of.

civilis, -e, civil.

civis, -is, *c.*, citizen.

civitas, -tatis, *f.*, community, citizenship.

clades, -is, *f.*, disaster.
clam, *adv.*, secretly.
clamito (1), cry repeatedly.
clamor, -oris, *m.*, shout, cry; uproar (41. 1).
clandestinus, -a, -um, hidden.
clangor, -oris, *m.*, scream.
clarus, -a, -um, famous, glorious.
classis, -is, *f.*, fleet, class (*in centuries*).
claudo, -ere, -si, -sum (3), shut.
clava, -ae, *f.*, club.
clemens, -ntis, merciful.
clipeum, -i, *n.*, *or* -us, *m.*, (round) shield.
clivus, -i, *m.*, slope.
cloaca, -ae, *f.*, sewer.
Cloelii, -orum, *m. pl.*, the Cloelii (*Alban family*).
Cluilius, -i, *m.*, Cluilius (*Alban king*).
Cluilius, -a, -um, of Cluilius.
coalesco, -ere, -alui, -alitum (3), combine, become united.
coepi, -isse, began.
coeptum, -i, *n.*, undertaking.
coerceo (2), restrain.
coetus, -us, *m.*, gathering, class.
cogitatio, -ionis, *f.*, thought.
cognatus, -a, -um, kindred, related; *also as noun*, kindred.
cognitio, -ionis, *f.*, legal investigation.
cognomen, -inis, *n.*, (*family*) name; surname; nickname.
cognosco, -ere, -novi, -nitum (3), learn, recognise.
cogo, -ere, coegi, coactum (3), collect, compel; force (58. 9).
Collatia, -ae, *f.*, Collatia (*a city*).
Collatinus, -a, -um, of Collatia; *as noun*, man of Collatia; *in* 57. 7, *etc.*, Tarquinius Collatinus.

colligo (1), tie together.
colligo, -ere, -legi, conlectum, gather together, collect.
collis, -is, *m.*, hill.
colloco (1), place, station.
colo, -ere, colui, cultum (3), cultivate, study; celebrate; serve.
colonia, -ae, *f.*, colony.
colonus, -i, *m.*, colonist.
columna, -ae, *f.*, pillar.
comes, -itis, *c.*, companion, comrade.
comis, -e, courteous, friendly.
comissatio, -ionis, *f.*, revelling, carousal.
comitas, -tatis, *f.*, courtesy.
comitatus, -us, *m.*, attendant.
comiter, *adv.*, courteously, politely; in a friendly spirit (22. 5).
comitia, -iorum, *n. pl.*, assembly; elections.
commeatus, -us, *m.*, furlough.
commentarius, -i, *m.*, memoranda.
commentum, -i, *n.*, invention.
commercium, -i, *n.*, intercourse.
commigro (1), settle at; remove (*intrans.*).
comminus, *adv.*, at close quarters.
committo, -ere, -misi, -missum (3), entrust.
commoditas, -tatis, *f.*, convenience.
commodum, -i, *n.*, gain, advantage.
communis, -e, common, shared.
communiter, *adv.*, in common; in co-operation (45. 2).
compar, -is, equal.
comparo (1), make ready; prepare for (war) (36. 2); procure.
compello, -ere, -puli, -pulsum (3), drive together; concentrate.
complector, -i, -exus (3), embrace.

compleo, -ere, -evi, -etum (2) fill.

comploratio, -ionis, f., lamentation.

compono, -ere, -posui, -positum (3), compose ; ex composito, by agreement, by preconceived plan.

compos, -otis, in possession or enjoyment of.

comprehendo, -ere, -di, -sum (3), seize ; arrest.

comprimo, -ere, -pressi, -pressum (3), crush ; quell (of riot).

conatus, -us, m., attempt.

concedo, -ere, -cessi, -cessum (3), yield.

concelebro (1), celebrate or keep (a festival).

concieo, -ere, -civi, -citum (2), collect (a crowd), draw together ; provoke (60. 2).

concilio (1), win over, win.

concilium, -i, n., assembly, meeting.

concipio, -ere, -cepi, -ceptum, conceive ; draw up, formulate.

concito (1), rouse, whip up (28. 10).

conclamo (1), shout ; lament, wail (58. 12).

concordia, -ae, f., harmony.

concors, -dis, in harmony or concord.

concupisco, -ere, -ii, -itum (3), long for, covet.

concurro, -ere, -curri, -cursum (3), charge (25. 3) ; muster.

concursus, -us, m., rush, encounter.

condemno (1), condemn ; find guilty (26. 8).

condico, -ere, -xi, -ctum (3), make demands on.

conditor, -oris, m., founder ; originator.

condo, -ere, -didi, -ditum (3), found; close.

confero, -ferre, -tuli, -latum, bring together, collect, compare ; contribute. signa conferre, to join battle.

confessio, -ionis, f., acknowledgment.

confestim, adv., immediately.

conficio, -ere, -feci, -fectum, make, accomplish ; dispatch (25. 10).

confido, -ere, -fisus sum (3), semidep., feel confident, trust.

conflagro (1), burn, be consumed (with fire).

confligo, -ere, -xi, -ctum (3), fight.

confluentes, -ium, m. pl., the confluence of the Tiber and the Anio.

confugio, -ere, -fugi, fly, flee for refuge ; have recourse.

confundo, -ere, -fudi, -fusum (3), confuse, merge.

congero, -ere, -gessi, -gestum (3), heap up.

congredior, -i, -gressus sum, meet.

congrego (1), collect ; in pass., flock together.

congressus, -us, m., meeting.

congruo, -ere, -ui (3), agree.

conicio, -ere, -ieci -iectum, hurl, fling ; se conicere, to plunge (12. 10).

conitor, -i, -nixus or nisus (3), exert oneself fully.

coniungo, -ere, -iunxi, -iunctum (3), unite ; join on to ; make to touch.

coniunx, -iugis, c., husband or wife

coniurator, -oris, m., conspirator.

coniuro (1), conspire.

conlaudo (1), praise highly.

conligo, *see* colligo.

conloquium, -i, *n.*, conference, parley.

conor (1), try, attempt.

conqueror, i, -questus (3), complain bitterly of.

conquiesco, -ere, -quievi, -quietum (3), remain at rest.

consaluto (1), salute, greet.

consanguinitas, -tatis, *f.*, blood relationship.

conscendo, -ere, -di, -sum (3), mount.

conscisco, -ere, -scivi, -scitum (3), approve.

conscius, -a, -um, conscious.

conscribo, -ere, -scripsi, -scriptum (3), enrol.

consecro (1), consecrate.

consensus, -us, *m.*, unanimity, harmony, agreement.

consentio, -ire, -si, -sum (4), agree ; *in pass.*, be agreed upon.

consequor, -i, -secutus (3), overtake.

consero, -ere, -ui, -tum (3), join ; manus conserere, to engage in fight.

consido, -ere, -sedi, -sessum (3), sit down, seat oneself.

consilium, -i, *n.*, design, plan, measure, counsel ; contrivance.

consisto, -ere, -stiti (3), take one's stand.

consocio (1), unite, assume as a body.

consolor (1), console.

conspectus, -us, *m.*, sight.

conspicio, -ere, -spexi, -spectum, behold ; look on (47. 5).

conspicuus, -a, -um, conspicuous.

constituo, -ere, -ui, -utum (3), determine, establish, institute ; settle (46. 5).

consto, -are, -stiti, -statum, become static ; *impersonal*, it is agreed *or* allowed.

construo, -ere, -xi, -ctum (3), construct, build.

Consualia, -ium, *n. pl.*, festival in honour of Consus.

consuesco, -ere, -suevi, -suetum (3), accustom; *in perf.*, be accustomed.

consul, -ulis, *m.*, consul.

consulo, -ere, -ui, -tum (3), consult (+ *acc.*) ; consult interests of (+ *dat.*).

consulto (1), consider.

consultus, -a, -um, learned.

contagio, -ionis, *f.*, infection.

contamino (1), pollute, stain.

contemno, -ere, -tempsi, -temptum (3), despise.

contemptus, -us, *m.*, contempt ; neglect (56. 7).

contendo, -ere, -di, -tum (3), contend, assert ; hasten, fight.

contentus, -a, -um, satisfied.

continens, -ntis, continuous, unbroken.

contineo, -ere, -ui, -tum (2), hold in check.

contingo, -ere, -tigi, -tactum (3), befall, fall to one's lot ; osculo contingere, to kiss.

continuo (1), make continuous.

continuus, -a, -um, continuous, successive.

contio, -ionis, *f.*, meeting, assembly.

contionor (1), address (*a meeting*).

contra, *prep. with acc. and adv.*, against ; on the other hand ;

opposite ; **contra intueri** (16. 6), gaze on him face to face.

contraho, -ere, -traxi, -tractum (3), draw together.

contumelia, -ae, *f.*, indignity, insult.

conubium, -i, *n.*, marriage.

convalesco, -ere, -ui (3), grow strong.

convallis, -is, *f.*, valley.

conveho, -ere, -vexi, -vectum (3), collect.

convenio, -ire, -veni, -ventum (4), come together ; (+ *acc.*), meet ; be agreed upon (3. 5, 24. 2).

converto, -ere, -ti, -sum (3), divert, attract attention of.

convivium, -i, *n.*, entertainment ; banquet.

coorior, -iri, -ortus (4), rise.

copia, -ae, *f.*, plenty ; *in pl.*, forces.

cor, cordis, *n.*, heart.

coram, *prep. with abl., and adv.*, in the presence (of).

Corinthius, -a, -um, Corinthian, of Corinth.

Corinthus, -i, *f.*, Corinth.

corneus, -a, -um, of horn.

corneus, -a, -um, of cornel-wood.

cornicen, -cinis, *m.*, horn-blower.

Corniculum, -i, *n.*, Corniculum.

cornu, -us, *n.*, horn, wing (*of an army*).

corpus, -oris, *n.*, person, body.

corrumpo, -ere, -rupi, -ruptum (3), bribe.

corruo, -ere, -ui, fall (*lifeless*).

cos, cotis, *f.*, whetstone.

cratis, -is, *f.*, hurdles.

creber, -bra, -brum, thick ; thickly (31. 2).

credo, -ere, -didi, -ditum (3), believe, trust ; believe in (*often with dat.*).

cremo (1), burn.

creo (1), elect, appoint.

cresco, -ere, crevi, cretum (3), grow.

Creusa, -ae, *f.*, Creusa (*wife of Aeneas*).

crimen, -inis, *n.*, accusation.

criminatio, -ionis, *f.*, incrimination.

criminor (1), accuse.

crinis, -is, *m.*, hair.

Croton, -is, *f.*, Croton (*S. Italian city*).

cruciatus, -us, *m.*, torture.

crudelis, -e, cruel.

crudelitas, -tatis, *f.*, cruelty.

cruentus, -a, -um, bloody.

cruor, -oris, *m.*, blood, gore.

Crustumerium, -i, *n.*, Crustumerium.

Crustumini, -orum, *m. pl.*, men of Crustumerium.

cubiculum, -i, *n.*, bedroom.

culmen, -inis, *n.*, top, roof.

culpa, -ae, *f.*, fault, error.

culter, -tri, *m.*, knife.

cultus, -us, *m.*, worship ; style, fashion (39. 3) ; use, occupation (44. 4).

cum, *conj.*, when, since, although.

cum . . . tum, not only . . . but also both . . . and.

cum, *prep. with abl.*, with, together with.

cumulus, -i, *m.*, heap.

cunctanter, *adv.*, with delay *or* hesitation.

cunctor (1), delay, hesitate.

cupiditas, -tatis, *f.*, desire, ambition.

cupido, -inis, *f.*, desire, ambition.

cupidus, -a, -um, desirous.

cupio, -ere, -ivi, -itum, desire.

cura, -ae, *f.*, care, anxiety, concern, attention ; management ; foreboding (56. 4).

Cures, -ium, *pl.*, *m. or f.*, Cures (*a Sabine town*).

curia, -ae, *f.*, curia, ward ; senate-house.

Curiatii, -orum, *m. pl.*, the Curiatii.

curo (1), carry out, deal with (20. 7) ; heal (*of wounds*).

curro, -ere, cucurri, cursum (3), run.

currus, -us, *m.*, chariot.

cursus, -us, *m.*, running, rush, phase ; effuso cursu (37. 4), in scattered rout.

Curtius, -i, *m.*, Mettius Curtius (*Sabine chief*).

curulis, -e, curule.

custodia, -ae, *f.*, custody, protection.

custos, -odis, *c.*, guard, sentinel.

Cyprius, -a, -um, Cyprius (*name of street in Rome*).

(daps) dapis, *f.*, (*not found in sg.*), feast.

de, *prep. with abl.*, from, concerning, for, about.

dea, -ae, *f.*, goddess.

debeo (2), owe.

decedo, -ere, -cessi, -cessum (3), die.

decem, ten.

deceo (2), *imperson.*, it becomes, befits.

decerno, -ere, -crevi, -cretum (3), decide, decide (*the issue*), fight it out ; decree.

decipio, -ere, -cepi, -ceptum, deceive.

declaro (1), declare.

declino (1), turn aside.

decoro (1), adorn ; decoratus (26. 10), trophy-laden.

decorus, -a, -um, appropriate, becoming, suitable.

decuria, -ae, *f.*, decury.

decurro, -ere, -curri, -cursum (3), run down.

decursus, -us, *m.*, charge.

decus, -oris, *n.*, ornament, honour, distinction.

decutio, -ere, -cussi, -cussum, strike off.

dedecus, -oris *n.*, disgrace ; the (threat of) dishonour (58. 4).

dedico (1), dedicate, appoint.

deditio, -ionis, *f.*, surrender.

dedo, -ere, -didi, -ditum (3), give up, surrender ; devote.

deduco, -ere, -duxi, -ductum (3), guide, conduct ; (*of colonies*) plant.

defectio, -ionis, *f.*, revolt.

defendo, -ere, -di, -nsum (3), defend.

defero, -ferre, -tuli, -latum, carry down *or* to ; offer ; report.

deficio, -ere, -feci, -fectum, fail ; fall away.

defigo, -ere, -fixi, -fixum (3), plunge; overwhelm (29. 3).

deformis, -e, hideous.

defungor, -i, -functus (3), finish off (*with abl.*).

degenero (1), degenerate.

dego, -ere, degi (3), live.

dehinc, *adv.*, from here.

deicio, -ere, -ieci, -iectum, throw *or* strike down.

dein, *see* deinde.

deinceps, *adv.*, next, successively.

deinde, *adv.*, then, next ; after that, therefore ; afterwards ; subsequently.

delabor, -i, -lapsus (3), glide down.

delenio (4), soothe, mitigate.

deliberabundus, -a, -um, plunged in thought.

deliberatio, -ionis, *f.*, reflection.

delictum, -i, *n.*, sin, wrong.

deligo, -ere, -legi, -lectum (3), select.

delinquo, -ere, -liqui, -lictum (3), offend.

Delphi, -orum, *m. pl.*, Delphi (in Greece).

delubrum, -i, *n.*, shrine.

demando (1), entrust.

Demaratus, -i, *m.*, Demaratus.

demergo, -ere, -si, -sum (3), send underground.

demitto, -ere, -misi, -missum (3), send down ; *in pass.*, descend ; sink (34. 8).

demo, -ere, dempsi, demptum (3), take away, remove.

demum, *adv.*, at last.

deni, -ae, -a, ten each.

denique, *adv.*, lastly, in short, finally.

densus, -a, -um, thick.

depono, -ere, -posui, -positum (3), lay down *or* aside.

deprehendo, -ere, -di, -sum (3), seize.

descendo, -ere, -di, -sum (3), descend ; penetrate, (19. 5).

descisco, -ere, -scivi, -scitum (3), revolt.

describo, *see* discribo, copy.

desero, -ere, -ui, -tum, abandon, neglect, desert.

deses, -idis, inactive.

desiderium, -i, *n.*, regret, loss.

desido, -ere, -sedi (3), sink.

designo (1), mark out.

desisto, -ere, -stiti (3), desist.

despondeo, -ere, -di, -sum (2), betroth.

destino (1), destine.

destituo, -ere, -ui, -tum (3), desert, baulk (51. 5).

desuetudo, -inis, *f.*, disuse.

desum, -esse, -fui, be wanting *or* lacking.

determino (1), mark off, delimit.

detineo, -ere, -ui, -tum (2), withhold, keep back.

deus, -i, *m.*, god.

deversorium, -i, *n.*, lodging.

deverticulum, -i, *n.*, lodging.

devinco, -ere, -vici, -victum (3), defeat utterly.

devolvo, -ere, -volvi, -volutum (3), roll down ; *in pass.*, sink.

dexter, -tra, -trum, right.

dextra, *or* dextera, -ae, *f.*, right hand.

dextere, *adv.*, skilfully.

Dialis, -e, of Jupiter.

Diana, -ae, *f.*, Diana.

Dianium, -i, *n.*, shrine of Diana.

dicio, -ionis, *f.*, sovereignty, power.

dico (1), dedicate.

dico, -ere, -xi, -ctum (3), say, call, give name.

dictator, -oris, *m.*, dictator ; Alban magistrate.

dictito (1), exclaim.

dictum, -i, *n.*, word ; dicto audiens, obedient.

dies, -ei, *m.* or *f.*, day ; in dies, day by day.

differo, -ferre, distuli, dilatum, put off, postpone.

difficilis, -e, difficult.

difficiliter, *adv.*, with difficulty.

diffido, -ere, -fisus sum (3), *semi-dep.*, distrust (*often with dat.*).

digitus, -i, *m.*, finger.

dignitas, -tatis, *f.*, worth, rank, honour, dignity.

dignus, -a, -um, worthy (*often with abl.*).

digredior, -i, -gressus, depart.

digressus, -us, *m.*, departure, withdrawal.

dilatio, -ionis, *f.*, delaying.

dimicatio, -ionis, *f.*, contest, struggle, fight ; trial of strength.

dimico (1), fight.

dimitto, -ere, -misi, -missum (3), dismiss.

dirigo, -ere, -exi, -ectum (3), arrange.

dirimo, -ere, -emi, -emptum (3), break off ; put off.

diruo, -ere, -ui, -utum (3), pull down, demolish.

disceptator, -oris, *m.*, arbitrator.

discerpo, -ere, -psi, -ptum (3), tear in pieces.

discindo, -ere, -scidi, -scissum (3), cleave.

disciplina, -ae, *f.*, discipline, system ; instruction (28. 9).

disco, -ere, didici (3), learn.

discribo, -ere, -psi, -ptum (3), divide.

discribo, -ere, -psi, -ptum (3), copy.

discrimen, -inis, *n.*, distinction ; decisive *or* critical point.

discurro, -ere, -curri, -cursum (3), dart.

dispar, -paris, unlike.

dispenso (1), order.

displiceo (2), displease (*often with dat.*).

dissero, -ere, -ui, -tum. discourse, utter.

dissimilis, -e, unlike.

dissimulo (1), conceal.

dissonus, -a, -um, discordant, different.

distendo, -ere, -di, -tum (3), stretch out.

disto (1), be separate *or* distant.

distraho, -ere, -xi, -ctum (3), pull asunder.

distribuo, -ere, -i, -utum (3), divide.

distributio, -ionis, *f.*, distribution.

dito (1), enrich ; *in pass.*, to enrich oneself (57. 1).

diu, *adv.*, by day ; for a long time.

diuturnus, -a, -um, of long duration.

divendo, -ere, -venditum (3), sell piecemeal.

diversus, -a, -um, diverse, opposite.

dives, divitis *or* ditis, rich.

divido, -ere, -visi, -visum (3), divide, allot.

divinitas, -tatis, *f.*, divinity.

divinitus, *adv.*, from the gods.

divinus, divine, sacred ; res divinae (8. 1), worship of the gods.

divinus, -i, *m.*, diviner, soothsayer.

divisus, -us, *m.*, a distributing.

divitiae, -arum, *f. pl.*, riches.

do, dare, dedi, datum (1), give, grant ; give away ; me obviam do (*with dat.*), I meet.

doceo, -ere, -ui, -tum (2), teach, tell ; explain (9. 14).

doctrina, -ae, *f.*, teaching.

documentum, -i, *n.*, example.

dolor, -oris, *m.*, pain, grief, resentment (40. 4).

dolus, -i, *m.*, deceit, stratagem ; dolus malus (24. 7), malice prepense.

domesticus, -a, -um, domestic, private.

domicilium, -i, *n.*, home, domicile.

domina, -ae, *f.*, mistress.

dominus, -i, *m.*, master, owner.

domo, -are, -ui, -itum (1), tame, subdue.

domus, -us, *f.*, home, house ; *loc.* domi, at home.

donec, *conj.*, until.

donum, -i, *n.*, gift.

dormio (4), sleep.

dorsum, -i, *n.*, ridge ; in dorso, along a ridge.

dubie, *adv.*, haud dubie, unmistakeably.

dubito (1), doubt.

dubius, -a, -um, doubtful.

ducenti, -ae, -a, two hundred.

duco, -ere, -xi, -ctum (3), lead ; marry ; deem ; build (*of walls*).

ductor, -oris, *m.*, leader.

duellum, *old form of* bellum.

dulcedo, -inis, *f.*, charm, sweetness.

dum, *with indic.*, while ; *with subj.*, provided that.

dummodo, *conj.*, provided that.

duo, duae, duo, two.

duodecim, twelve.

duodeni, -ae, -a, twelve each.

duodequadragesimus, -a, -um, thirty-eighth.

duplex, -icis, twofold, double.

duplico (1), double.

duro (1), last, endure.

duumviri, -orum, *m. pl.*, duumvirs.

dux, ducis, *m.*, leader.

e, ex, *prep. with abl.*, from, out of, in accordance with, in consequence of, after.

ea, *adv.*, on that side.

ecqui, -quae, -quod, *interrog. adj.* any.

ecquis, -quid, any, anyone or thing.

edico, -ere, -xi, -ctum (3), make proclamation.

edictum, -i, *n.*, proclamation.

edo, -ere, -didi, -ditum (3), bring forth, produce ; perform, do ; give out, name.

edoceo, -ere, -ui, -tum (2), prescribe.

educo (1), rear, bring up.

educo, -ere, -xi, -ctum (3), lead out.

effero, -ferre, extuli, elatum, carry out ; copy (32. 2.)

effero (1), make savage.

efficax, -acis, effective.

efficio, -ere, -feci, -fectum, make, do ; cause.

effigies, -ei *f.*, image, symbol.

effor (1), pronounce.

effringo, -ere, -fregi, -fractum (3), break open.

effugio, -ere, -fugi, escape.

effundo, -ere, -fudi, -fusum (3), pour forth ; *in pass.*, stream out ; effusus, scattered *or* headlong.

effuse, *adv.*, in scattered flight.

egens, -entis, poor, needy.

egeo (2), be in need (*often with abl.*).

Egeria, -ae, *f.*, Egeria (*wife of Numa and Roman muse*).

Egerius, -i, *m.*, Egerius (*nephew of Lucumo*).

ego, I.

egredior, -i, -gressus, go out, leave ; land.

egregius, -a, -um, noble, peerless, goodly, outstanding.

eicio, -ere, -ieci, -iectum, turn *or* fling out.

elabor, -i, -lapsus (3), slip out, escape.

elanguesco, -ere, -langui (3), grow feeble, languish.

elicio, -ere, -licui, -licitum, elicit.

Elicius, -i, *m.*, Elicius (*title of Jupiter*).

eludo, -ere, -si, -sum (3), mock at.

eluvies, -ei, *f.*, overflow, flood.

ementior (4), lie, assert falsely.

emergo, -ere, -si, -sum (3), extricate ; *in pass.*, get out, emerge (13. 5).

emineo (2), be prominent.

emitto, -ere, -misi, -missum (3), send forth ; utter.

emo, -ere, emi, emptum (3), buy.

Eneti, -tum, *m. pl.*, the Eneti.

enim, *conj.*, for.

enimvero, *adv.*, then indeed, of course.

eniteo (2), shine forth, be conspicuous.

eo, *adv.*, thither, there ; to such a pitch.

eo, *adv.*, for that reason, on this *or* that account.

eo, ire, ii (ivi), itum, go.

eodem, *adv.*, to the point *or* place.

Ephesius, -a, -um, Ephesian, of Ephesus.

eques, -itis, *m.*, horseman, knight.

equester, -tris, -tre, equestrian, of cavalry.

equidem, *adv.*, indeed, truly, surely.

equitatus, -us, *m.*, cavalry.

equus, -i, *m.*, horse.

erga, *prep. with acc.*, towards, for.

ergo, *adv.*, therefore.

ergo, *prep. with gen.*, by way of.

erigo, -ere, -rexi, -rectum (3), rouse ; excite (25. 2) ; raise on high (27. 8).

eripio, -ere, -ripui, -reptum, rescue.

erogo (1), draw.

errabundus, -a, -um, wandering.

erro (1), err.

error, -oris, *m.*, wandering, confusion.

erudio (4), educate.

escendo, -ere, -di, -sum (3), ascend, climb.

Esquiliae, -arum, *f. pl.*, the Esquiline or Esquiline Hill.

Esquiliarius, -a, -um, Esquiline.

Esquilinus, -a, -um, Esquiline.

et, *conj.*, and ; et . . . et, both . . . and ; also.

etiam, *adv.*, also, even.

Etruria, -ae, *f.*, Etruria.

Etruscus, -a, -um, of Etruria, Etruscan ; *as noun*, Etruscan.

etsi, *conj.*, although, even if.

Euganei, -orum, *m. pl.*, the Euganei.

Evander, -dri, *m.*, Evander.

evado, -ere, -si, -sum (3), escape ; turn out to be (39. 4).

eveho, -ere, -xi, -ctum (3), carry up *or* away ; *in pass.*, ascend.

evenio, -ire, -veni, -ventum (4), happen, turn out.

eventus, -us, *m.*, issue, result ; fulfilment (39. 1).

evoco (1), call out *or* forth.

ex, *see* e.

exaedifico (1), complete building of.

exanimis, -e, lifeless, breathless.

exaudio (4), hear clearly ; overhear.

exauguratio, -ionis, *f.*, deconsecration.

exauguro (1), deconsecrate, withdraw from consecration.

excello, -ere, -lui, -sum (3), excel.

excelsus, -a, -um, lofty.

excidium, -i, *n.*, destruction, demolition.

excieo (2)⎱ rouse, draw out, summon ;
excio (4) ⎰ attract (7. 9).

excipio, -ere, -cepi, -ceptum, take up, welcome ; engage in (53. 4).

excito (1), provoke, rouse.

excludo, -ere, -si, -sum (3), shut out, exclude.

excurro, -ere, -(cu)curri, -cursum (3), sally out.

exemplum, -i, *n.*, example, pattern, type, exemplar.

exeo, -ire, -ii (ivi), -itum, go out, land ; expire (*of truce*).

exerceo (2), train ; conduct (49. 4) ; make to work (56. 3).

exercitus, -us, *m.*, army.

exhaurio, -ire, -si, -stum (4), exhaust, drain out, cleanse.

exigo, -ere, -egi, -actum (3), drive out.

exiguus, -a, -um, small, meagre.

eximius, -a, -um, choice.

eximo, -ere, -emi, -emptum (3), take away ; waste (50. 8).

exinde, *adv.*, thereupon.

existimo (1), think.

exitus, -us, *m.*, ending, issue.

exordium, -i, *n.*, beginning.

exorior, -iri, -ortus (4), rise up.

expeditio, -ionis, *f.*, expedition.

expergiscor, -i, -perrectus (3), awake.

experior, -iri, -tus (4), try, test ; experience ; *perf. part. in passive meaning* (17. 3 ; 34. 12).

expers, -tis, without a share of ; free from (*often with gen.*).

expeto, -ere, -petivi (ii), -petitum (3), demand ; inflict ; *intrans.*, fall.

expio (1), atone for.

expleo, -ere, -evi, -etum (2), fill up, complete.

explico, -are, -avi (ui), -atum (itum) (1), organise ; deploy (27. 6).

expono, -ere, -posui, -positum (3), expose.

exposco, -ere, -poposci (3), implore, demand.

expugno (1), storm.

exsanguis, -e, lifeless.

exscribo, -ere, -psi, -ptum (3), write out.

exsecror (1), curse.

exsequor, -i, -secutus (3), carry out · pursue, punish.

exsigno (1), register, note down.

exsilium, -i, *n.*, exile.

exspecto (1), wait for.

exspiro (1), breathe one's last.

exsto, -are (1), remain ; may be seen (25. 14).

exsul, -ulis, *c.*, exile.

exsulo (1), be an exile.

exsupero (1), overcome ; exceed the costs of (55. 9). ·

exta, -orum, *n. pl.*, vitals.

extemplo, *adv.*, at once, on the instant.

externus, -a, -um, external, foreign.

exterreo (2), terrify.

extra, *prep. with acc.*, outside of.

extraho, -ere, -xi, -ctum (3), draw out.

extremum, -i, *n.*, end.

extremus, -a, -um, outermost, extreme.

extrinsecus, *adv.*, outside.

exulto (1), exult, triumph.

faber, -bri, *m.*, workman.

Fabius, -i, *m.*, Fabius Pictor (*historian*).

fabricor (1), construct.

fabula, -ae, *f.*, story.

facesso, -ere, -i, -itum (3), *intr.*, retire.

facies, -ei, *f.*, features.

facile, *adv.*, easily.

facilis, -e, easy.

facinorosus, -a, -um, bold, daring.

facinus, -oris, *n.*, deed.

facio, -ere, feci, factum, do, act ; make, offer ; appoint, create (26. 5).

factio, -ionis, *f.*, faction, party.

factum, -i, *n.*, deed ; *in pl.*, conduct.

facultas, -tatis, *f.*, opportunity.

fallo, -ere, fefelli, falsum (3), deceive.

falso, *adv.*, falsely.

falsus, -a, -um, false.

fama, -ae, *f.*, reputation, glory : tradition ; story, news ; **famā ferre**, to celebrate.

familia, -ae, *f.*, household.

familiaris, -e, familiar, intimate ; *as noun*, a domestic, attendant.

familiaritas, -tatis, *f.*, intimacy.

fanum, -i, *n.*, shrine.

fas, *indecl. n.*, right ; permitted ; religion (9. 13).

fastigium, -i, *n.*, top ; downward slope (38. 6).

fastus, -a, -um, propitious for speech.

fateor, -eri, fassus (2), acknowledge, confess.

fatigo (1), weary, beset (11.2).

fatiloquus, -a, -um, prophetic.

fatum, -i, *n.*, destiny, fate.

Faustulus, -i, *m.*, Faustulus.

faustus, -a, -um, favoured, blessed.

fautor, -oris, *m.*, supporter, patron.

faveo, -ere, favi, fautum (2), be favourable to (*with dat.*).

favor, -oris, *m.*, favour, support.

felix, -icis, successful, fortunate.

femina, -ae, woman.

fenestra, -ae, *f.*, window.

fera, -ae, *f.*, wild animal.

ferculum, -i, *n.*, frame.

fere, *adv*, nearly, almost.

Ferentina, -ae, *f.*, Ferentina (*Latin goddess*).

Feretrius, title of Jupiter.

feriae, -arum, *f. pl.*, festival.

ferio, -ire (4), strike.

ferme, *adv.*, about, pretty much.

fero, ferre, tuli, latum, bear, carry ; say ; give out (30. 6) ; **prae se ferre**, to assert ; **ad populum ferre**, bring *or* submit a proposal before the people.

ferociter, *adv.*, fiercely, truculently.

Feronia, -ae, *f.*, Feronia (*Italian deity*).

ferox, -ocis, bold, warlike ; high-spirited ; aggressive (51. 7) ; emboldened ; desperate (40. 5).
ferramentum, -i, *n.,* implement (*of iron*).
ferratus, -a, -um, shod with iron.
ferrum, -i, *n.,* iron, weapon, sword.
fessus, -a, -um, weary.
festino (1), hasten.
fetialis, -e, fetial ; *as noun,* Fetial priest.
Ficana, -ae, *f.,* Latin city.
Ficulea, -ae, *f.,* Ficulea.
ficus, -i (us), *f.,* fig-tree.
fidelis, -e, faithful, trusty.
Fidenae, -arum, *f. pl.,* Fidenae.
Fidenas, -atis, of Fidenae ; **Fidenates, -ium,** *m. pl.,* people of Fidenae.
fides, -ei, *f.,* trust, good faith ; allegiance ; loyalty ; pledge, protection ; credibility ; reliability, honour (9. 13).
fiducia, -ae, *f.,* confidence.
fidus, -a, -um, faithful, reliable.
figo, -ere, -xi, -xum (3), fix, hang up.
filia, -ae, *f.,* daughter.
filius, -i, *m.,* son.
filum, -i, *n.,* thread, band.
finio (4), finish, limit, fix, fix upon.
finis, -is, *m.,* boundary ; *pl.,* territory.
finitimus, -a, -um, neighbouring ; *as noun,* neighbour.
fio, fieri, factus sum, am made, am held ; am committed ; **ut fit, as** happens, as is usual.
firmo (1), strengthen.
firmus, -a, -um, strong, firm.
flamen, -inis, *m.,* flamen, priest.
flamma, -ae, *f.,* flame.

flebiliter, *adv.,* tearfully, weeping.
flecto, -ere, -xi, -xum (3), bend, turn ; **viam flectere,** make a circuit.
floreo (2), flourish.
fluctuo (1), waver.
fluito (1), float.
flumen, -inis, *n.,* river.
fluvius, -i, *m.,* river, stream.
foede, *adv.,* foully, hideously.
foeditas, -tatis, *f.,* hideousness, horror.
foedus, -a, -um, foul, detestable, shameful.
foedus, -eris, *n.,* treaty.
fons, fontis, *m.,* spring.
foras, *or* **foris,** *adv.,* out of doors, abroad ; outwards.
foris, -is, *f.,* door.
forma, -ae, *f.,* form, beauty.
formo (1), shape, model.
formula, -ae, *f.,* form.
fors, fortis, *f.,* chance ; **forte, by** chance, at haphazard.
forsitan, *adv.,* perhaps.
fortis, -e, brave, courageous.
fortuna, -ae, *f.,* fortune, fate ; *pl.,* property, state.
forum, -i, *n.,* forum.
forus, -i, *m.,* bench.
fossa, -ae, *f.* ditch, trench.
fragor, -oris, *m.,* crash.
frango, -ere, fregi, fractum (3), break.
frater, -tris, *m,* brother.
fraus, fraudis, *f.,* deceit, harm : **fraude,** treacherously (11. 9).
fremo, -ere, -ui, -itum (3), murmur.
frenum, -i, *n.,* rein.
frequens, -ntis, crowded, in crowds *or* numbers.

frequenter, *adv.*, in large numbers ; *compar.*, frequentius, more populously.

frequentia, -ae, *f.*, large number.

fretum, -i, *n.*, strait, channel.

fretus, -a, -um, relying on (*with abl.*).

frugifer, -era, -um, (fruit-bearing), remunerative.

fruor, -i, fructus (3), enjoy (*with abl.*).

frustror (1), disappoint, cheat.

Fufetius, -i, *m.*, Mettius Fufetius.

fuga, -ae, *f.*, flight, exile.

fugio, -ere, fugi, flee.

fugo (1), put to flight.

fulgeo, -ere, -si, -sum (2), shine, glitter.

fulmen, -inis, *n.*, lightning, thunderbolt.

funda, -ae, *f.*, sling.

fundamentum, -i, *n.*, foundation.

fundo, -ere, fudi, fusum (3), rout, put to flight.

funebris, -e, of funerals ; *in n. pl.*, funeral rites.

fungor, -i, functus (3), (*with abl.*) perform ; hold.

funus, -eris, *n.*, funeral, death.

furca, -ae, *f.*, fork ; props.

furia, -ae, *f.*, desire, frenzy ; avenging spirit.

Fusius, -i, *m.*, Spurius Fusius.

futurus, -a, -um, *fut. part. of* sum, future.

Gabii, -orum, *m. pl.*, Gabii.

Gabini, -orum, *m. pl.*, the men of Gabii.

galea, -ae, *f.*, helmet.

gaudium, -i, *n.*, joy, rejoicing.

Geganii, -orum, *m. pl.*, the Geganii.

gemino (1), double.

geminus, -a, -um, twin.

gemmatus, -a, -um, jewelled.

gener, -eri, *m.*, son-in-law.

genitus, *see* gigno.

gens, gentis, *f.*, tribe, nature, race, people, family.

genus, -eris, *n.*, kind, race.

gero, -ere, gessi, gestum (3), do, wage (*of war*) ; display (25. 3).

Geryon, -onis, *m.*, Geryon.

gigno, -ere, genui, genitum (3), beget, produce ; genitus, -a, -um, born.

gladius, -i, *m.*, sword.

globus, -i, *m.*, body (5. 7) ; band (12. 9), gang.

glomero (1), form into a ball.

gloria, -ae, *f.*, glory, renown.

glorior (1), boast.

Graecia, -ae, *f.*, Greece.

Graecus, -a, -um, Greek.

Gradivus, title of Mars.

gradus, -us, *m.*, step ; gradation (43. 10).

gramen, -inis, *n.*, grass.

grando, -inis, *f.*, hail, hailstones.

gratia, -ae, *f.*, affection, favour ; gratiam inire, to win favour. gratias agere, to thank.

gratuitus, -a, -um, without pay *or* effect ; ineffective.

gratulor (1), congratulate (*acc. of thing ; dat. of person*).

gratus, -a, -um, pleasing, dear.

gravatim, *adv.*, reluctantly.

gravidus, -a, -um, pregnant.

gravis, -e, heavy, weighty ; formidable (40. 4).

gravo (1), burden, make heavy.

gravor (1), be reluctant, regard as a burden (56. 1).
grex, gregis, m., troop.

habeo (2), have, hold.
habito (1), live, inhabit.
habitus, -us, m., bearing ; possession (42. 5).
Hadriaticus, -a, -um, Adriatic.
haereo, -ere, -si, -sum (2), stick.
haruspex, -icis, m., soothsayer, diviner.
hasta, -ae, f., spear, lance.
haud, adv., not.
haudquaquam, adv., by no means.
Helena, -ae, f., Helen.
Heraclea, -ae, f., Heraclea (a city).
herba, -ae, f., grass.
herbidus, -a, -um, grassy.
Hercules, -is, m., Hercules.
Herdonius, -i, m., Turnus Herdonius.
heres, -edis, c., heir.
Hernici, -orum, m. pl., the Hernici.
Hersilia, -ae, f., Hersilia.
hesternus, -a, -um, yesterday's ; of yesterday.
hic or hice, haec, hoc, this ; he, she, it ; pl., they ; the other (cf. ille).
hic, adv., here.
hinc, adv., hence, from here, on this side ; hinc . . . hinc, on one side . . . on the other.
hodie, adv., today.
hodiernus, -a, -um, today's.
homo, hominis, c., human being, man.
honestas, -tatis, f., honourableness.
honestus, -a, -um, honourable, respectable.

honoro (1), honour.
honos, -oris, m., honour, advancement ; respect ; rank (8. 7).
hora, -ae, f., hour.
Horatia, -ae, f., Horatia.
Horatii, -orum, m. pl., the Horatii.
Horatius, -i, m., Horatius (Publius), (i) father of the three Horatii, (ii) the survivor of the three Horatii.
Horatius, -a, -um, of the Horatii.
horrendus, -a, -um, dread, dreadful.
horreo (2), shudder, dread.
horror, -oris, m., horror, shudder, awe.
hortus, -i, m., garden.
hospes, -itis, m., host or guest ; stranger.
hospitalis, -e, hospitable ; used for a guest.
hospitaliter, adv., hospitably.
hospitium, -i, n., hospitality ; tie of hospitality.
hostia, -ae, f., victim.
hostilis, -e, hostile, of the foe.
hostiliter, adv., in hostile manner.
Hostilius, -i, m., Tullus Hostilius.
Hostilius, -a, -um, of Hostilius.
hostis, -is, c., enemy.
Hostius, -i, m., Hostius Hostilius.
huc, adv., hither.
humanus, -a, -um, human, profane.
humilis, -e, humble, lowly.

iaceo (2), lie.
iacio, -ere, ieci, iactum, throw, lay (foundations).
iacto, (1), discuss,

iam, *adv.*, now, already; then (6. 1); iam ab inde initio, from the very first.

Ianiculum, -i, *m.*, the Janiculum.

Ianus, -i, *m.*, Janus.

ibi, *adv.*, there.

ico, -ere, ici, ictum (3), strike, smite; foedus icere, make a treaty.

ictus, -us, *m.*, blow.

idem, eadem, idem, same, he too, likewise.

identidem, *adv.*, repeatedly.

igitur, *conj.*, therefore.

ignarus, -a, -um, ignorant.

ignavia, -ae, *f.*, cowardice.

ignis, -is, *m.*, fire.

ignoro (1), not know

ignotus, -a, -um, unknown.

Ilium, -i, *n.*, Ilium (Troy).

ille, illa, illud, that; he, she, it; the one (cf. hic).

imago, -inis, *f.*, image, likeness; mask.

imbellis, -e, unwarlike.

imbuo, -ere, -i, -tum (3), imbue, impregnate.

imitatio, -ionis, *f.*, imitation.

imitor (1), copy, imitate.

immaturus, -a, -um, unseasonable.

immemor, -oris, *m.*, forgetful, unreasonable; making no mention of (34. 3).

immensus, -a, -um, infinite.

immigro (1), penetrate.

immineo (2), overlook; imminens, impending, threatening.

imminuo, -ere, -i, -tum (3) diminish, reduce.

immitto, -ere, -misi, -missum (3), send into, loose against.

immo, *adv.*, on the contrary.

immolo (1), sacrifice.

immortalis, -e, immortal.

immortalitas, -tatis, *f.*, immortality.

immunis, -e, exempt (from).

impar, -paris, unequal, unlike.

impedio (4), hinder.

impello, -ere, -puli, -pulsum (3), break.

impensa, -ae, *f.*, outlay.

impense, *adv.*, fiercely, vehemently; *compar.*, impensius.

imperator, -oris, *m.*, commander; emperor.

imperfectus, -a, -um, unaccomplished.

imperito (1), rule.

imperitus, -a, -um, ignorant.

imperium, -i, *n.*, order, authority, dominion; sovereignty, government, power.

impero (1), order, command (*with dat.*).

impetro (1), obtain (request).

impetus, -us, *m.*, attack, charge; pushing (41. 4).

impie, *adv.*, impiously.

impiger, -gra, -grum, active, energetic; *adv.*, impigre.

impingo, -ere, -pegi, -pactum (3), strike against.

impius, -a, -um, undutiful, unnatural.

impleo, -ere, -plevi, -pletum (2), fill, fulfil.

implico (1), involve.

impono, -ere, -posui, -positum (3), place in *or* on.

impudens, -entis, immodest.

impudicus, -a, -um, unchaste.

impune, *adv.*, with impunity.

in, *prep. with abl.*, in, on ; *with acc.*, into, on to, to, towards, for ; over (in urbem).

inaedifico (1), build on.

inambulo (1), walk in.

inaugurato, *adv.*, after taking auspices.

inauguro (1), take auspices ; consecrate, instal, inaugurate..

incalesco, -ere, -ui (3), grow hot.

incautus, -a, -um, off one's guard.

incedo, -ere, -cessi, -cessum (3), advance ; (*transit.*) attack, seize.

incendo, -ere, -di, -sum (3), set on fire, inflame.

incensus, -a, -um, not registered ; *as noun*, unregistered person.

inceptus, -us, *m.*, undertaking, beginning.

incertus, -a, -um, uncertain, indecisive ; as yet undecided ; illegitimate (4. 2) ; bewildered (7. 6).

inceste, *adv.*, impurely.

incido, -ere, -cidi, -casum (3), happen ; encounter.

incipio, -ere, -cepi, -ceptum, begin.

incito (1), incite, stir.

inclamo (1), cry, call out to.

inclino (1), make to waver (58. 4) ; predispose (51. 7) ; make to fall back (27. 11) ; transfer (27. 6, 43. 9, 47. 12) ; *pass.*, waver (12. 3) ; *intrans.*, incline.

inclitus, -a, -um, famous.

includo, -ere, -si, -sum (3), shut up.

incoho (1), begin.

incolo, -ere, -ui (3), dwell, inhabit.

incolumis, -e, unhurt, unharmed ; unimpaired, intact.

incorruptus, -a, -um, genuine, pure, incorruptible.

incrementum, -i, *n.*, addition, growth.

increpito (1), speak angrily.

increpo, -are, -ui, -itum (1), clash. speak angrily ; upbraid (26. 3) ; rebuke (27. 8) ; taunt (47. 6).

incresco, -ere, -crevi, -cretum (3), grow.

incurro, -ere, -curri, -cursum (3), charge.

incursio, -ionis, *f.*, incursion.

incuso (1), blame, protest against.

incutio, -ere, -cussi, -cussum, strike into ; inspire.

inde, *adv.*, thence, from that point ; then ; in consequence of that.

index, -icis, *c.*, indicator.

indico (1), signify, show.

indico, -ere, -xi, -ctum (3), proclaim, declare.

indictus, -a, -um, not pleaded.

indiges, -etis, born in the country.

indignatio, -ionis, *f.*, indignation.

indignitas, -tatis, *f.*, indignity, outrage.

indignor (1), be indignant at, resent.

indignus, -a, -um, unworthy ; shameful.

indo, -ere, -didi, -ditum (3), place *or* put on, give to.

indoles, -is, *f.*, natural qualities, character, capacity.

induco, -ere, -xi, -ctum (3), draw over ; in animum inducere, make up the mind.

indulgentia, -ae, *f.*, indulgence ; solicitude.

induo, -ere, -i, -tum (3), put on.

industria, -ae, *f.*, diligence ; **ex** *or*
de ind., purposely.

indutiae, -arum, *f. pl.*, truce.

ineo, -ire-ii, (ivi), -itum, enter into ;
in gratiam inire, gain favour ;
in viam (rationem), adopt a
method *or* plan; suffragium inire,
to begin voting.

inermis, -e, unarmed.

iners, -tis, useless.

infandus, -a, -um, unspeakable,
abominable.

infans, -fantis, *c.*, infant.

infeliciter, *adv.*, unsuccessfully.

infelix, -icis, unfruitful, barren
(26. 6) ; unsuccessful.

infensus, -a, -um, hostile.

inferior, -us, lower.

infernus, -a, -um, of the lower
world.

infero, -ferre, -tuli, -latum, bring
on, to, into. se inferre, go ;
arma inferre, attack ; bellum
inferre, *with dat.*, make war on.

infestus, -a, -um, hostile, dangerous ; in danger (47. 1) ; infestis
armis, with drawn swords.

infidus, -a, -um, faithless.

infimus, -a, -um, lowest, end of ;
foot of ; ex infimo, from the
humblest beginnings.

infit, *defect. vb.*, begins to speak.

infortunium, -i, *n.*, misfortune.

infra, *prep. with acc., and adv.*, below.

ingenium, -i, *n.*, nature, disposition ; temper (57. 7).

ingens, -tis, enormous, large,
mighty.

ingigno, -ere, -genui, -genitum (3),
implant ; ingenitus, innate.

ingratus, -a, -um, displeasing.

ingredior, -i, -gressus, enter.

inhaereo, -ere, -si, -sum (2), be
fastened.

inhibeo (2), check, pull up.

inhumanus, -a, -um, inhuman.

inicio, -ere, -ieci, -iectum, fasten
on ; instil.

inimicus, -a, -um, unfriendly : *as
noun*, foe.

iniquus, -a, -um, uneven, dis-
advantageous.

initium, -i, *n.*, beginning ; ab
initio, from the first.

iniuria, -ae, *f.*, injury, injustice,
outrage, injurious treatment.

iniussu, *adv.*, without orders or
election.

iniustus, -a, -um, unjust.

inligo (1), bind on to.

inlucesco, -ere, -xi (3), dawn.

inlustris, -e, clear.

innoxius, -a, -um, innocent.

innubo, -ere, -psi, -ptum (3), marry
into.

inopia, -ae, *f.*, want, poverty ;
lack.

inops, -opis, needy, poor.

inquam (*defect. v.*), say ; inquit,
he said.

inquietus, -a, -um, restless.

inrito (1), provoke.

inritus, -a, -um, in vain.

inrumpo, -ere, -rupi, -ruptum (3),
burst in.

insanabilis, -e, incurable.

inscius, -a, -um, ignorant, un-
knowing.

insectatio, -ionis, *f.*, attack ; abuse,
railing.

insepultus, -a, -um, unburied.

insideo, -ere, -sedi, -sessum (2), abide with.

insidiae, -arum, *f. pl.*, ambush.

insidior (1), lay ambush (*with dat.*).

insigne, -is, *n.*, distinctive mark ; *in pl.*, dress, insignia.

insignis, -e, distinctive, distinguished, conspicuous, known.

insitus, -a, -um, innate.

insons, -ntis, innocent.

insperatus, -a, -um, unlooked for ; ex insperato, unexpectedly.

inspicio, -ere, -spexi, -spectum, examine.

instigo (1), stimulate, work upon.

instinguo, -ere, -xi, -ctum (3), incite, animate.

instituo, -ere, -i, -tum (3), appoint, institute ; establish (*custom*) ; lay down ; institutum, -i, *n.*, institution.

insto, -are, -stiti, -statum (1), press on, insist ; press hard upon (*with dat.*).

instructe, *adv.*, magnificently.

instruo, -ere, -xi, -ctum (3), draw up, marshall ; train ; form, fashion.

insulto (1), trample on (*with dat.*) ; behave insolently.

insum, -esse, -fui, am in.

intactus, -a, -um, untouched, unhurt.

integer, -gra, -grum, intact, unwounded, unhurt ; de integro, afresh.

integro (1), renew.

intelligo, -ere, -lexi, -lectum (3), understand.

intendo, -ere, -di, -tum (sum) (3), stretch deepen (57. 8) ; *in pass.*

concentrate ; intentus, eager for (*with dat.*) ; intent on, engrossed in.

inter, *prep. with acc.*, between, among, within, amid, in the midst of ; inter se, together.

intercalarius, -a, -um, intercalary.

intercludo, -ere, -si, -sum (3), cut off.

interdiu, *adv.*, by day.

interdum, *adv.*, sometimes, from time to time.

interea, *adv.*, meanwhile.

intereo, -ire, -ii (ivi), -itum, perish.

interficio, -ere, -feci, -fectum, kill.

intericio, -ere, -ieci, -iectum, interpose ; *pass.*, lie between ; intervene (58. 1).

interim, *adv.*, in the meantime, meanwhile.

interimo, -ere, -emi, -emptum (3), destroy.

interior, -us, inner.

interluceo, -ere, -xi (2), shine between.

interpono, -ere, -posui, -positum (3), insert.

interpres, -etis, *c.*, interpreter.

interpretor (1), interpret, explain ; lay it down.

interregnum, -i, *n.*, interregnum.

interrex, -regis, *m.*, interrex.

interrogo (1), ask.

intersaepio, -ire, -si, -tum (4), fence ; hide from (27. 9).

intersum, -esse, -fui, be between ; take part in ; be interested in ; (*often with dat.*).

intervallum, -i, *n.*, interval, lapse.

intervenio, -ire, -veni, -ventum (4), interrupt (*often with dat.*).

intestinus, -a, -um, domestic, intestine.

intimus, -a -um, inmost.

intolerabilis, -e, unbearable.

intra, *prep. with acc.*, within.

intro (1), enter.

intueor (2), gaze at, look at, behold.

inultus, -a, -um, unavenged.

Inuus, -i, *m.*, Inuus (name of Lupercus).

invado, -ere, -si, -sum (3), attack.

inveho, -ere, -xi, -ctum (3), carry in ; *in pass.*, ride into *or* upon *or* against ; (50. 3) inveigh against.

invenio, -ire, -veni, -ventum (4), find.

invideo, -ere, -vidi, -visum (2), be jealous.

invidia, -ae, *f.*, jealousy, unpopularity ; discontent, resentment.

inviso, -ere, -i, -um (3), go to see.

invisus, -a, -um, hated, hateful.

invito (1), invite, entertain.

invitus, -a, -um, unwilling ; with reluctance.

invoco (1), call upon, invoke.

involvo, -ere, -vi, -utum (3), wrap, cover.

iocus, -i, *m.*, joke, sport.

Iovem, *see* Iuppiter.

ipse, -a, -um, self.

ira, -ae, *f.*, anger, animosity.

irascor, -i, iratus, be angered.

iratus, -a, -um, angry.

is, ea, id, he, she, it ; that ; such.

iste, -a, -ud, that (of yours) ; this.

istic, *adv.*, there ; in your case (47. 3).

ita, *adv.*, thus, so.

Italia, -ae, *f.*, Italy.

Italicus, -a, -um, Italian.

itaque, *conj.*, and so, accordingly.

item, *adv.*, likewise.

iter, itineris, *n.*, journey, route, passage.

itero (1), repeat.

iterum, *adv.*, the second time, twice ; again.

iubeo, -ere, -iussi, -iussum (2), order, bid ; ordain ; elect.

iudicium, -i, *n.*, trial ; court ;

iudico (1), judge ; find guilty of ; pass judgment upon.

iugulo (1), cut throat of ; kill.

iugulum, -i, *n.*, throat.

ingum, -i, *n.*, yoke.

Iulius, -a, -um, of Julius, Julian.

Iulius, -i, *m.*, (Proculus) Iulius (*a senator*).

Iulus, -i, *m.*, Iulus (*son of Aeneas*).

iumentum, -i, *n.*, carriage-horse.

iungo, -ere, -xi, -ctum (3), join, unite, link ; make (*a treaty or alliance*).

iuniores, -um, *m. pl.*, juniors.

Iuppiter, Iovis, *m.*, Jupiter.

iuro (1), swear.

iure, rightly, justly.

ius, iuris, *n.*, right, privilege (56. 8), law, justice ; *quasi adj.*, lawful (2. 6).

ius iurandum, iuris iurandi, *n.*, oath ; the sworn oath (21. 1).

iussus, -us, *m.*, only *in abl.*, by the order, election, consent (of).

iuste, *adv.*, justly.

iustitia, -ae, *f.*, justice.

iustus, -a, -um, just, regular.

iuvenalis, -e, youthful.

iuvenis, -is, young ; *as noun*, young man, youth.

iuventa, -ae, *f.*, youth.

iuventus, -utis, *f.*, youth.
iuvo, -are, iuvi, iutum, help, assist.
iuxta, *adv.*, equally.

labor, -oris, *m.*, labour, toil.
labor, -i, lapsus (3), glide, slip.
laboro (1), work ; be distressed *or* in difficulties.
lacer, -era, -rum, torn.
lacrima, -ae, *f.*, tear.
lacus, -us, *m.*, lake.
laetus, -a, -um, glad, rejoicing, pleased ; abundant (7. 4).
laeva, -ae, *f.*, left hand.
laevus, -a, -um, left.
lambo, -ere, -i (3), lick.
lana, -ae, *f.*, wool.
languidus, -a, -um, languid, inert, still.
lapicida, -ae, *m.*, stone-cutter.
lapideus, -a, -um, of stone.
lapis, -idis, *m.*, stone.
laqueus, -i, *m.*, noose.
lar, laris, *m.*, household god.
Larentia, -ae, *f.*, Larentia (*wife of Faustulus*).
largior (4), bestow lavishly.
largitio, -ionis, *f.*, grant, distribution.
lascivia, -ae, *f.*, merriment, frolic.
late, *adv.*, far and wide, extensively.
lateo (2), lie hid, lurk.
Latine, *adv.*, in Latin ; **Latine scire,** to understand Latin.
Latinus, -a, -um, of Latium, Latin ; *as noun,* a Latin.
Latinus, -i, *m.*, Latinus (*King*).
Latinus, -i, *m.*, Silvius Latinus (*Alban king*).
Latium, -i, *n.*, Latium.
latro, -onis, *m* , robber.

latus, -eris, *n.*, side, flank.
laudo (1), praise.
Laurens, -tis, Laurentine.
Laurentes, -ium, *m. pl.*, the Laurentes.
Laurentinus, -a, -um, Laurentine.
laus, laudis, *f.*, praise, honour.
Lavinia, -ae, *f.*, Lavinia.
Lavinium, -i, *n.*, Lavinium.
lectus, -i, *m.*, bed.
legatio, -ionis, *f.*, embassy.
legatus, -i, *m.*, ambassador, envoy.
legio, -ionis, *f.*, levy.
legitimus, -a, -um, lawful.
lego, -ere, legi, lectum (3), send, select, choose, elect, enrol.
lego (1), commission, bequeath.
lenio (4,) soothe.
lenis, -e, gentle, quiet ; stagnant (4. 4).
leniter, *adv.*, gently.
lente, *adv.*, slowly.
lentus, -a, -um, slow, tedious.
letum, -i, *n.*, death.
levis, -e, light, easy.
leviter, *adv.*, lightly.
levo (1), raise.
lex, legis, *f.*, law, terms.
libenter, *adv.*, willingly.
liber, -era, -um, free.
liberalis, -e, liberal, generous.
liberaliter, *adv.*, generously.
liberator, -oris, *m.*, deliverer.
liberi, -orum, *m. pl.*, children.
libero (1), free.
libertas, -tatis, *f.*, liberty, freedom.
libido, -inis, *f.*, desire, lust.
licentia, -ae, *f.*, license, leave.
licet (2), *impers.*, it is allowed.
lictor, -oris, *m.*, lictor.
ligneus, -a, -um, of wood.

lignum, -i, *n.*, wood.

limen, -inis, *n.*, doorway.

lingua, -ae, *f.*, tongue.

liqueo, -ere, liqui (licui) (2), be clear.

lis, litis, *f.*, dispute, suit.

littera, -ae, *f.*, letter.

lituus, -i, *m.*, lituus (*augur's staff*).

loco (1), place, establish, pitch.

locuples, -etis, rich.

locus, -i, *m.*, place, room, position ; *pl.*, loca, -orum, *n. pl.*, parts, site.

longe, *adv.*, far, by far ; longe ante, far beyond.

longinquus, -a, -um, protracted.

longitudo, -inis, *f.*, length.

longus, -a, -um, long.

loquor, -i, locutus (3), speak.

lorica, -ae, *f.*, cuirass.

Luceres, -um, *m. pl.*, the Luceres.

Lucretia, -ae, *f.*, Lucretia.

Lucretius, -i, *m.*, Spurius Lucretius.

luctus, -us, *m.*, grief, mourning.

lucubro (1), work by lamplight.

Lucumo, -onis, *m.*, Lucumo (= L. Tarquinius).

lucus, -i, *m.*, grove.

ludibrium, -i, *n.*, mockery (7. 2) ; joke.

ludicrum, -i, *n.*, show, sport, festival.

ludificor (1), make sport of.

ludus, -i, *m.*, game. ludos facere, to hold games.

lugeo, -ere, -xi, -ctum (2), mourn.

lumen, -inis, *n.*, light.

luna, -ae, *f.*, moon.

luo, -ere, lui (3), atone for, expiate.

lupa, -ae, *f.*, she-wolf.

Lupercalia, -um, *n. pl.*, festival of Lupercus.

lustralis, -e, purificatory.

lustro (1), purify.

lustrum, -i, *n.*, purification (*of city*).

lusus, -us, *m.*, play, sport.

lux, -cis, *f.*, light. prima lux, dawn.

luxuria, -ae, *f.*, luxury, indulgence.

luxurio (1), be luxuriant *or* indulgent ; run riot.

luxus, -us, *m.*, luxury.

Lycaeus, -a, -um, Lycaean.

Macedonia, -ae, *f.*, Macedonia.

machina, -ae, *f.*, engine.

machinator, -oris, *m.*, contriver, plotter.

machinor (1), contrive, plot.

maculo (1), stain.

Maesius, -a, -um, Maesian.

maestitia, -ae, *f.*, sadness.

maestus, -a, -um, sad, gloomy, sorrowful ; griefstricken (58. 5).

magis, *adv.*, more ; rather.

magister, -tri, *m.*, master.

magistratus, -us, *m.*, magistrate.

magnificentia, -ae, *f.*, splendour.

magnificus, -a, -um, splendid.

magnitudo, -inis, *f.*, greatness, size.

magnopere, *adv.*, greatly, very much.

magnus, -a, -um, great.

maiestas, -tatis, *f.*, majesty.

maior, -us, greater ; maior natu, elder.

male, *adv.*, badly.

maledictum, -i, *n.*, abuse.

Malitiosa (Silva), the Malitiosa forest.

malo, malle, malui, prefer.

malum, -i, *n.*, curse, disaster.

malus, -a, -um, bad, evil.

Mamilius, -i, *m.*, Octavius Mamilius.

mamma, -ae, *f.*, dug.

mandatum, -i, *n.*, commission, order.

mando (1), entrust.

maneo, -ere, mansi, mansum (2), remain, wait ; endure.

Manes, -ium, *m. pl.*, shades *or* spirits (*of the departed*).

manifestus, -a, -um, caught red-handed (7. 9) ; flagrant (26. 12).

manipulus, -i, *m.*, company.

Manlius, -i, *m.*, Titus Manlius.

mano (1), spread ; drip.

manubiae, -arum, *f. pl.*, prize-money.

manus, -us, *f.*, hand ; power.

Marcius, -i, *m.*, Ancus Marcius.

Marcius, -i, *m.*, Numa Marcius (*a pontiff*).

Marcus, -i, *m.*, Marcus.

mare, -is, *n.*, sea.

maritus, -i, *m.*, husband.

Mars, Martis, *m.*, Mars (*god of war*) ; aequato Marte, on equal terms.

Martius, -a, -um, of Mars.

mater, -tris, *f.*, mother.

materia, -ae, *f.*, opportunity ; means ; cause (39. 3) ; stuff (46. 6).

maternus, -a, -um, maternal, mother's.

matrimonium, -i, *n.*, marriage ; in matrimonium ducere, to marry.

maturo (1), hasten, expedite ; maturatum, prompt action.

maturus, -a, -um, ripe ; quickly.

maxime, *adv.*, chiefly, particularly, especially, mainly.

maximus, -a, -um, greatest, very great ; eldest.

medium, -i, *n.*, midst, centre, middle.

medius, -a, -um, middle, midst of.

Medullia, -ae, *f.*, Medullia (*town*).

melior, -us, better.

melius, *adv.*, (*of above*), better.

membrum, -i, *n.*, member, limb.

memini, -isse, remember.

memor, -oris, mindful, remembering.

memoria, -ae, *f.*, memory ; recollection (5. 6) ; tradition.

memoro (1), record, relate.

mens, mentis, *f.*, mind, heart, attention.

mensis, -is, *m.*, month.

mentio, -ionis, *f.*, mention.

mercatus, -us, *m.*, market.

merces, -edis, *f.* pay.

mereor (2), earn, deserve ; meritus deserved, due ; meritum, -i, *n.*, service.

mergo, -ere, -si, -sum (3), plunge, drown.

meridies, -ei, *f.*, south.

meta, -ae, *f.*, goal ; position (19. 6).

Metapontum, -i, *n.*, Metapontum.

metor, (1), mark.

Mettius Fufetius, Mettius Fufetius (*Alban dictator*).

metuo, -ere, -i, -tum (3), fear; (*sometimes with dat.*).

metus, -us, *m.*, fear.

meus, -a, -um, my.

Mergentius, -i, *m.*, Mergentius.

mico, -are, -ui (1), flash.

migro (1), migrate.

miles, -itis, *m.*, soldier.

milia, -um, *n. pl.*, thousands.

militaris, -e, military ; res militaris, warfare.

militia, -ae, *f.*, military service ;
loc., militiae, on active service,
in war, on the field.

milito (1), serve as a soldier.

mille, thousand.

mina, -ae, *f.*, threat.

minax, -acis, threatening.

minime, *adv.*, least, not at all.

minimus, -a, -um, least, smallest ;
youngest.

minister, -tri, *m.*, servant, agent,
tool.

ministerium, -i, *n.*, office, service.

minor, -us, less, lesser ; younger.

minus, *adv.*, less ; less than.

minuo, -ere, -i, -tum (3), lessen,
diminish.

mirabilis, -e, astonishing.

miraculum, -i, *n.*, marvel, miracle ;
the supernatural.

mirandus, -a, -um, wonderful.

mire, *adv.*, wonderfully.

miror (1), wonder, admire ; be
surprised.

mirus, -a, -um, wonderful, strange.

misceo, -ere, -ui, -stum *or* -xtum (2),
mix, mingle, unite ; confuse
(29. 2).

miserabilis, -e, pitiable, plaintive ;
deplorable.

miseratio, -ionis, *f.*, pity.

miseria, -ae, *f.*, misery.

missilis, -e, for throwing.

mitigo (1), soften.

mitis, -e, gentle, mild, merciful.

mitto, -ere, misi, missum (3), send ;
throw, hurl.

moderatus, -a, -um, moderate,
temperate.

modicus, -a, -um, small.

modo, *adv.*, only.

modus, -i, *m.*, manner, way.

moenia, -ium, *n. pl.*, walls, fortifications.

moles, -is, *f.*, power, might ; effort
(38. 5).

molior (4), strive for, plan, devise.

mollio (4), soften, mitigate.

momentum, -i, *n.*, weight ; momentum facere, to exert influence.

moneo (2), warn, advise.

monitus, -us, *m.*, advice, counsel.

mons, montis, *m.*, mountain, hill.

monumentum, -i, *n.*, monument,
memorial (12. 6) ; reminder.

mora, -ae, *f.*, delay.

morbus, -i, *m.*, illness.

moribundus, -a, -um, dying.

morior, -i, mortuus, die.

moror (1), delay, linger ; nihil
morari, pay no attention to
(53. 10).

mors, mortis, *f.*, death.

mortalis, -e, mortal ; *in pl.*, men.

mortuus, -a, -um, dead.

mos, moris, *m.*, custom, manner ;
observance ; *in pl.*, character.

motus, -us, *m.*, movement ; rising
(59. 5, 60. 1).

moveo, -ere, movi, motum (2),
move, agitate, affect, rouse ;
numen movere, exert their divine
power ; arma movere, begin war.

mox, *adv.*, soon, presently.

mugio (4), roar, bellow ; low.

muliebris, -e, of a woman, a woman's.

mulier, -is, *f.*, woman.

multiplex, -icis, manifold, multi-
plied.

multiplico (1), multiply.

multitudo, -inis, *f.*, population, people, populace ; band (59. 6) ; multitude.

multo (1), fine, mulct, reprove ; bonis multare, to punish by confiscation.

multo, *adv.*, much.

multus, -a, -um, much ; *pl.*, many.

munia, *pl., only in nom. and acc.*, duties.

munifice, *adv.*, generously.

munificus, -a, -um, generous.

munimentum, -i, *n.*, fortification.

munio (4), build (8. 4) ; strengthen, protect.

munitio, -ionis, *f.*, fortification.

munus, -eris, *n.*, duty.

Murcia, title of Venus.

murus, -i, *m.*, wall.

mussito (1), mutter, grumble.

muto (1), change.

mutuus, -a, -um, mutual, reciprocated.

nam, for.

namque, for.

nanciscor, -i, nactus (3), obtain, get.

nascor, -i, natus (3), be born, arise, begin (9. 3) ; natus, born.

natus, -i, *m.*, son, child.

navis, -is, *f.*, ship.

Navius, -i, *m.*, Navius.

ne, *adv.*, not ; *conj.*, lest, that . . not ; ne . . . quidem, not even.

-ne, *enclitic particle to introduce direct questions ; in indirect questions,* whether.

nec, neque, not, nor, and not, but not ; neque . . . neque, neither . . . nor.

necdum, and not yet.

necessarius, -a, -um, imperative, necessary.

necesse, *only in nom. acc., sing. neut.*, essential.

necessitas, -tatis, *f.*, necessity ; inevitable course (42. 2).

necne, or not.

neco (1), kill, slay.

necopinatus, -a, -um, unexpected.

necto, -ere, -xui (xi), -xum, weave, concert (5. 7.).

nefandus, -a, -um, impious, unnatural.

nefas, *n., indecl.*, impiety.

nefastus, -a, -um, unpropitious for speech.

negligo, -ere, -exi, -ectum (3), neglect.

nego (1), refuse, deny.

negotiator, -oris, *m.*, trader.

negotium, -i, *n.*, task, work.

nemo, neminem, nullius, nemini, nullo, no one, nobody.

nepos, -otis, *m.*, grandson.

Neptunus, -i, *m.*, Neptune.

nequaquam, *adv.*, by no means.

nequiquam, *adv.*, to no purpose, in vain.

neuter, -tra, -trum, neither of two.

neutro, *adv.*, neither way, to neither side.

neve *or* neu, nor, and not.

nex, necis, *f.*, death.

ni = nisi, unless.

nihil, *neut. indecl.*, nothing

nihilo, *adv.*, by nothing, in no wise.

nimbus, -i, *m.*, cloud.

nimis, *adv.*, too much, too.

nimius, -a, -um, excessive ; nimio, by too much, far.

nisi, unless, if not ; *adv.*, except.

no (1), swim.
nobilis, -e, well-known, famous, noble.
nobilitas, -tatis, f., high fame, distinction ; advancement.
nobilito (1), make famous, obtain wide currency for.
nocturnus, -a, -um, at night.
nodus, -i, m., knot.
nolo, nolle, nolui, wish not, am unwilling, refuse.
nomen, -inis, n., name, reputation ; renown (9. 3) ; people bearing a name ; race.
Nomentum, -i, n., Nomentum.
nomino (1), nominate.
non, not.
nondum, not yet.
nos, we.
nosco, -ere, novi, notum (3), get to know, learn ; novi, I know.
noster, -tra, -trum, our.
notus, -a, -um, known, familiar.
notitia, -ae, f., acquaintance.
novacula, -ae, f., razor.
novem, nine.
novendialis, -e, of nine days.
noverca, -ae, f., step-mother.
novitas, -tatis, f., strangeness, novelty, newness.
novo (1), revolutionise.
novus, -a, -um, new, strange ; in superl., novissimus, last.
nox, noctis, f., night.
noxa, -ae, f., guilt.
nubes, -is, f., cloud.
nubo, -ere, -psi, -ptum (3), marry (of woman marrying a man), (with dat.).
nudo (1), expose ; uncover (of flank) (27. 7).

nudus, -a, -um, naked, exposed.
nullus, -a, -um, no ; as noun, no one.
Numa, -ae, m., Numa Pompilius.
numen, -inis, n., deity, divine power or will.
numero (1), count, reckon.
numerus, -i, m., number.
Numicus, -i, m., Numicus (a river).
Numitor, -oris, m., Numitor.
nunquam, adv., never.
nunc, adv., now, to this day.
nuncupo (1), call, name, solemnly declare.
nuntia, -ae, f., (female) messenger.
nuntius, -i, m., messenger ; news, message.
nuper, adv., lately.
nuptiae, -arum, f. pl., marriage.
nuptialis, -e, wedding (as adj.).
nurus, -us, f., daughter-in-law.
nusquam, nowhere.
nutrio (4), nurse, foster.

ob, prep. with acc., on account of, for.
obeo, -ire, -ii (ivi), -itum, discharge, perform.
obicio, -ere, -ieci, -iectum, throw or oppose against.
obiratus, -a, -um, angered, angry at (with dat..)
oblivio, -ionis, f., oblivion ; oblivioni dare, to consign to oblivion.
obliviscor, -i, oblitus (3), with gen., forget ; be careless of.
obloquor, -i, -locutus (3), interrupt.
obnoxius, -a, -um, slave to.
obnubo, -ere, -psi, -ptum (3), veil, cover.
oborior, -iri, -ortus (4), rise, well up.

obruo, -ere, -i, -tum (3), over-whelm.

obscurus, -a, -um, obscure.

obsequium, -i, *n.*, obedience.

obsero, -ere, -sevi, -situm (3), over-grow.

observantia, -ae, *f.*, respect.

observo (1), observe, respect.

obsideo, -ere, -sedi, -sessum (2), besiege, blockade.

obsidio, -ionis, *f.*, blockade.

obstino (1), set firmly ; obstinatus, resolute, obdurate.

obsto, -are, -stiti, -statum (1), stand in way of ; counteract, tell against (*often with dat.*).

obstrepo, -ere, -ui, -itum (3), drown.

obtentus, -us, *m.*, cover, shelter.

obtineo, -ere, -ui, -tentum (2), oc-cupy, keep, maintain, secure.

obtrunco (1), cut down, kill.

obverso (1), present to ; *in pass.*, occur to (25. 3).

obviam, *adv.*, in the way ; to meet (*with* ire, *etc.*).

obvius, -a, -um, in the way ; obvius fieri *or* esse, to meet, encounter ; obvium se dare, to meet (*often with dat.*).

occasio, -ionis, *f.*, opportunity.

occasus, -us, *m.*, west.

occido, -ere, -cidi, -casum (3), fall, set (*of sun*) ; disappear, perish.

occido, -ere, -cidi, -cisum (3), kill.

occipio, -ere, -cepi, -ceptum (3), begin.

occulo, -ere, -ui, -tum (3), hide.

occultus, -a, -um, secret ; **ex** occulto (37. 1), secretly.

occumbo, -ere, -cubui, -cubitum (3), fall prostrate *or* dead.

occupo (1), occupy ; *with infin.*, take the initiative, be the first to; occupatus, occupied.

occurro, -ere, -curri, -cursum (3), meet (*with dat.*).

ocrea, -ae, *f.*, greave.

octingenti, -ae, -a, eight hundred.

octo, eight.

octoginta, eighty.

oculus, -i, *m.*, eye.

odium, -i, *n.*, hatred.

offero, -ferre, obtuli, oblatum, offer, vouchsafe.

officio, -ere, -feci, -fectum, eclipse (*with dat.*).

officium, -i, *n.*, duty ; **officia** civilia, offices of state.

olim, *adv.*, formerly, once.

omen, -inis, *n.*, omen.

omitto, -ere, -misi, -missum (3), dismiss.

omnis, -e, all, every.

onus, oneris, *n.*, burden.

onustus, -a, -um, laden.

opacus, -a, -um, shady, dark.

opera, -ae, *f.*, work, aid, service ; operae est, it is worth while.

operio, -ire, -ui, -tum (4), cover.

operor (1), be busied.

opifex, -ficis, *m.*, workman.

opimus, -a, -um, rich.

opinio, -ionis, *f.*, belief.

opinor (1) think.

oportet (2), it is proper ; ought.

opperior (4), wait for, bide.

oppidum, -i, *n.*, town.

opportunus, -a, -um, suitable.

opprimo, -ere, -pressi, -pressum (3) crush, overwhelm, suppress, hold down.

[ops], opis, *f.* (*not in nom. and dat.*

sing.), aid ; energy, remedy ; *in pl.*, wealth, power ; **summa ope** (56. 11), with all possible care.

optimus, -a, -um, best.

opulente, *adv., compar.,* **opulentius,** on a richer scale.

opulentus, -a, -um, rich, powerful.

opus, operis, *n.,* work, deed, labour.

opus, *n., indecl.,* need ; **opus est,** there is need of (*with abl.*).

ora, -ae, *f.,* coast, region.

oraculum, -i, *n.,* oracle.

oratio, -ionis, *f.,* speech ; **orationem habere,** deliver a speech.

orator, -oris, *m.,* spokesman.

orbis, -is, *m.,* circle, cycle ; revolution ; **orbis terrarum,** the world.

orbitas, -tatis, *f.,* bereavement.

orbus, -a, -um, orphan, childless ; bereft (*with abl.,* 54. 10).

ordior, -iri, -orsus (4), begin, set out.

ordo, -inis, *m.,* order, class, rank ; senatorial order (49. 6) ; racial strain ; **ordine,** in order.

oriens, -tis, *m.,* east.

origo, -inis, *f.,* origin, foundation ; *pl.,* early history.

orior, -iri, ortus (4), arise, spring, be born.

oriundus, -a, -um, sprung *or* descended (from).

orno (1), equip.

oro (1), pray, beg, plead.

orsum, -i, *n.,* beginning.

os, oris, *n.,* mouth.

osculum, -i, *n.,* kiss.

ostendo, -ere, -di, -sum *or* **tum** (3), show, point out ; declare. **se ostendere,** to appear.

ostentator, -oris, *m.,* displayer.

ostento (1), display, point to.

Ostia, -ae, *f. or n. pl.,* Ostia.

otium, -i, *n.,* peace, rest ; free *or* spare time.

ovo (1), rejoice, exult.

pabulum, -i, *n.,* food.

pacisco, -ere, -pactus (3), betroth.

paciscor, -i, pactus (3), agree ; *perf. part. used in pass. meaning.*

pacatus, -a, -um, at peace.

paco (1), make peaceful.

pactum, -i, *n.,* bargain ; **way.**

paene, *adv.,* almost.

paenitet (2), it repents, discontents.

pagus, -i, *m.,* district.

palam, *adv.,* openly.

Palatinus, -a, -um, Palatine.

Palatius, -i, *m.,* the Palatine Hill.

Palatium, -i, *n.,* the Palatine Hill (old name **Pallantium,** 5. 1).

Pallanteum, -i, *n.,* Pallanteum (*in Arcadia*).

pallor, -oris, *m.,* pallor.

palor (1), struggle.

paludamentum, -i, *n.,* cloak (*military*).

palus, -udis, *f.,* swamp.

Pan, Panos, *m.,* Pan.

pando, -ere, -di, -nsum (-ssum) (3), dishevel.

pango, -ere, pepigi, pactum (3), fix ; bargain for (11. 8).

papaver, -is, *m.,* poppy.

Paphlagonia, -ae, *f.,* Paphlagonia.

par, paris, equal, a match for ; steadfast (26. 12).

parco, -ere, peperci (3), *with dat.,* spare.

parens, -ntis, parent, father.

pareo (2), *with dat.,* obey.

pario, -ere, peperi, partum, gain, win.

pariter, *adv.*, equally alike.

paro (1), make ready, prepare, prepare for ; paratus, prepared, ready.

parricidium, -i, *n.*, parricide, murder of kin.

pars, partis, *f.*, part, direction ; branch (30. 2) ; ab una parte, in one respect.

parsimonia, -ae, *f.*, frugality.

particeps, -cipis, *c.*, partner.

partus, -us, *m.*, motherhood (3. 11) ; offspring.

parum, *adv.*, too little, not enough.

parvus, -a, -um, small, little.

passim, *adv.*, in different directions, everywhere.

passus, -us, *m.*, step, pace : mille passus, mile.

pastor, -oris, *m.*, shepherd.

pateo (2), be open (to), be evident.

pater, -tris, *m.*, father, senator.

paternus, -a, -um, of a father, father's.

patientia, -ae, *f.*, patience.

patior, -i, passus, suffer, endure, allow.

patria, -ae, *f.*, fatherland, home ; native city.

patricius, -a, -um, patrician.

patrius, -a, -um, of a father, ancestral.

patro (1), accomplish, execute.

paucitas, -tatis, *f.*, fewness.

paucus, -a, -um, few, small.

paulatim, *adv.*, little by little.

paulo, *adv.*, a little.

pauper, -eris, poor.

paupertas, -tatis, *f.*, poverty.

pavidus, -a, -um, alarmed.

pavor, -oris, *m.*, fear, panic, terror.

pax, pacis, *f.*, peace.

peccatum, -i, *n.*, sin.

pecco (1), sin.

pectus, -oris, *n.*, breast ; heart.

pecunia, -ae, *f.*, money.

pecus, -oris, *n.*, cattle.

pedes, -itis, *m.*, foot-soldier ; *pl., or in sing.*, infantry.

pedester, -tris, -tre, on foot ; infantry.

peior, -us, worse.

peius, *adv.*, worse.

Peloponnesus, -i, *m.*, the Peloponnese.

pello, -ere, pepuli, pulsum (3), drive back.

Penates, -ium, *m. pl.*, the Penates (*gods of the store-chamber*).

pendo, -ere, pependi, pensum (3), pay.

penes, *prep. with acc.*, in power of; with.

penitus, *adv.*, deep, deeply.

penuria, -ae, *f.*, want, shortage.

per, *prep. with acc.*, through, throughout ; during, by, among, over.

perago, -ere, -egi, -actum (3), complete, finish, accomplish ; go through (24. 9) ; recite.

peragro (1), roam.

percello, -ere, -culi, -culsum (3), dismay.

percontor (1), ask.

percutio, -ere, -cussi, -cussum, strike, smite.

perdo, -ere, -didi, -ditum (3), destroy.

perduco, -ere, -duxi, -ductum (3), lead *or* carry through.

perduellio, -ionis, *f.*, high treason.

pereg in is, -a, -um, foreign ; *as noun*, a foreigner.

perennis, -e, perennial.

pereo, -ire, -ii (ivi), -itum, perish, be lost.

pererro (1), wander through.

perfero, -ferre, -tuli, -latum, convey ; *in pass.*, reach.

perficio, -ere, -feci, -fectum, finish, complete.

perfidia, -ae, *f.*, disloyalty.

perfidus, -a, -um, treacherous.

perfugio, -ere, -fugi, escape, flee.

perfundo, -ere, -fudi, -fusum (3), bathe ; paralyse (16. 6).

pergo, -ere, -rexi, -rectum (3), proceed, hasten.

periclitor (1), prove, test.

periculosus, -a, -um, dangerous.

periculum, -i, *n.*, danger.

perimo, -ere, -emi, -emptum (3), destroy.

peritus, -a, -um, skilled ; instructed in (*with gen.*).

perlustro (1), traverse, examine ; oculis perlustrare, to survey, glance over.

permitto, -ere, -misi, -missum (3), entrust.

perobscurus, -a, -um, very obscure.

peropportune, *adv.*, very opportunely.

perpello, -ere, -puli, -pulsum (3), drive, urge.

perperam, *adv.*, wrongly.

perpetro (1), finish ; attend to (8. 1).

perpetuitas, -tatis, *f.*, perpetuity.

perpetuus, -a, -um, perpetual ; in perpetuity.

persaepe, *adv.*, very often.

perscribo, -ere, -scripsi, -scriptum (3), write fully.

persequor, -i, -secutus (3), pursue.

persolvo, -ere, -solvi, -solutum (3), pay, perform.

perstringo, -ere, -strinxi, -strictum (3), graze ; chill, paralyse (25. 4).

persuadeo, -ere, -suasi, -suasum (2), persuade (*with dat.*).

perterreo (2), terrify.

pertineo, -ere, -ui (2), affect, belong to, concern.

perturbo (1), agitate, alarm.

pervagor (1), wander through.

pervenio, -ire, -veni, -ventum (4), arrive, reach ; extend.

pes, pedis, *m.*, foot ; foot (= 12 inches) (35. 9).

pessimus, -a, -um, worst, foul.

pestifer, -era, -erum, deadly.

pestilentia, -ae, *f.*, pestilence.

peto, -ere, -ivi (ii), -itum (3), seek, attack, make for ; beg, beseech.

piacularis, -e, purificatory, propitiatory.

piaculum, -i, *n.*, atonement, expiation.

Pictor, -oris, *m.*, Fabius Pictor.

pictus, *see* pingo.

pie, *adv.*, rightfully, righteously.

pietas, -tatis, *f.*, sense of duty, piety.

piget (2), *imperson.*, dislike, regret.

pigritia, -ae, *f.*, reluctance.

pila, -ae, *f.*, column.

Pila Horatia, the Horatian Column.

pilleus, -i, *m.*, *or n.*, pilleum, (felt) cap.

pilum, -i, *n.*, javelin.

Pinarii, -orum, *m. pl.*, the Pinarii (*Roman gens*).

pingo, -ere, pinxi, pictum (3), paint, embroider.

Piso, -onis, *m.*, Piso (*Roman historian*).

pius, -a, -um, dutiful, righteous, religious.

placeo (2), be pleasing, find favour with (*with dat.*) ; *imperson.*, it is decided.

placo (1), appease.

planus, -a, -um, plain, level.

plebs, plebis, *f.*, plebs, commons.

plenus, -a, -um, full ; completed ; crowded (*of gates*, 14. 8).

plerumque, *adv.*, for the most part.

plerusque, -aque, -umque, *in pl.*, the most.

pluo, -ere, -i (vi) (3), *imperson.*, it rains.

plurimum, *adv.*, most, mostly.

plurimus, -a, -um, very many.

plus, pluris, more.

plus, *adv.*, more.

poena, -ae, *f.*, punishment.

poeta, -ae, *m.*, poet.

poeticus, -a, -um, of a poet.

Politorium, -i, *n.*, Politorium.

polleo (2), be powerful.

polliceor (2), promise.

pomerium, -i, *n.*, the pomerium.

Pometinus, -a, -um, of Pometia.

Pompilius, -i, *m.*, Numa Pompilius.

pondo, *adv.*, by weight.

pondus, -eris, *n.*, weight.

pono, -ere, posui, positum (3), place, pitch, put ; lay *or* set aside.

pons, pontis, *m.*, bridge.

pontifex, -ficis, *m.*, priest, high priest.

populabundus, -a, -um, bent on raiding.

popularis, -e, of the people.

populor (1), lay waste.

populus, -i, *m.*, people, nation ; tribe.

porcus, -i, *m.*, pig.

porrigo, -ere, -rexi, -rectum (3), stretch out : porrectus, extending.

porro, *adv.*, forward, onwards.

porta, -ae, *f.*, gate.

portendo, -ere, -di, -ntum (3), hold out ; mean, portend.

portentum, -i, *n.*, portent.

porticus, -us, *f.*, colonnade.

porto (1), carry.

posco, -ere, poposci (3), demand.

possessio, -ionis, *f.*, right of holding.

possideo, -ere, -sedi, -sessum (2), hold, possess.

possum, posse, potui, be able, can.

post, *adv., and prep. with acc.*, after, since.

postea, *adv.*, afterwards.

posterus, -a, -um, after, next ; *in pl.*, posterity.

postmodum, *adv.*, afterwards.

postmoerium, the part behind the wall.

postquam, *conj.*, after, when.

postremo, *adv.*, finally.

postremus, -a, -um, last.

postulatum, -i, *n.*, demand.

postulo (1), demand.

potens, potentis, powerful ; rich (33. 5) ; sui potens, one's own master.

potestas, -tatis, *f.*, authority, power; opportunity.
potior, -ius, preferable.
potior (4), gain possession of (*with abl.*).
potissimum, most of all, especially.
potissimus, -a, -um, most suitable.
Potitii, -orum, *m. pl.*, the Potitii (*Latin gens*).
potius, *adv.*, rather.
poto (1), drink.
prae, *prep. with abl.*, before ; compared with ; prae se ferre, assert.
praebeo (2), afford, offer.
praeceps, -cipitis, headlong.
praecipio, -ere, -cepi, -ceptum, instruct.
praecipue, *adv.*, especially.
praecipuus, -a, -um, special.
praeco, -onis, *m.*, herald.
praeda, -ae, *f.*, plunder, booty.
praedor (1), plunder.
praefectus, -i, *m.*, prefect.
praefero, -ferre, -tuli, -latum, put . . . before, (*acc. and dat.*).
praeficio, -ere, -feci, -fectum, place over, appoint.
praefluo, -ere, -uxi, -uxum (3), flow by.
praemitto, -ere, -misi, -missum (3), send on in advance.
praemium, -i, *n.*, reward.
praeparo (1), get ready beforehand ; prepare.
praepolleo (2), be very powerful.
praesagio (4), have presentiment of.
praesens, -ntis, present, in person ; of the moment, immediate.
praeses, -idis, *c.*, protector, guardian.

praesidium, -i, *n.*, protection, guard ; garrison.
praesto, *adv.*, ready, present.
praesto, -are, -stiti, -stitum (statum) (1), excel (*with dat.*).
praesum, -esse, -fui, preside over (*with dat.*).
praeter, *prep. with acc.*, besides, except ; in addition to (57. 2).
praeterea, *adv.*, besides.
praetereo, -ire, -ii (ivi), -itum, go by *or* past ; pass ; praeteritum, past.
praeterquam, except ; praeterquam quod, besides the fact that.
praetexta, -ae, *f.*, (toga) praetexta.
praeuro, -ere, -ussi, -ustum (3), burn at the end ; harden in the fire.
praevaleo (2), predominate.
prave, *adv.*, improperly.
pravus, -a, -um, evil, improper.
precatio, -ionis, *f.*, prayer, entreaty.
precor (1), pray, entreat.
premo, -ere, pressi, pressum (3), press hard (57. 3).
prenso (1), solicit.
pretium, -i, *n.*, price, value.
[prex], prece, *f.*, *defect.*, prayer, entreaty.
pridem, *adv.*, long since.
primo, *adv.*, at first.
primordium, -i, *n.*, very beginning.
primores, -um, *m. pl.*, first rank (12. 7) ; leading men.
primum, *adv.*, first, in the first place ; quam primum, as soon as possible.
primus, -a, -um, first.
princeps, -ipis, foremost ; *as noun*, chief man.

principium, -i, *n.*, beginning.

prior, -us, former, first ;   last (58. 8).

priscus, -a, -um, old, former.

prius, *adv.*, first.

priusquam, *conj.*, before ;   *after neg.*, until.

privatim, *adv.*, in private ; unofficially.

privatus, -a, -um, private ; *as noun*, private citizen.

pro, *prep. with abl.*, instead of, for, before ; pro certo, for certain, as certain.

Procas (Proca), -ae, *m.*, Procas (*Alban king*).

procedo, -ere, -cessi, -cessum (3), advance, succeed.

procella, -ae, *f.*, storm, squall.

proceres, -um, *m. pl.*, chieftains, leading men.

proclamo (1), proclaim.

procreo (1), beget.

Proculus, -i, *m.*, Proculus.

procul, *adv.*, far, from afar.

procumbo, -ere, -cubui, -cubitum (3), lie down.

procuro (1), arrange.

prodeo, -ire, -ii (ivi), -itum, come forward.

prodigium, -i, *n.*, portent.

proditio, -ionis, *f.*, treason, treachery.

proditor, -oris, *m.*, traitor.

prodo, -ere, -didi, -ditum (3), hand down ; set (*an example*).

proelium, -i, *n.*, battle.

profecto, *adv.*, certainly, assuredly.

profero, -ferre, -tuli, -latum, extend.

proficiscor, -i, -fectus (3), start, set out.

profluo, -ere, -xi, -xum (3), flow forward.

profugio, -ere, -fugi, -fugitum (3), fly.

profugus, -a, -um, banished, an exile.

profundus, -a, -um, deep.

progenies, -ei, *f.*, offspring, descendants.

prognatus, -a, -um, born, descended.

prohibeo (2), check, hinder, prevent.

proinde, *adv.*, accordingly.

prolabor, -i, -lapsus (3), fall forward.

proles, -is, *f.*, offspring, stock.

promisce, *adv.*, without distinction.

promiscuus, -a, -um, promiscuous.

promptus, -a, -um, ready, handy ; bold (54. 2).

prope, *adv., and prep. with acc.*, near, almost.

prope diem, *adv.*, soon.

propere, *adv.*, hastily.

propinquitas, -tatis, *f.*, nearness.

propinquus, -a, -um, near, neighbouring ; *as noun*, relative.

propior, -us, nearer.

propitius, -a, -um, propitious, gracious.

propius, *adv.*, nearer.

propono, -ere, -posui, -positum (3), put forth ; display.

proprius, -a, -um, one's own.

propter, *prep. with acc.*, on account of.

propulso (1), repel.

prospectus, -us, *m.*, view.

prosper, -a, -um, successful.

protraho, -ere, -traxi, -tractum (3), draw forth, produce.

providentia, -ae, *f.*, foresight, providence.

provoco (1), appeal.

provolo (1), fly *or* rush forward.

proxime, *adv.*, very near ; quam proxime, as near as possible.

proximus, -a, -um, nearest, last ; very near.

prudentia, -ae, *f.*, knowledge.

puber (pubes), -eris, grown up, adult ; of manhood ; puberes, adult males.

pubes, -is, *f.*, youth (young man) ; soldiery.

publice, *adv.*, publicly ; at the public expense ; officially (26. 13).

publicum, -i, *n.*, state *or* public treasury.

publicus, -a, -um, public, the nation's, official ; in publico, in public.

pudicitia, -ae, *f.*, modesty.

puella, -ae, *f.*, girl.

puer, -i, *m.*, boy.

puerilis, -e, of a boy, boy's.

pugil, -is, *m.*, boxer.

pugna, -ae, *f.*, fighting, battle, combat ; attack.

pugno (1), fight.

pulchritudo, -inis, *f.*, beauty.

pulso (1), beat ; maltreat (14. 1).

pulvis, -eris, *m.*, dust.

Punicus, -a, -um, Carthaginian, Punic.

purgamentum, -i, *n.*, refuse.

purgo (1), clear, excuse ; make apologies (22. 6).

purus, -a, -um, pure, clear ; innocent.

puto (1), think, suppose.

Pylaemenes, -ae, *m.*, Pylaemenes.

Pythagoras, -ae, *m.*, Pythagoras.

Pythicus, -a, -um, Pythian.

qua, *adv.*, where, on which side.

quacumque, *adv.*, wherever.

quadrageni, -ae,-a, forty each.

quadraginta, forty.

quadrifariam, *adv.*, in four parts.

quadrigae, -arum, *f. pl.*, teams of four.

quadringenti, -ae, -a, four hundred.

quadro (1), square ; quadratus, -a, -um, squared, hewn.

quaero, -ere, quaesivi, quaesitum (3), seek, ask.

qualis, -e, *interrog.*, of what kind ; *relative*, as, (of such a kind) as.

quam, *adv.*, as, then, how ; how much.

quamquam, *conj.*, although.

quamvis, *conj.*, although ; however.

quando, when?

quando, ever (*after* si, nisi, ne, num).

quandoque, quandocumque, whenever.

quantus, -a, -um, how great *or* much ; (as great) as.

quartus, -a, -um, fourth.

quasi, *adv.*, as if, as though.

quattuor, four.

-que, and ; -que . . . -que, both . . . and.

quercus, -us, *f.*, oak.

querella, -ae, *f.*, lamentation.

queror, -i, questus (3), complain.

qui, quae, quod, *rel. pron.*, who, which, that ; what.

qui, quae, quod, *interrog. adj.*, what; *indefin. adj.*, any.

quia, *conj.*, because.
quicumque, quae-, quod-, whatever, whoever, whatsoever.
quid, *adv.*, why, how.
quidam, quaedam, quoddam, a certain.
quidem, indeed ; ne ... quidem, not even.
quies, quietis, *f.*, rest, quiet, respite ; hush.
quietus, -a, -um, quiet, at rest.
quilibet, quae-, quod-, any.
quin, *conj.*, but that ; that ... not, without ; *as adv.*, nay, why ... not.
Quinctii, -orum, *m. pl.*, the Quinctii.
quinquaginta, fifty.
quinque, five.
quippe, for, for of course.
Quirinalis, -e, Quirinal.
Quirinus, -i, *m.*, Quirinus (*Romulus*).
Quirites, -ium, *m. pl.*, the Quirites (= *Romans*).
quis, quid, who? what?
quis, quid, *indefin.*, anyone, anything.
quisnam, quaenam, quidnam, who (*pray*)?
quisquam, quicquam, anyone, any.
quisque, quaeque, quidque (quodque), cach.
quisquis, quicquid (quidquid), *adj.*, quodquod, whoever, whatever.
quo, whither?, to which?
quo, *relat. adv.*, whither, to which.
quoad, *adv.*, as long as.
quod, *conj.*, because, that ; quod si, but if.
quondam, *adv.*, formerly ; one day ; at one time.

quoniam, *conj.*, since.
quoque, *adv.*, also, too, even.

Ramnes (Ramnenses), -ium, *m. pl.*, the Ramnenses *or* Ramnes.
rapina, -ae, *f.*, robbery, plunder.
rapio, -ere, -ui, -tum, seize, carry off ; whirl ; rapta, -orum, *n. pl.*, plunder.
raptim, *adv.*, hurriedly, swiftly.
raro, *adv.*, rarely, seldom.
rarus, -a, -um, rare.
ratio, -ionis, *f.*, method.
ratis, -is, *f.*, raft, boat.
ratus, *from* reor.
ratus, -a, -um, fixed, valid ; ratum efficere, to ratify.
Rea, -ae, *f.*, Rea Silvia.
rebello (1), rebel, renew war.
recens, -ntis, new, recent.
recenseo, -ere, -ui, -um (2), review.
receptaculum, -i, *n.*, refuge, receptacle.
recipero (1), recover.
recipio, -ere, -cepi, -ceptum, receive, capture (55. 1) ; se recipere, betake oneself, make one's way, return.
recito (1), read aloud.
reconcilio (1), win back ; in gratiam reconciliare, reconcile.
recte, *adv.*, justifiably, rightly.
rectus, -a, -um, straight, right, upright, honest (27. 1) ; clear (24. 7).
recuso (1), refuse, object.
reddo, -ere, -didi, -ditum (3), give back, return ; answer (7. 7, 56. 10) ; iura reddere, administer justice.
redintegro (1), renew, begin afresh.

reduco, -ere, -xi, -ctum (3), lead back.

refello, -ere, -i (3), prove false, refute.

refero, -ferre, rettuli, relatum, bring back, report; relate (59. 10); referre gradum (14. 8), retreat.

reficio, -ere, -feci, -fectum, refresh (7. 4); make (of money).

regalis, -e, regal.

regia, -ae, f., palace, royal house, court.

regio, -ionis, f., district, quarter.

regius, -a, -um, royal, of a king or prince; kingly.

regno (1), reign, am king.

regnum, -i, n., kingdom, throne (46. 3), sovereign power; royal power, reign, monarchy.

rego, -ere, -xi, -ctum (3), rule.

religio, -ionis, f., religious scruple, observance, piety; in pl., worship.

relinquo, -ere, -liqui, -lictum (3), leave, abandon, give up.

reliquus, -a, -um, remaining.

remedium, -i, n., remedy.

Remus, -i, m., Remus.

renovo (1), renew.

renuntio (1), report.

reor, reri, ratus (2), think, believe.

repens, -ntis, sudden, fresh.

repente, adv., suddenly.

repentinus, -a, -um, sudden.

repeto, -ere, -ivi (ii), -itum (3), seek back or again; attack again; demand.

repono, -ere, -posui, -positum (3), place back.

reputo (1), reflect.

requiro, -ere, -quisivi, -quisitum (3), desire to regain.

res, rei, f., thing, affair, matter, deed, government, state; property; res repetere, to demand restitution or satisfaction; res militaris, warfare; rem divinam facere, to offer sacrifice.

reservo (1), keep back, reserve.

residuus, -a, -um, remaining over from (+gen.).

resisto, -ere, -stiti (3), resist (+dat.); rally; stop short (48. 6).

respergo, -ere, -si, -sum (3), besprinkle.

respicio, -ere, -spexi, -spectum, look back, regard.

respondeo, -ere, -di, -sum (2), reply, answer.

responsum, -i, n., answer.

restinguo, -ere, -xi, -ctum (3), extinguish.

restis, -is, f., rope.

retineo, -ere, -ui, -tum (2), detain, keep.

retro, adv., back, backwards.

reus, -i, m., accused person.

reveho, -ere, -vexi, -vectum (3), carry (home), bring back.

revereor (2), stand in awe of.

revoco (1), recall.

rex, regis, m., king.

rigo (1), water.

ripa, -ae, f., bank.

rite, adv., duly.

ritus, -us, m., rite, due form; ritual.

rixa, -ae, f., fight, quarrel.

robur, -oris, n., strength, toughness.

rogito (1), question, ask frequently.

rogo (1), ask; propose (17. 9).

Roma, -ae, *f.,* Rome.

Romanus, -a, -um, Roman.

Romularis, -e, of Romulus.

Romulus, -i, *m.,* Romulus.

Romulus, -i, Silvius, -i, *m.,* Romulus Silvius.

rudimentum, -i, *n.,* beginning, first attempt.

rudis, -e, uncivilised, unacquainted with (7. 8).

ruina, -ae, *f.,* downfall ; *pl.,* ruin, desolation (29. 6).

Ruminalis, -e, of Rumina.

rumpo, -ere, rupi, ruptum (3), break.

ruo, -ere, -i, -tum (3), rush.

ruptor, -oris, *m.,* breaker.

rursus, *adv.,* again.

Rutuli, -orum, *m. pl.,* the Rutuli.

Sabinus, -a, -um, Sabine ; *as noun,* a Sabine.

sacellum, -i, *n.,* chapel.

sacer, -cra, -crum, sacred, holy.

sacerdos, -otis, *c.,* priest, priestess.

sacerdotium, -i, *n.,* priestly office.

sacrarium, -i, *n.,* sanctuary, shrine.

sacratus, -a, -um, sacred.

sacrificium, -i, *n.,* sacrifice.

sacro (1), consecrate.

sacrum, -i, *n.,* sacred rite, sacrifice, religious observance.

saeculum, -i, *n.,* generation, age ; *pl.,* period, age.

saepe, *adv.,* often.

saepio, -ire, -psi, -ptum (4), enclose, hem in.

saevire in, show no mercy to.

saevitia, -ae, *f.* cruelty.

sagmen, -inis, *n.,* tuft (of sacred herbs).

Salii, -orum, *m. pl.,* the Salii.

salinae, -arum, *f. pl.,* salt pits or pans.

saltatus, -us, *m.,* leaping.

saltem, *adv.,* at least.

saltus, -us, *m.,* glade.

salubris, -e, healthy, salutary.

salus, -utis, *f.,* safety.

salutatio, -ionis, *f.,* salutation.

saluto (1), salute.

salveo (2), be well.

salve, *adv.,* well.

salvus, -a, -um, safe.

Samius, -a, -um, of Samos.

sancio, -ire, -xi, -ctum (4), ratify, solemnise.

sanctus, -a, -um, inviolable ; sacred (28. 9) ; binding (8. 2).

sane, *adv.,* certainly, by all means.

sanguineus, -a, -um, bloody.

sanguis, -inis, *m.,* blood.

satis, *adv.,* enough, adequately, well enough, sufficiently, quite.

saxum, -i, *n.,* stone.

sceleratus, -a, -um, of crime ; wicked.

scelus, -eris, *n.,* crime, guilt.

scilicet, *adv.,* of course.

scindo, -ere, scidi, scissum (3), rend.

scio (4), know.

sciscitor (1), question, ask.

scisco, -ere, scivi, scitum (3), resolve.

scitum, -i, *n.,* decision.

scribo, -ere, scripsi, scriptum (3), enrol ; write.

scriptor, -oris, *m.,* author, historian.

scutum, -i, *n.,* shield.

se, sui, sibi, se, *reflex. pronoun,* himself, herself, itself, themselves.

secerno -ere, -crevi, -cretum (3), separate.

secretus, -a, -um, separate ; in secretum, into a private place, apart.

secundum, *prep. with acc.*, after, next to ; following on, in accordance with.

secundus, -a, -um, second, victorious.

securis, -is, *f.*, axe, hatchet.

sed, but.

sedeo, -ere, sedi, sessum (2), sit.

sedes, -is, *f.*, habitation, home ; seat.

seditio, -ionis, *f.*, insurrection ; civil commotion.

seditiosus, -a, -um, turbulent.

sedo (1), calm.

sedulo, *adv.*, busily, diligently.

segnis, -e, inactive.

segrego (1), separate ; break up ; divide.

sella, -ae, *f.*, chair.

semel, *adv.*, once.

semen, -inis, *n.*, seed, lineage.

semper, *adv.*, always.

senator, -oris, *m.*, senator.

senatus, -us, *m.*, senate.

senectus, -tutis, *f.*, old age.

senesco, -ere, senui (3), grow old, decay, decline.

senex, senis, *m.*, old man ; *compar.*, senior.

sensim, *adv.*, gradually.

sensus, -us, *m.*, feeling, perception.

sententia, -ae, *f.*, opinion ; in sententiam inire, to vote in favour of a proposal.

sentio, -ire, -si, -sum (4), feel, perceive.

sepelio, -ire, -ivi (ii), -ultum (4), bury.

sepono, -ere, -posui, -positum (3), set aside.

septem, seven.

septentrio, -ionis, *m.*, *usually pl.*, the north.

septingentesimus, -a, -um, seven-hundredth.

septuaginta, seventy.

sepulcrum, -i, *n.*, sepulchre.

sepultura, -ae, *f.*, burial.

sequor, -i, secutus (3), follow, attend, pursue.

serenus, -a, -um, bright.

serius, -a, -um, serious ; *n. pl.*, seria, business.

sermo, -onis, *m.*, language.

serus, -a, -um, late.

serva, -ae, *f.*, female slave.

Servilii, -orum, *m. pl.*, the Servilii.

servilis, -e, slave-like.

servio (4), be a slave.

servitium, -i, *n.*, slavery.

servitus, -tutis, *f.*, servitude.

Servius, -i, *m.*, Servius.

servo (1), save, keep, observe.

servus, -i, *m.*, slave.

sese = se.

seu = sive.

sex, six.

si, *conj.*, if.

Sibylla, -ae, *f.*, the Sibylla.

sic, *adv.*, thus, so.

sicco (1), dry, drain.

siccus, -a, -um, dry.

Sicilia, -ae, *f.*, Sicily.

Siculus, -a, -um, Sicilian.

sicut, just as.

Signia, -ae, *f.*, Signia.

significo (1), signify ; indicate.

signum, -i, *n.*, standard, sign, land-mark ; **ad prima signa,** in the van, thick of the fray.

silentium, -i, *n.*, silence.

silex, -icis, *m.*, flint.

silva, -ae, *f.*, wood, forest.

Silvius, -i, *m.*, Silvius (*Alban king*).

similis, -e, like (*followed by dat. and gen.*).

similitudo, -inis, *f.*, likeness, simi-larity.

simul, *adv.*, together, at the same time.

simulatio, -ionis, *f.*, assumed ap-pearance.

simulo (1), pretend.

simultas, -tatis, *f.*, feud.

sin, *conj.*, if however.

sine, *prep. with abl.*, without.

singuli, -ae, -a, one each ; one at a time (25. 7) ; individual.

sinister, -tra, -trum, left.

sino, -ere, sivi, situm (3), bury (2. 6) ; let, allow ; situs, placed.

sinus, -us, *m.*, bay, gulf.

sisto, -ere, stiti, statum (3), stay, check, stop.

sitio (4), be thirsty.

situs, -us, *m.*, position, situation.

sive (seu), or if : sive (seu) . . . sive (seu), whether . . . or.

socer, -eri, *m.*, father-in-law.

societas, -tatis, *f.*, alliance, associa-tion.

socius, -a, -um, allied ; *as noun,* ally.

socorditer, *adv.*, carelessly ; *com-par.,* socordius, less promptly.

socors, -dis, senseless, careless.

socrus, -us, *f.*, mother-in-law.

sol, solis, *m.*, sun.

soleo, -ere, solitus sum (2), am wont, accustomed.

solidus, -a, -um, complete.

solitudo, -inis, *f.*, desert, wilderness.

solium, -i, *n.*, throne.

sollemnis, -e, yearly, customary ; ceremonial ; solemn.

sollemne, -is, *n.*, festival, cere-mony ; custom (31. 4).

sollicito (1), stimulate ; disturb, irritate.

sollicitus, -a, -um, distracted.

solstitialis, -e, solar.

solum, -i, *n.*, ground.

solum, *adv.*, only.

solus, -a, -um, alone.

solvo, -ere, -i, solutum (3), loosen, pay ; discontinue (49. 7).

somnus, -i, *m.*, sleep.

sopio (4), put to asleep ; **sopitus,** stunned (41. 5) ; asleep (58. 2).

sopor, -oris, *m.*, sleep.

sordidus, -a, -um, low, base, mourning (10. 1).

soror, -oris, *f.*, sister.

sororius, -a, -um, of a sister.

sors, sortis, *f.*, lot, inheritance, share ; fate, chance (56. 11) ; *pl.,* oracle.

sospito (1), protect.

spatium, -i, *n.*, full course, space, period, respite.

species, -ei, *f.*, sight ; pret·xt ; beauty (7. 4).

speciosus, -a, -um, having a good appearance, plausible.

spectaculum, -i, *n.*, spectacle, sight; stand (*at a show*, 35. 8).

spectator, -oris, *m.*, spectator.

specto (1), watch, view ; **alio spectare,** to have another bear-

ing ; **spectatus,** tested, proved ;
spectatissimum, the decisive
proof.
specus, -us, *m.,* cave.
spelunca, -ae, *f.,* cave.
sperno, -ere, sprevi, spretum (3),
despise, spurn.
spero (1), hope, hope for.
spes, spei, *f.,* hope ; **spem facere,** to
inspire hope.
spiritus, -us, *m.,* breath ; *pl.,* spirits.
spolio (1), spoil.
spolium, -i, *n.,* spoil.
sponsus, -i, *m.,* betrothed,
sponte, *adv.,* of one's own accord.
stabilis, -e, firm, permanent.
stabulum, -i, *n.,* stall, cottage.
stagnum, -i, *n.,* pool.
statim, *adv.,* immediately.
stativus, -a, -um, stationary ;
castra stativa, permanent camp.
Stator, Statoris, *m.,* the Stayer.
statua, -ae, *f.,* statue.
statuo, -ere, -i, -tum (3), set,
determine, assign.
status, -us, *m.,* state.
sterno, -ere, stravi, stratum (3),
overthrow, breach (29. 2).
stimulo (1), stimulate, urge on,
provoke, goad.
stipendium, -i, *n.,* stipend, pay ;
stipendia mereri, to serve campaigns.
stipo (1), throng ; **stipatus,** attended
(by).
stirps (stirpis), -is, *f.,* family, breed,
stock ; offspring, issue.
sto, -are, steti, statum (1), stand,
stand secure (29. 6).
strages, -is, *f.,* slaughter.
strenuus, -a, -um, active.

strepitus, -us, *m.,* noise, din.
stringo, -ere, -nxi, -ctum (3), draw,
unsheathe.
struo, -ere, -xi, -ctum (3), draw up,
array.
studeo (2), be eager, desire anxiously.
studium, -i, *n.,* eagerness, desire ;
pl., learning (18. 2).
stultitia, -ae, *f.,* folly ; idiocy (56. 8).
stupeo (2), be amazed, stunned.
stupro (1), debauch.
stuprum, -i, *n.,* defilement.
sub, *prep. with acc. and abl.,* under ;
of time, with acc., just before, at.
subeo, -ire, -ivi (ii), **-itum,** go up ;
draw off to (28. 5).
subicio, -ere, -ieci, -iectum, put
under ; make subject ; suggest
(59. 11).
subigo, -ere, -egi, -actum (3), compel.
subito, *adv.,* suddenly.
subitus, -a, -um, sudden.
sublica, -ae, *f.,* pile.
sublicius, -a, -um, resting on piles.
sublimis, -e, on high, aloft.
submergo, -ere, -si, -sum (3),
drown.
submitto, -ere, -misi, -missum (3),
let down, lower.
subsido, -ere, -sedi, -sessum (3), sit
down, lie.
subsisto, -ere, -stiti (3), stand firm ;
encounter, face.
subsum, -esse, remain.
succedo, -ere, -cessi, -cessum (3),
retreat ; succeed (48. 8).
successus, -us, *m.,* advance.
Suessa, -ae, Pometia, -ae, *f.,* Suessa
Pometia.

suffragium, -i, *n.*, vote, voting, suffrage ; inire suffragium, begin voting.

sum, esse, fui, am, exist.

summa, -ae, *f.*, sum ; **summa rerum**, administration.

summus, -a, -um, top of, greatest, supreme ; **summa rerum**, the most important undertakings (36. 6).

sumo, -ere, sumpsi, sumptum (3), take, gain, undertake.

sumptus, -us, *m.*, expense.

suopte, -apte = suo, sua.

suovetaurilia, -um, *n. pl.*, sacrifice of pig, sheep, and bull.

super, *adv., and prep. with acc., and abl.*, above, over, on.

superbe, *adv.*, haughtily.

superbia, -ae, *f.* pride.

superbus, -a, -um, proud ; overbearing (50. 3).

superior, -us, high, upper ; former.

superne, *adv.*, from above, downwards.

supero (1), cross, surpass.

superpono, -ere, -posui, -positum (3), place upon (+ *dat.*).

superstes, -stitis, surviving.

superstitio, -ionis, *f.*, superstition.

supersum, -esse, -fui, remain, survive ; be excessive.

suppedito (1), suffice (55. 7).

supplementum, -i, *n.*, accretion of numbers.

supplex, -icis, suppliant.

supplicium, -i, *n.*, punishment.

supra, *adv., and prep. with acc.*, above, beyond.

uprascando (3), climb over, pass.

suscipio, -ere, -cepi, -ceptum, undertake, adopt ; recognise as such (20. 7).

suspendo, -ere, -di, -sum (3), hang ; suspensus, anxious, in suspense (25. 2) ; outspread (34. 8).

suspicio, -ere, -spexi, -spectum, look up to ; suspectus, suspected.

sustineo, -ere, -tinui, -tentum (2), support, hold firm ; withstand (41. 4).

suus, -a, -um, his, her, their (own).

suuspte, *emphatic form of* suus.

T. = Titus.

taberna, -ae, *f.* shop.

tabula, -ae, *f.*, (writing) tablet.

taceo (2), am silent ; conceal (56. 11).

tacitus, -a, -um, silent.

taedet (2), *impers.*, be wearied.

taedium, -i, *n.*, weariness, loathing.

Talassius, -i, *m.*, Talassius.

talentum, -i, *n.*, a talent.

talis, -e, such.

tam, so.

tamen, nevertheless, however, yet.

tamquam, as if.

Tanaquil, -ilis, *f.*, Tanaquil.

tandem, *adv.*, at length.

tango, -ere, tetigi, tactum (3), touch ; strike (5. 6).

tantisper *adv.*, meanwhile.

tantus, -a, -um, so great. tantum, *adv.*, so much, only.

Tarpeius, -i, *m.*, Tarpeius (Spurius).

Tarpeius, -a, -um, Tarpeian.

Tarquinia, -ae, *f.*, Tarquinia.

Tarquinii, -orum, *m. pl.*, Tarquinii.

Tarquinius, -a, -um, of Tarquinii.

Tarquinius, -i, *m.*, Tarquinius ;
  (1) Lucius Tarquinius Priscus,
  (2) Lucius Tarquinius Superbus,
  (3) Arruns Tarquinius,
  (4) Sextus Tarquinius,
  (5) Titus Tarquinius,
  (6) Tarquinius Conlatinus.
Tatius, -i, *m.*, Titus Tatius.
tectum, -i, *n.*, house, building.
tego, -ere, texi, tectum (3), cover ;
  protect (53. 8).
tegumen, -inis, *n.*, covering.
tegumentum, -i, *n.*, covering.
Tellena, -orum, *n. pl.*, Tellena
  (*Latin city*).
telum, -i, *n.*, weapon.
temere, *adv.*, without good reason
  or design.
temeritas, -tatis, *f.*, recklessness.
tempero (1), regulate, discipline ;
  spare (*with dat.*, 29. 6).
tempestas, -tatis, *f.*, season, time,
  period ; storm.
templum, -i, *n.*, temple.
tempto (1), attempt, prove.
tempus, -oris, *n.*, time.
tendo, -ere, tetendi, tensum (3),
  direct one's course.
tenebrae, -arum, *f. pl.*, darkness.
teneo, -ere, tenui, tentum (2), hold,
  keep ; sail (1. 4), prevail (4. 6).
tenuis, -e, thin, scanty.
tergum, -i, *n.*, back, **terga vertere,**
  flee.
terminus, -i, *m.*, boundary.
Terminus, -i, *m.*, Terminus.
terni, -ae, -a, three each *or* apiece.
tero, -ere, trivi, tritum (3), wear,
  waste ; spend (*of time*).
terra, -ae, *f.*, land, ground ; **in
  terris,** on earth.

terrestris, -e, of the earth.
terribilis, -e, terrible.
terror, -oris, *m.*, terror, danger
  (2. 3) ; **ad terrorem,** to intimi-
  date.
tertius, -a, -um, third.
testamentum, -i, *n.*, will.
testis, -is, *c.*, witness.
testor (1), call to witness ; make a
  will (34. 3).
tetricus, -a, -um, austere.
Tiberinus, -a, -um, Tiberinus.
Tiberis, -is, *m.*, the Tiber.
tigillum, -i, *n.*, little beam.
timeo (2), fear.
timor, -oris, *m.*, fear.
Titienses, -ium, *m.*, Titienses.
Titus, -i, Tatius, -i, *m.*, Titus Tatius.
toga, -ae, *f.*, toga.
tollo, -ere, sustuli, sublatum (3),
  raise ; recover (32. 3) ; remove.
tonitrus, -us, *m.*, thunder.
torpeo (2), be torpid, paralysed.
tot, so many.
totidem, just so many.
totiens, so often.
totus, -a, -um, whole, entire.
trabea, -ae, *f.*, robe of state.
trado, -ere, -didi, -ditum (3), hand
  down *or* over, record.
traduco, -ere, -duxi, -ductum (3),
  transfer.
tragicus, -a, -um, fit for tragedy,
  tragic.
traho, -ere, traxi, tractum (3), draw;
  claim(7. 1), attract (30. 7).
traicio, -ere, -ieci, -iectum, cross.
traiectus, -us, *m.*, crossing.
tranquillus, -a, -um, calm, serene.
transeo, -ire, -ii (ivi), -itum, caoss :
  desert (27. 5).

transfero, -ferre, -tuli, -latum, transfer, shift.

transfigo, -ere, -fixi, -fixum (3), transfix, pierce.

transfugio, -ere, -fugi, -fugitum, flee over to, desert.

transigo, -ere, -egi, -actum (3), transact.

transilio (4), leap over.

transitio, -ionis, f., desertion.

transmitto, -ere, -misi, -missum (3), send or throw across.

transversus, -a, -um, in flank.

trecenti, -ae, -a, three hundred.

trepidatio, -ionis, f., alarm.

trepido (1), be excited, waver.

trepidus, -a, -um, agitated ; alarming (48. 1) ; alarmed (60. 1).

tres, tria, trium, three.

tribunus, -i, m., tribune.

tribus, -us f., a tribe.

tributum, -i, n., tax, tribute.

triceni, -ae, -a, thirty each.

tricesimus, -a, -um, thirtieth.

Tricipitinus, -i, m., Tricipitinus.

trigeminus, -a, -um, triplet ; triple (of spoils).

triginta, thirty.

tripudium, -i, n., dance.

tristis, -e, sad, gloomy.

triumpho (1), celebrate (a triumph).

Troia, -ae, f., Troy.

Troianus, -a, -um, Trojan ; as noun, Trojan.

trucido (1), kill cruelly.

tu, te, tui, tibi, te, thou.

tubicen, -cinis, m., trumpeter.

Tullia, -ae, f., Tullia.

Tullii, -orum, the Tullii.

Tullius, -i, Servius, -i, m., Servius Tullius.

Tullus, -i, m., Tullus Hostilius.

tum, adv., then, on that occasion ; cum . . . tum, not only . . . but also, both . . . and.

tumultuarius, -a, -um, hastily levied.

tumultuose, adv., in or with confusion ; superl., with as much noise (as possible) (40. 5).

tumultuosus, -a, -um, noisy.

tumultus, -us, m., uproar, rush, tumult (29. 2), stampede, confusion (59. 6).

tunc, adv., then.

tunica, -ae, f., tunic.

turba, -ae, f., crowd, mob.

turbidus, -a, -um, stormy.

turbo (1), disturb, throw into confusion, violate.

turma, -ae, f., squadron.

Turnus, -i, m., Turnus.

Tusci, -orum, m. pl., Etruscans.

Tusculanus, -a, -um, of Tusculum.

tutela, -ae, f., preservation, regency (3. 1).

tutor (1), secure, keep.

tutor, -oris, m., guardian.

tutus, -a, -um, safe.

tuus, -a, -um, your.

tyrannus, -i, m., tyrant, despot.

ubertas, -tatis, f., productiveness.

ubi, adv., where? relat. adv., in which, where ; conj., when.

ubicumque, adv., wheresoever.

ulciscor, -i, ultus (3), take revenge.

Ulixes, -is, m., Ulysses (Odysseus).

ullus, -a, -um, any.

ultimus, -a, -um, last, decisive (15. 3), final ; distant (29. 4) ;

ad ultimum, at last (34. 5, 53. 10, 54. 2).

ultor, -oris, *m.,* avenger, revenger.

ultra, *prep. with acc., and adv.,* beyond ; longer.

ultro, *adv.,* actually, of one's own accord.

umerus, -i, *m.,* shoulder.

umquam, *adv.,* ever.

unde, *adv.,* whence ; *relat. adv.,* whence, from where ; from this cause (31. 5).

undecim, eleven.

undique, from *or* on every side.

unicus, -a, -um, unique.

universus, -a, -um, whole, all together.

unus, -a, -um, one ; **ad unum,** to a man.

urbanus, -a, -um, belonging to *or* of the city.

Urbius, -a, -um, (of) Urbius.

urbs, -is, *f.,* city.

usquam, *adv.,* anywhere.

usque, *adv.,* right on ; **usque ad,** right up to, as far as, down to.

usurpo (1), exercise.

usus, -us, *m.,* employment (56. 3), need.

ut, *conj.,* as, when ; (in order) that, so that. *relat. adv.,* as, how. **ut qui,** as one who.

utcumque, however.

utensilia, -ium, *n. pl.,* utensils.

uter, utra, utrum, which of the two ; *pl.,* which of two parties, sides *or* lots.

uterque, -traque, -trumque, each *or* both (of two), both : *in pl.,* each of two sides *or* lots.

uti = ut.

utilis, -e, useful, expedient.

utilitas, -tatis, *f.,* advantage.

utique, anyhow, certainly.

utor, -i, usus (3), use, find (by experience) (9. 15) *with abl.*

utrimque, *adv.,* on either side, from *or* by both sides.

utroque, *adv.,* to both places.

uxor, -oris, *f.,* wife.

vacuus, -a, -um, empty.

vado, -ere (3), go.

vadum, -i, *n.,* shallow, ford.

vagitus, -us, *m.,* crying, wailing.

vagus, -a, -um, unsettled.

valeo (2), be strong, have influence, prevail.

Valerius, -i, *m.,* (1) Marcus Valerius, (2) Publius Valerius.

validus, -a, -um, strong, powerful.

vallis, -is, *f.,* valley.

vanus, -a, -um, empty (8. 5), useless, untrue ; weak (27. 1) ; groundless ; ineffectual (10. 4).

vario (1), vary ; *imperson.,* there is a difference of opinion.

varie, *adv.,* variously.

varius, -a, -um, different ; **deinde varius,** diverging from that point.

vas, vasis, *n.,* vessel; emblems, badge (24. 5).

vastatio, -ionis, *f.,* devastation.

vasto (1), lay waste.

vastus, -a, -um, vast.

vates, -is, *c.,* prophet, soothsayer.

-ve, *enclitic conj.,* or.

vehiculum, -i, *n.,* carriage.

veho, -ere, vexi, vectum (3), carry.

Veiens, -ntis, of Veii ; **Veientes, -ium,** *m. pl.,* men of Veii.

vel, either ; **vel . . . vel,** either . . . or.

velamen, -inis, *n.*, covering, band.

velo (1), veil, cover, bind round.

velut, as if ; as it were.

venerabilis, -e, revered.

venerabundus, -a, -um, full of awe.

veneror (1), worship ; do honour to (5. 2).

Veneti, -orum, *m. pl.*, the Veneti.

venia, -ae, *f.*, pardon.

venio, -ire, veni, ventum (4), come.

venor (1), hunt.

venter, -tris, *m.*, belly ; **ventrem ferre,** be with child.

ventus, -i, *m.*, wind.

Venus, -eris, *f.*, Venus.

verbena, -ae, *f.* sprig.

verber, -eris, *m.*, lash, blow.

verbero (1), flog.

verbum, -i, *n.*, word.

vere, *adv.*, truly.

verecundia, -ae, *f.*, respect.

veridicus, -a, -um, truthful.

vero, *adv.*, indeed, really.

verso (1), turn, occupy.

versus, *prep. with acc.*, towards.

verto, -ere, -ti, -sum (3), turn ; **versus,** facing ; devoted (21. 2).

verus, -a, -um, true, genuine. **verum,** *n. sg. or n. pl.*, **vera,** truth.

verutum, -i, *n.*, dart, javelin.

vescor, -i (3), feed on.

Vesta, -ae, *f.*, Vesta.

Vestalis, -e, Vestal, of Vesta ; *as noun,* a Vestal virgin.

vester, -tra, -trum, your.

vestibulum, -i, *n.*, vestibule.

vestigium, -i, *n.*, footprint, trace.

vestis, -is, *f.*, clothing, robe, dress.

veteranus, -a, -um, veteran.

veto, -are, -ui, -itum (1), forbid.

vetus, -eris, of long standing, ancient, old.

vetustas, -tatis, *f.*, lapse of time.

vetustus, -a, -um, ancient, old.

via, -ae, *f.*, road, way ; means.

vicem, -is, -e, *pl.*, **-es, -ibus,** office ; **in vicem,** in turn.

vicesimus, -a, -um, twentieth.

vicinus, -a, -um, neighbouring, near.

victima, -ae, *f.*, victim.

victoria, -ae, *f.*, victory.

victor, -oris, conqueror, victorious.

victrix, -icis, *fem.* of **victor.**

vicus, -i, *m.*, street.

video, -ere, vidi, visum, see ; *pass.,* seem, seem good.

vidua, -ae, *f.*, widow.

viduus, -a, -um, widowed.

viginti, twenty.

vigor, -oris, *m.*, vigour.

Viminalis, -e, Viminal.

vincio, -ire, -nxi, -nctum (4), bind.

vinco, -ere, vici, victum (3), defeat, outdo, overcome, be victorious.

vinculum, -i, *n.*, chain, bind ; cord.

vindico (1), liberate ; protect (4. 3).

vinum, -i, *n.*, wine.

violentus, -a, -um, violent.

violo (1), violate.

vir, viri, *m.*, man, hero ; husband.

virginitas, -tatis, *f.*, virginity.

virgo, -inis, *f.*, virgin, maiden.

virgultum, -i, *n.*, bush ; *pl.*, brush-wood, thicket.

virilis, -e, manly ; **stirpis virilis** male issue, son.

viritim, *adv.*, individually.

virtus, -utis, *f.*, worth (7. 14), merit, good quality, virtue; valour (1. 5).

vis, vim, vi, *pl.*, vires, *f. pl.*, force, quantity; violence (attack); vi et armis, by force of arms; *in pl.*, strength.

viso, -ere (3), view.

visus, -us, *m.*, apparition (56. 5), phenomenon.

vita, -ae, *f.*, life.

vitium, -i, *n.*, fault, vice.

vito (1), avoid.

vivo, -ere, vixi, victum (3), live.

vivus, -a, -um, alive, living.

vix, *adv.*, hardly, scarcely.

vociferor (1), shout, raise one's voice.

voco (1), call, summon.

Volesius, -i, *m.*, Volesius, father of Publius Valerius (58. 6).

volgo, *adv.*, commonly, generally.

volito (1), fly (quickly).

volo, velle, volui, wish, be willing; volens, gracious, willing.

volo (1), fly.

Volsci, -orum, *m. pl.*, the Volsci.

voluntarius, -i, *m.*, volunteer.

voluntas, -tatis, *f.*, will, wish, desire; opinion (28. 8).

voluptas, -tatis, *f.*, pleasure.

volvo, -ere, -vi, -utum (3), turn over (*of page*).

vos, *pl.*, you.

votum, -i, *n.*, vow.

voveo, -ere, -vi, -tum (2), vow.

vox, vocis, *f.*, voice, cry; *pl.*, words, expressions.

Vulcanus, -i, *m.*, Vulcan.

vulgo (1), make common (10. 7); prostitute (4. 7); vulgatus, common.

vulgo, *adv.*, = volgo.

vulgus, -i, *n.*, common people, the commons.

vulnero (1), wound.

vulnus, -eris, *n.*, wound.

vultur, -uris, *m.*, vulture.